# LONG ISLAND

Produced in Coooperation with the
Society for the Preservation of Long Island Antiquities


With contributions from Geoffrey L. Rossano, Carol A. Traynor,
Gaynell Stone and Roger W. Lotchins


American Historical Press
Sun Valley, California

# LONG ISLAND

# An Illustrated History

Edited By
Robert B. MacKay and Richard F. Welch

*Previous Page:* The Northport
Thimble Factory, 1880. *Water-
color on paper by Edward
Lange. Courtesy, Society for
the Preservation of Long Island
Antiquities*

*Opposite page: With over 500
acres and numerous manmade
lakes, bridle paths, and bicycle
paths, Prospect Park represented a new concept in
recreation—municipally
planned, open spaces within
an urban center. Courtesy,
Brooklyn Historical Society*

*Page 6: To get around a lack
of water power, many millers
built tidal mills that twice daily
trapped the rising tide water,
channeling it over a water wheel
to produce power. Photo by
Paul J. Oresky*

Photos attributed to Long Island Historical Society,
now Brooklyn Historical Society.

© American Historical Press
All Rights Reserved
Published 2000
Printed in the United States of America

Library of Congress Catalogue Card Number: 00-108798
ISBN: 1-892724-14-6

Bibliography: p. 286
Includes Index

# Contents

# Introduction

Long Island has always been a land of contrast —of Europeans and native Americans—of Dutch and English—of lords of the manor and tenant farmers—of fashionable watering places and agrarian villages—of suburbia and potato fields. Its rich experience has given it a layering of history comparable to few other regions. Today, Long Island remains a place of many separate realities. There are the Northeast corridor problems of deteriorating neighborhoods, suburban sprawl, and an aging infrastructure, but there is also a strong technology-based economy and an entrepreneurial climate, fostering the growth of hundreds of emerging companies. Long Island also plays host to a significant concentration of institutions of higher learning and remarkable amenities—the great legacy of the Moses parkway system, the estate era museums and preserves, the myriad recreational facilities and, despite the movement of the twentieth-century development, unsuspected natural beauty. Here are found 90 percent of New York's wetlands, its most productive agricultural county, and twenty-one state parks.

Long Island's habitation by native Americans, which predates the arrival of the Europeans by at least 5,000 years, is at least as noteworthy, since "Seawanhaka" (land of shell beads) was a major center of wampum production for the Algonkian peoples. In the intervening years the history of our Island has been exciting, if often contentious. Positioned in the stream of events taking place between New England and the middle colonies, Long Island experienced just about everything except for the brunt of the Industrial Revolution and it bypassed that era only for the lack of falling water necessary to power mill turbines. Most strikingly, it has been the cradle of so many developments now synonymous with American life. It was here that many of the nation's recreational pursuits, including thoroughbred racing, came of age; that aviation spread its wings; and that suburbia was first realized on a large scale.

# Acknowledgments

No fewer than twenty persons have made major contributions to *Long Island: An Illustrated History,* making this project very much a team effort. I would like to thank those who assisted with an earlier version of this book.

C. W. Post Professor Richard Welch provided the chapter, "Into The Millennium" and served as co-editor of this edition.

Geoffrey L. Rossano, co-editor, author of five chapters and several sidebars, received his Ph.D. in American urban history from the University of North Carolina-Chapel Hill in 1980. He has published numerous articles. Raised in the Huntington area and currently residing in Connecticut where he teaches history at the Salisbury School.

Carol A. Traynor SPLIA's former publications coordinator, was co-editor or an earlier edition and author of several sidebars.

Roger W. Lotchin, author of the chapters on Brooklyn, received his Ph.D in 1969 from the University of Chicago and his special interests include American urban history and politics. He has written extensively and published numerous articles on these topics.

Gaynell Stone, author of the first chapter, received her anthropology doctorate from the State University of New York-Stony Brook.

Councilman Bradley L. Harris of Smithtown wrote the essay on Richard Smythe; Dr. Steven Kesselman, manager of the William Floyd Estate, authored the William Floyd essay; Carolyn Marx, SPLIA's curator and Custom House administrator provided the profile on Henry Packer Dering; Robert Farwell, former director of the Whaling Museum in Cold Spring Harbor, wrote the essay on Walter R. Jones; Linda Day, former curator of the Black History Museum of Nassau County, authored the essay on Samuel Ballton; the late Dr. Roger G. Gerry of the Roslyn Landmarks Society and Anthony Cucchiara, co-authored the side-bar on William Cullen Bryant; Malcolm MacKay, author of *A History of Brooklyn Heights*, wrote the sidebars on Hezekiah B. Pierrepont, Charles Pratt, and Seth Low; Marilyn Oser wrote the essay on the poet; John Gable, director of the Theodore Roosevelt Association, contributed the sidebar on our twenty-sixth President; Edward J. Smits, Nassau County Historian and author of *Nassau Suburbia, U.S.A.*, authored the A.T. Stewart essay; Timorth O'Brien, formerly with Long Island Heritage, wrote the essays on Leroy R. Grumman and Robert Moses; and Kimberly Greer of *Newsday* and Stuart Diamond of the *New York Times* co-authored the sidebars on Alicia Patterson Guggenheim, William Levitt, and the Doubledays.

Robert B. MacKay

# CHAPTER ONE

# Long Island before the Europeans

About 12,000 years ago, when the last Wisconsinan Glacier was retreating across the Northeast, it left behind a small lake (now Long Island Sound) and a landmass that stretched from New Jersey to Cape Cod. Except for Long Island, the land mass is presently underwater as part of the Continental Shelf. The Island, residue of two glacial deposits, is itself almost a series of islands. It is nearly cut through at Hashamomuck and Mattituck on the North Fork, at Amagansett and Canoe Place on the South Fork, where the Nissequogue and Connetquot rivers almost meet in mid-Island, and by the Flushing Creek estuary in Queens County.

Thus, native inhabitants of the last 6,000 years had one of the most beneficent environments in the region: a continental humid climate with the Northeast's longest growing season, 220 days, and a landmass warmed by the Gulf Stream. The area contained abundant marine resources—fish, shellfish, waterfowl, seals, porpoises, and whales—as well as animals, fowl, plants, nuts, tubers, berries, and seeds. These resources fell into various ecological niches and weather zones, with the East End—like two fingers poking out into the Atlantic—subject to highly changeable marine weather and heavier snowfall. The coastline is punctuated by innumerable creeks and rivers providing food, transportation, and fresh water for humans and animals. Lakes in kettleholes (a depression remaining after the melting of buried ice) and ponds—strung strategically across the broader parts of the Island and at the head of every estuary—made it a well-watered land. The islands, marshes, and peninsulas evident on early maps illustrate why the Dutch called Long Island "Gebroken (broken) Landt."

The earliest native Americans had crossed the

*In 1524 Florentine explorer Giovanni Verrazano described the native Americans in New York as handsome and tall in stature, "clothed with the feathers of birds of various colors," their hair "fastened back in a knot, of olive color."* From Adams, History of the Town of Southampton, *Hampton Press, 1917*

*Left: Long Island's first inhabitants hunted caribou, using spears with chipped stone projectile points. Courtesy, New York State Museum/ The State Education Department*

*Below: Among native American hunting and butchering tools, projectile points are most often used to define cultural periods because of their varied styles. The Wading River (#3) and Orient (#10) points were first found and identified on Long Island. Photo by Daniel H. Kaplan. Courtesy, Nassau County Museum*

Bering Strait land bridge or come by boat or raft from Asia in several migrations more than 12,000 years ago. They followed the retreating glacier across North America and into the Long Island area. In a cold tundra environment, these early peoples hunted animals and gathered plant foods. Indians of the Northeastern United States hunted caribou and elk. Although mastodon and mammoth teeth are still dredged from Continental Shelf waters off Long Island, there is no evidence that these animals were hunted here. As the climate warmed and the glacier retreated, sea levels rose about 350 feet. An evergreen forest slowly developed, then changed to a boreal, or northern zone, parkland. Sea levels 8,000 years ago were about 100 feet lower than they are today, but this later environment was an oak-hickory forest much as we know it today.

A more varied native culture was evolving, but our knowledge of local Indian lifestyles before the seventeenth century (and the availability of written records) is based on information from archaeological excavation. Although abundant wood, bone, and

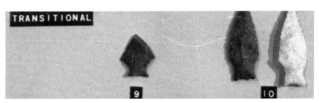

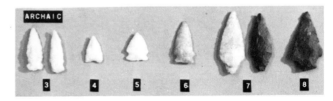

textile products existed from the earliest human life, this material has not survived well in the archaeological record. This is due to a number of factors, including rising sea levels, acid soil, rapid urban expansion, relic-hunting by collectors, and the small number of trained archaeologists active on Long Island.

It is, nevertheless, reasonable to assume that prehistoric Long Islanders had the same needs—food and shelter—and the same preoccupations—

The Pipestave Hollow excavations of 1976 and 1977 uncovered a Late Archaic habitation site at Mt. Sinai on Long Island's North Shore. In addition to studying artifacts and settlement pattern remains, the excavators collected and analyzed over seventy bushels of shell and bone fragments in order to establish an accurate picture of prehistoric life and diet. Courtesy, Gaynell Stone

understanding the unknown and regulating human interaction—that we have today. Human life and culture are a continuous process, but for convenience this long period has been placed in time categories generally based on evidence of technological change. Dating from about 12,000 to 9,000 years ago, the earliest Paleo-Indian period is known on Long Island only from the fluted spear points found scattered from Queens County to Greenport in Suffolk County. No actual Paleo-Indian sites have been discovered here, although there is evidence of one on Staten Island. Any remains of local campsites are now probably underwater on the Continental Shelf.

More types of tools were developed by native inhabitants during the Archaic period, about 9,000 to 3,000 years ago, to meet the expanding subsistence opportunities of a deciduous forest and more temperate climate. Artifacts typical of this era include: new types of spear points and the *atlatl,* which made spear-throwing more effective; more cutting implements and knives; fishing equipment, such as stone sinkers for fishing nets, fish hooks, and harpoon points; and woodworking tools—gouges, axes, adzes, hammerstones, drills, and scrapers. In fact, every type of tool we use today was developed in stone by the Archaic, and possibly earlier, peoples. Dugout canoes, wooden bowls, ropes, and nets of hemp and other fibers, as well as baskets, folded

bark bags, and mats, were made, but generally have not survived. Archaic sites have been studied at Stony Brook, Wading River, Mt. Sinai, Shelter Island, and other spots. These sites provide evidence of a people who lived close to the marine resources available after about 6,000 years ago. According to archaeological excavations, they dwelled around marshes or river estuaries, and had specialized areas for a sweat hut, houses, food processing, and toolmaking. Post-molds (remains of saplings in the ground) indicate the Indians lived in round and oval wigwams covered with bark or mats.

Long Island's short Transitional period, about 3,300 to 3,000 years ago, is identified by evidence of a new ritual or religious behavior and is called the Orient Burial Cult. These few ceremonial burials in large pits contained grave offerings such as paintstones, fire-making kits, and tools. The bones, sometimes cremated, were usually covered with red ochre (hematite) powder; this probably meant that the dead enjoyed high status. Period artifacts include pots made from steatite, a form of stone from Connecticut; smoking pipes; and the Orient Fishtail projectile point. Trade networks enabled Pennsylvania jasper, Hudson Valley flint, and Great Lakes and Connecticut copper to be used for Long Island Indian artifacts.

The Woodland period, from 3,000 years ago until about 500 years ago (A.D. 1500), was a continuation

*Opposite page: The Island's swamp-like areas provide excellent hiding places for fish and fowl. Photo by Barbara C. Harrison*

*Below: Long Island Indian groups hunted deer, which can still be found in the Island's state parks. Photo by Paul J. Oresky*

*Left: As one of the commonest wild geese in North America, the Canada goose is abundant on Long Island's streams and open tundra. It feeds by grazing or by sounding for aquatic vegetation in streams and ponds. Photo by Paul J. Oresky*

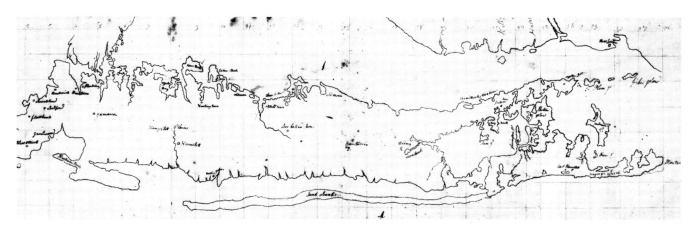

*Above: The islands and peninsulas evident on early maps illustrate why the Dutch called Long Island "Gebroken Landt." Courtesy, William L. Clements Library, University of Michigan*

*At the time of European contact the New England coast was an area of rich and varied resources. These illustrations from a 1502 map of New En-gland, the earliest visual record of the area, depict Indians hunting and smoking meat. Courtesy, New York Public Library*

of the diversified gathering, fishing, and hunting strategies of earlier times, augmented by the harvesting of sunflowers, Jerusalem artichokes, groundnuts, and other plants. These plant resources were expanded in the late Woodland with the introduction of cultivated plants—corn, beans, squash, pumpkins, melons, and gourds—from their Central American origins. However, the extent of corn horticulture on Long Island is unknown. Hoes and mortars found on archaeological sites indicate gardening to some degree. The development of pottery at this time also enhanced cooking and storage possibilities.

The development of village sites in the Woodland period possibly reflects trade contact with Europeans as well as increased gardening activity. Since no Long Island Woodland or Contact period Indian villages have been scientifically examined, we have little firm information on this period. Yet Indian villages existed where most of the original Colonial towns were later built. In fact, Indian settlements served as environmental predictors—the best spots for settlers wanting village sites.

The era of contact with Europeans, the Historic period, disrupted the Indians' comfortable subsistence, relatively complex social life, and varied material culture. The Indians adopted iron pots for cooking and guns for hunting. They cut brass kettles into projectile points and tools, adorned themselves with glass trade beads, and chose duffel (blanket) cloth and European clothes over skins. European furniture was added to wigwams, and American wood houses were used by the latter eighteenth century. This radical change took place within 150 years after Giovanni Verrazano's visit to the New World in 1524. After a storm drove the Italian explorer out of New York Bay, he skirted Long Island and Block Island, finally arriving at Newport Harbor. There he found natives, similar to those on Long Island, who

*excel us in size; they are of bronze color, some inclining more to whiteness, others to tawny color; the face sharply cut, the hair long and black, upon which they bestow the greatest study in adorning it; the eyes black and alert, the bearing kind and gentle.*

Verrazano describes leaders who wore stag skins adorned with colorful embroideries like damask (probably dyed porcupine quills) and broad, stone-encrusted chains of many colors at the neck. In addition, he observed the women to be graceful and comely, similarly dressed, and sporting lynx skins on their arms and pendants in their ears. Both sexes preferred earrings of copper plates to those of gold. They also had a fondness for the colors blue and red. Single women braided their hair on both sides of the head, while married women let their locks—either short or long—hang loose.

Other early observers found that young maidens reaching reproductive age decked themselves in wampum: bands of it circled the head, wampum strings covered the hair, and strands also served as necklaces and earrings. The festively-clad girls positioned themselves in a central point in the village where they might be viewed by all those seeking a wife. Van der Donck noted in the 1640s that "they usually carry small bags of paints with them . . . such as red, blue, green, brown, white, black, yellow, etc . . . that they were generally disposed to paint and ornament their faces with several brilliant colors." Indians of the area also frequently tattooed their bodies and faces, often with the clan totem represented by bears, wolves, turtles, and eagles.

In 1609 Robert Juet, a member of Henry Hudson's crew, described the area's Indians wearing "deer skins loose, well dressed . . . some in mantles of feathers, some in skins of divers sorts of good furs . . . They had red copper tobacco pipes, and other things of copper they did wear about their necks." The first Indian leader they met was Penhawitz or Pennewits, the one-eyed *sachem* of the Canarsies. Although the Vikings may have coasted through Long Island Sound around A.D. 1000, and Europeans had been fishing along the New England coast for several hundred years, the Canarsies were the first Indians documented in regional history to make contact with foreigners from across the sea. This early meeting hastened the swift demise of the Long Island natives through disease, malnutrition, and the effects of alcohol on a people who possessed

no physiological tolerance for it. New World natives also lacked immunity to European diseases such as smallpox, measles, and others. Thus, the Northeastern aboriginal population dwindled to a small fraction of its prehistoric size before the first colonists settled in the region. The Long Island natives had no hinterland to retreat to, as mainland groups had. The settlers' view of this unfortunate situation was characterized in 1670 by Daniel Denton, who felt it

*is to be admired, how strangely they have decreast by the Hand of God, since the English first settling of those parts . . . it hath been generally observed, that where the English come to settle, a Divine Hand makes way for them, by removing or cutting off the Indians, either by Wars one with the other, or by some raging mortal Disease.*

The inability to tolerate alcohol, exploited by some settlers, led to malnutrition and drunkenness. Rum flowed whenever colonists traded with the Indians or wanted them to sign deeds. Indian leaders requested that no liquor be sold to their people and early town laws prohibited the sale of rum and guns to the natives. Nevertheless, traders and land speculators honored the regulation against weapons better than that against alcohol.

Daniel Denton noted that "in their wars they fight no pitcht fields . . . but endeavor to secure their wives and children upon some Island . . . and then with their guns and hatchets they way-lay their enemies . . . and it is a great fight when seven or eight is slain." Given their traditions, the Indians were amazed by the tactics of the Europeans, who killed everyone, including women and children. Areas of disagreement among tribes were generally resolved not by war, but by protocols of behavior. A Shinnecock leader, for example, stroked the back of a Montauk *sachem* to show obeisance, and an Iroquois family who had lost a father or son often adopted a captive to fill his place. However, the Dutch under Governor William Kieft killed Indians of the area for little reason. Taking peaches from an orchard seemed natural to the communally-oriented natives, but to property-conscious Europeans, this act meant theft. Murder, which was relatively rare among the Indians, could often be assuaged by paying the bereaved family wampum or other remuneration.

*Long Island Indians be-
friended the early European
settlers, as depicted in this
idealized mural of the Hempstead settlement painted by
Peppino Mangravite in 1937.
Courtesy, National Archives*

Native Americans had no idea they were "selling" their land, but thought that the Europeans were giving them gifts for being allowed to use its resources. Sharing and gift-giving were an integral part of the aboriginal culture, a behavior which enabled groups to survive in times of scarcity. Due to the Indians' communal use of the land, they thought that they would be sharing their territory with the settlers. When the colonists "purchased" Indian lands and developed farms, they removed most of the food sources from the native diet; this created malnutrition, which heightened disease and hastened death. In addition, one regional native American tradition foretold the arrival of a great, white-skinned *Manitto* (Supreme Being) from the East. Verrazano recorded in 1524 that "they came toward us with evident delight, raising loud shouts of admiration, and showing us where we could most securely land . . ." Furthermore, a stone technology, however sophisticated, was no match for the Europeans' "magical" and much more powerful firearms and metal implements.

The settlers actually invaded inhabited land, since the earth was choice wherever the native Americans had settled and cleared gardens. Europeans needed only to push the Indians into less

desirable areas to inherit already cultivated land, multiple food resources, and water for people, animals, and the mills which soon dotted the landscape. Thus, beneath most historical sites on Long Island are prehistoric ones.

There were never "thirteen tribes" on Long Island. Each suitable habitation area had an extended family group or band living there. Each Indian group had a geographically descriptive name for their area; the settlers gave this name for the area to the native group, thereby creating the "tribal name." Thirteen appears to be an average of the numbers of groups named in various historic accounts, which range from two to twenty. Whatever their number, native bands did not constitute separate tribes with different cultures.

Long Island Indian life was fundamentally egalitarian, but an archaeological clue to possible social differentiation is found in the Orient Burial Cult of the Transitional period. This Red Ochre Burial Cult was widespread throughout the Northeast during Archaic times, and occurred during the Paleo period in North Dakota. Performed with red ochre and grave goods for the afterworld, the rites were probably organized by a ritual specialist, such as a *powawa* or *shaman;* his role was essential and, therefore, possibly marked the beginning of social ranking. Although its evolution is uncertain, the *sachem,* another status role, was evident in one form at Contact, where his power was related to his family or band. Aboriginal *sachems* were not absolute rulers in the European sense; rather, they were consensual leaders who emerged by displaying skill. Several accounts report an experienced general leader and a younger coordinator of military activities.

In some cases leadership may have been hereditary, but this interpretation also could be attributed to European misconceptions. Settlers actually fostered a "hereditary ruler" to ensure that property transactions needed to be approved by only one Indian authority. Wyandanch and Tackapausha—historic "leaders" of East End and West End Long Island Indian "confederations"—even signed over lands which they did not actually control. In fact, half of the "Shinnecock"—including the *sachem*—who signed a 1703 deed with the early Southampton purchasers did not appear on the 1698 census.

Long Island's prehistoric artifacts provide some clues to the Indian belief system, as well as to other cultural facets of life. Thunderbird and Great Horned Serpent figures carved on stone, for example, hint at a complex religion and philosophy revolving around and attempting to explain nature. However, descriptions of aboriginal beliefs, especially by the

*The outline of a bird figure on this pottery fragment from the Shinnecock site at Sebonac is a representation of the god of the upperworld in the Algonkian belief system. Courtesy, American Museum of Natural History*

colonial clergy, proved more subjective, even hostile. The Indians were considered heathens and their actions, illogical. In fact, the "powwow," a gathering which could include healing ceremonies, group dances, trances, and decision-making sessions, was perceived by colonists only as wild, dangerous behaviour. Samuel Taylor, a Quaker traveling on Shelter Island in 1659, observed the ritual:

*In came a great many lusty proper men . . . and sat down; and every one had a short truncheon stick in*

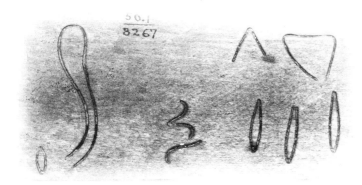

*Stone tablets with pictograph symbols found at Dosoris (Glen Cove), the Sebonac Shinnecock site, and Orient provide evidence of a complex comunication system. Early records note that carved wood slabs were used to record a group's family history or a warrior's deeds. Photo by Kay C. Lenskjold. Courtesy, American Museum of Natural History*

# WYANDANCH

A little known and even less understood commodity was to have a major impact on early relations between the English and the Indians on Long Island during the seventeenth century. Wampum, along with land, was among the chief objects of attraction to early colonial leaders. As sachem of the wampumrich Montauk Peninsula, Wyandanch played a pivotal role in these complex and often strained relations. Interacting with such prominent colonial figures as Lion Gardiner and Richard Smythe and assuming a strong position of leadership over the other native American groups on the east end of Long Island, he was able to exert a degree of political control unusual for the time—a control that was both shaped and limited by the political and economic climate established by the English.

The production of wampum, or shell beads, can be considered Long Island's first industry. As early as 1633, John Winthrop, governor of Massachusetts Colony, considered Long Island the best place for obtaining wampum for trade. The Dutch even called the Island "Seawanhackey," or "place of shell beads," after the Indian custom. Wampum was produced from two species of shell, whelk and quahog, especially abundant in Long Island waters, but was also produced by other coastal Indian groups as well. The cylindrical beads were fashioned from the

*Wampum was used as personal adornment, a unit of exchange in barter, currency in the colonial fur trade, tribute to avoid war, and to ritually finalize agreements. The whelk shells from which it was made were especially abundant on Long Island. Photo by Harvey Weber. Courtesy, Suffolk County Historical Society*

shells in a time-consuming process using sharpened stone drills. After contact with the settlers, the Indians were soon supplied with iron drills to speed manufacture. While the Indians had produced wampum before contact and used it for a variety of functions including tribute, ransom, marriage gifts, and adornment, the introduction of Europeans with their different economic concepts caused subtle shifts in the use and value of this commodity. The early colonists began to use wampum as a form of

currency as it was durable, lightweight, fairly uniform in size, and could be grouped in various increments from a single bead to what was called a "fathom" consisting of 540 beads. The Dutch and English traded goods for wampum from the coastal Indians and in turn traded it to inland and northern Indians for furs in a trade network that extended as far as Nova Scotia—a process which amassed a great deal of wealth for the early white traders as American furs had become quite fashionable in Europe. By the 1630s the English and Dutch had established "trade houses" along the trading network and the colonial government attempted to regulate and monopolize wampum production by controlling the areas of production and the Indians who owned and produced it. Wyandanch, as sachem of a rich wampum producing area, was right in the midst of these developments. His backing of the English in their war against the Pequot Indians of Connecticut in 1636-1637 produced a shift in the balance of wampum control and established a new basis for future relations with the English.

Wyandanch was able to exert a great deal of authority over his own group of Montauks, as well as the other eastern Long Island groups of Shinnecocks, Corchaugs, and Manhassets. This authority was based on three factors: the traditional Indian custom of group leaders governing by consensus; the Montauks' apparent strength in terms of numbers; and, most importantly, the influence of the English. It was advantageous to the English in their wampum trading and land deals to negotiate with one individual instead of the whole group. Their influence brought about a shift in power from numerous local "troublesome" sachems, each representing one or a few settlements, to a few "cooperative" chiefs who controlled many settlements. These chiefs became directly responsible for payments of wampum, were the first to be approached in securing land titles, and were often backed by Dutch and English authority in settling disputes. Wyandanch had made no secret of his respect and regard for the Europeans, whom he considered friends, and he was early placed by the English in the role of chief negotiator for the other eastern Long Island Indians.

Previous to contact, the Montauks had been paying wampum tribute to the stronger and more aggressive Pequots across the Sound. After the Pequots' defeat in 1637 Wyandanch petitioned the English through his friend Lion Gardiner and offered to pay wampum to them for protection and trade rights, like the Montauks' previous agreement with the Pequots. In 1644 the four sachems from eastern Long Island requested and received certificates from the English acknowledging them to be tributaries of the English. While this might have been thought to be an astute political move by Wyandanch—a new allegiance for protection and trade with the dominant power—subsequent developments proved otherwise. The Montauks were not completely protected from assaults by other Indian groups and the English were slow to come to their aid. Wyandanch often found himself in conflict with the Narragansetts of New England and he was now forced to pay tribute to them as well as the English. With his prosperity diminished by these obligations, Wyandanch began to sell Montauk and other Indian land on Long Island to his land-hungry English friends, particularly Lion Gardiner. Gardiner had especially attached himself to Wyandanch through his efforts to ransom the sachem's daughter from the Narragansetts, who had held her captive for a number of years, and Wyandanch showed his appreciation to Gardiner with gifts of land. Gardiner, in turn, sold large parcels to other early settlers, such as Richard Smythe and John Cooper, and it can be questioned whether Gardiner used his influence over Wyandanch to obtain Indian land for others.

Wyandanch was eventually to sell or give away lands occupied by the Shinnecocks, Corchaugs, and Montauks, including areas of present-day Smithown, Huntington, Hempstead, and North Hempstead, as well as much of Montauk. While Wyandanch's authority to dispose of land and wampum for other groups was apparently not questioned in his own lifetime, after his death in 1659 (some claim he was poisoned), many disputes arose over his right to have dealt for other groups and countless lawsuits ensued.

*By this deed dated East Hampton, July 14, 1659, Wyandanch conveyed as a gift to Lion Gardiner a tract of land in what is now Smithtown. Wyandanch's mark can be seen at bottom right, along with that of his son and his wife, known as "the Sunck Squa." Courtesy, The Long Island Historical Society*

Carol A. Traynor

*his hand . . . So they began to pow-wow, as they called it . . . the sick man sitting up as well as he could, and having a dish or calabash of water . . . he supped a little of it . . . spirted it with his mouth into his hands, and threw it over his head and naked body . . . and beating himself with his arms and clapping his hands till he was all of a foam with sweat and did speak something in his own tongue very loud; and as he spoke they all spoke very loud, as with one voice, and knocked on the ground with their truncheons, so that it made the very woods ring and the ground shake . . .*

Powwows were banned by town governments, a political act intended to erode the power of the *pow-awa*, the keeper of traditional beliefs.

The Indians also had an effective healing system based on herbs. Indeed, "green medicine" was the only kind known throughout human history until Pasteur proposed the germ theory in the late 1800s. Van der Donck observed of the Indians in the 1640s that "they can heal fresh wounds and dangerous bruises in a most wonderful manner. They also have remedies for old sores and ulcers . . . and venereal affections . . . All their cures are from herbs, roots, and leaves . . ." This aspect of native life received universal admiration from Europeans otherwise critical of this strange, new world and people. The efficacy of the Indian healing methods, including sweat baths, fasting, light-weight rawhide casts for broken limbs, and herbal medicines, was superior to that of the European intruders. Over 75 percent of the U.S. Pharmacopoeia today is still based on these empirically-tested herbal remedies.

Minerals, too, held a special place in the native culture. Paint pots (concretions of red ochre), plus remains of yellow limonite and black graphite found at archaeological excavations, indicate their use for body painting and pictographs. Face and body painting were done daily for both pleasure and for certain ritual occasions, such as war and death.

Historical accounts of mourning practices tell of much lamenting, many visits to the gravesite, and of the family painting their faces black for a year. Ten-day burial feasts cemented ancestral ties and social relations. According to some observers, the dead were buried "sitting up" in a flexed position with the knees under the chin. Christian influence after Contact changed the position to the European

style of lying prone. On western Long Island, a small structure of mat-covered saplings was erected around the grave, which was kept free of grass during yearly or more frequent visits. In Montauk territory, mounds of stones marked Historic period graves.

Effigy representations of faces and eyes have been found on rocks and shells. The ritual and religious importance of these objects was noted by Azariah Horton, a traveling Presbyterian missionary to the natives, who wrote in 1741:

*This day conversed with a Squaw [Shinnecock], who had the possession of two wooden Gods, but could by no means persuade her to part with them. She said, being askt, that she did not worship them, but kept them, because her father gave them to her.*

David Gardiner observed of the Montauk that "they had small idols or images and a regular priesthood . . . by whom these idols were consulted." The same effigy faces have been found on some Long Island pots as well. Commemorating their winter Twelve Nights ceremony, Delaware Indians carved similar facial images on the drumsticks and houseposts of the lodge.

Though Indians have generally been thought preliterate, pictographs on Long Island stones give testimony to a complex communication system. Historic records state that men kept visual accounts of their exploits on planks in their wigwams. A wooden slab in the village center documented the group's history and genealogy. In addition, hunting parties left messages along the trail as to their size, destination, and the prey sought. None of these artifacts survived, but early records have preserved this aspect of the area's prehistoric life.

As part of the large body of Indians who lived from Canada to Virginia, Long Island natives spoke variants of the Algonkian language family. If Thomas Jefferson and James Madison had not visited William Floyd in 1791 and documented Poosepatuck words, and if John Lion Gardiner had not recorded a Montauk vocabulary list in 1798, we would not know that Long Island Indians communicated in several closely-related languages. Those of western Long Island spoke the Munsee form of Delaware, as did their neighbors on Manhattan, Staten Island, and New Jersey. These Long Islanders were dispersed

*While early missionary efforts were sporadic and largely unsuccessful, by the eighteenth and nineteenth centuries a large number of native Americans had been converted to Christianity. Courtesy, East Hampton Free Library*

by colonists before any language was recorded, but it can be recreated from New Jersey linguistic materials. The word lists of the East End Montauk and Shinnecock indicate they spoke a version of Mohegan-Pequot, and the Poosepatuck (Unkechaug), a variant of Naugatuck-Quiripi. It is not known if the Matinecock and other mid-Island peoples used an Unkechaug or Delaware language, but Long Island Indians generally spoke the language of the group directly across the Sound from them. The Sound proved to be a conduit, rather than a barrier, and facilitated linguistic and social interaction.

In addition to cultural remains, the legends and myths of Long Island's natives have survived, often through the recorded history of neighboring Indians. When asked from where his people came, a New Jersey Indian visiting the Flemish Labadist missionary, Jasper Danckaerts, in 1679

*took a piece of coal . . . and began to write upon the floor. He first drew a circle, a little oval, to which he made four paws or feet, a head and a tail. This . . . is a tortoise, lying in the water around it . . . This was or is all water, and so at first was the world or earth, when the tortoise gradually raised its round back up high, and the water ran off of it, and thus the earth became dry . . . and there grew a tree in the middle of the earth, and the root of this tree sent forth a sprout beside it and there grew upon it*

*a man, who was the first male. This man was then alone, and would have remained alone; but the tree bent over until its top touched the earth, and there shot therein another root, from which came forth another sprout, and there grew upon it the woman, and from these two are all men produced.*

This is the origin myth known by Long Island Indians. All peoples have their own version, just as ours is the story of Adam and Eve.

Life for Long Island Indians was not one unbroken round of struggle for subsistence. Contemporary gathering and hunting groups around the world, for example, spend about twenty hours a week securing food. The longer "workweek" began with an increasing focus on horticulture. Extended family groups on Long Island lived near rivers and estuaries where a wealth of food resources existed throughout the year; they also sought what they needed from various spots as the season permitted. Additional time was spent gathering plants for baskets, clay for pottery, grasses for mats, wood for certain implements, and stone for tools. Toolmaking itself took a great deal of time. The fish trapping season ran from March to May; vegetal foods, as well as berries, tubers, and groundnuts, were collected in spring and summer. Crabs, fish, and shellfish were gathered, smoked, and dried in the summer for winter use. Historic records note that area In-

*Left: Because preservation of objects made from materials other than stone or bone is particularly poor on Long Island, the full picture of our prehistoric predecessors' lifestyles is distorted. Leatherworking, textile and clothing manufacturing, basketry, and woodworking frequently produced objects such as these circa 1900 Shinnecock baskets that could be both functional and beautiful. Photo by Kay C. Lenskjold. Courtesy, American Museum of Natural History*

*Opposite page: The development of fired clay pots around 1000 B.C. was an important technological innovation. This pot was made during the Woodland period, A.D. 1200 to 1500. Photo by Harvey Weber. Courtesy, Suffolk County Historical Society*

dians planted corn, beans, squash, gourds, melons, pumpkins, and tobacco in spring and harvested them in summer and autumn. Nuts were collected and stored in the fall. Hunting drives for deer occurred during the autumn, and small game trapping took place throughout the year. The colder seasons also lent themselves to the pursuit of wild fowl, and seals and whales could be harvested in winter. Although there is uncertainty as to the extent of maize horticulture in pre-Contact Long Island, all historic accounts discuss the fields of "Turkish wheat" or "Indian corn"—its amount, storage, and purchase by the traders and colonists. Later, when they became dependent on the European economy, the Indians purchased corn from the settlers. Early records also tell of "Old Fields" in some of the major habitation areas. Planted in "mounds" with bean and squash vines climbing the cornstalks, these Indian gardens were cleared by burning the forests. Settlers invariably saved time and energy by claiming as theirs these already cultivated plots. The hamlet of Old Field, above Stony Brook, is a

reminder of this practice.

Play, sports, and celebrations broke up the seasonal round of work. Children's games, too, fostered practical adult skills such as shooting, weaving, or making pots. Denton (1670) states that the Indians' favorite recreational activities were football and cards. Gaming balls and markers from Mt. Sinai and Nissequogue suggest a form of bowling and "board" games, and a stone puzzle from Montauk sharpened problem-solving skills. Early accounts also refer to seasonal gatherings where matchmaking occurred. At the time of the Winter Solstice, for example, the people held *canticas* or dancing celebrations. Wassenaer found in the 1620s that

*the first full moon following that at the end of February is greatly honored by them. They watch it with great devotion, and as it rises, they compliment it with a festival; they collect together from all quarters, and revel in their way, with wild game or fish, and drink clear river water to their fill,*

25

# STEPHEN PHAROAH

Stephen Pharoah, a Montauk Indian who was born in 1819 and died in 1879, participated in adapting the Long Island Indians' economic, social, and technological cultures to life in the nineteenth century, and he is certainly one of the most interesting of these native participants. Also known as Steve Talkhouse, Pharoah became a legend in his own time, as well as today, because of his combinations of abilities and strength of character. He had various careers as a whaler, hunter, circus performer, and champion cross-country walker, and was a veteran of the Civil War, serving in the 29th Connecticut Volunteers. This multifaceted figure captured the imagination of the period and stories of his exploits have been passed on to later generations.

Stephen Pharoah lived during an era when life for native Americans was not particularly easy or pleasant. Decimated in numbers by contact with European diseases and the forced migration of many of their groups to other areas, exploited of most of their land through confusing and misunderstood land use rights, and with their former culture and livelihood greatly eroded, the Indians who remained on eastern Long Island survived by adapting their skills to a new lifestyle. These Indians became an integral part of their community and worked in many of the industries of the period, including whaling,

*In addition to his other abilities, Stephen Pharoah was a legendary long-distance walker who won a number of competitions across the country. This portrait was taken circa 1875. Courtesy, Smithsonian Institution*

craft production, and farming, functioning as agricultural laborers and as noted guides and hunters. As such they contributed to the economic development of the east end of Long Island during the nineteenth century.

Stephen Pharoah was born into this changing environment. He was a descendant of the Montauks (or Meantacuts), one of the Indian groups of the Algonkian culture inhabiting Long Island. Stephen himself was highly regarded in the East Hampton area and the name of Pharoah had a long and important place in Montauk history. Claimed to be descendants of the seventeenth-century sachem of the Montauks, Wyandanch, Pharoahs appear in early documents and town records as active participants in Indian land use disputes involving their property in Montauk. Erroneously called the "King of the Montauks," Stephen's family was considered to be titular leader of that group. Stephen's father, Sylvester, who died in 1870, had reigned as tribal leader, as had other members of his family, and Stephen assumed the role for one year in 1878.

During Stephen's childhood, there is evidence that he was bound out as a farmhand to a Colonel William Parsons. The settlers early encouraged Indians to become indentured servants because of the severe shortage of manpower. As a young man, Stephen, like other Montauk Indians, roamed the Montauk Peninsula hunting ducks and geese to sell to nearby communities. Many of the local Indians were valued for their traditional skills as hunters and fishermen and were employed as guides by wealthy sportsmen who frequented such early resorts as the Southside Sportsmen's Club in Oakdale. Stephen was also known to have participated in the whaling industry for a time, and his son was to follow him in this field. Skilled Indian fishermen were much in demand by whalers as early as the seventeenth century and it is believed that the Indians were the first to teach the settlers the skill of shore whaling. Stephen also worked for wages on nearby farms. Forced off much of their own land due to expansion of the white population, and needing money to purchase the goods and necessities they were now dependent upon, many Indians became wage laborers. Stephen Pharoah was highly regarded as an able and dependable worker by the farmers of his community. He was known to have walked from Montauk to East Hampton, which is quite a distance on foot, perform a full day's work as a farmhand, and walk home again.

In fact, Stephen's walking prowess was legendary in East Hampton and helped to bring him the attention of a larger public than his immediate community. He was a great cross-country walker and was known to walk twenty-five miles to mail a letter, for which he charged twenty-five cents. The year before his death he walked from Brooklyn to Montauk in one day, a distance of over 100 miles. One local story has him refusing a lift in a horse and carriage because he said he was in a hurry to get to town. He participated in several walking races and won one particular race from Boston to Chicago against fifty others. It was through these athletic exploits that P.T. Barnum heard of him, and Stephen was persuaded to join his circus for a time billed as "King of the Montauks."

Stephen died in 1879 and was buried in Indian Field Cemetery in Montauk. A stone monument marks his birthplace and his grave in Montauk contains the only headstone in this traditional Indian cemetery, evidence of his stature in the community. During the year of his death Montauk was partitioned off and sold to Arthur Benson for development, and in 1885 Montauk was closed to the Meantacuts.

Carol A. Traynor

*without being intoxicated . . . this moon being a harbinger of the spring . . . they celebrate the new August moon by another festival, as their harvest then approaches.*

The prehistoric population of Long Island was probably denser than that of the surrounding region. One scholar believes it to have been around 3,000 people, though other sources set the figure at 6,000 or more. Verrazano noted how populous the area was by the many fires seen along the coast at night. Recurring epidemics which spread across the Northeast around the time of Verrazano's contact, however, rapidly reduced Long Island Indians to less than one-tenth their former number. An estimated 500 survived by 1658. Azariah Horton listed 400 Long Island native Americans in the 1740s, but a 1785 census counted 765, possibly including those who "married in." Some local Indians were made slaves; still more became indentured servants until reaching twenty-one years of age. Daniel Tredwell's early nineteenth-century diary mentions intermarriage between Indian men and local south shore women.

Besides intermarriage with the Europeans, the Indians left other imprints on American culture. The notable surveyor and mediator Cockenoe-de-Long

Island also served as the first Indian teacher and translator of Mohegan-Pequot for John Eliot, who later produced America's first Bible. This was written in Narragansett so that the New England tribes could understand it. The Shinnecock, too, presumably helped the Reverend John Pierson prepare his *Some Helps for the Indian,* a Quiripi-language book, just as the Montauk aided the Reverend Thomas James with his *Catechism.*

Samson Occum, the Mohegan-Pequot who married Mary Fowler of Montauk, became that group's teacher and minister. One of the most notable clerics in America and the outstanding Indian preacher of his time, he even traveled to England, raising funds for Dartmouth, the college for Indians he helped to found. The eloquence of the Reverend Paul Cuffee, a Shinnecock who served after Occum and ministered to a Congregational chapel in the Shinnecock Hills during the late 1700s, also was noted by Harriet Beecher Stowe in *Uncle Tom's Cabin.*

In spite of many contributions and the value of their labor, Indians were continually pushed onto smaller plots of land. Since East Hampton Town deported all Montauk who did not marry within the group—a decree which meant limited survival on Long Island—Occum ultimately led many Montauk and some Shinnecock to Brothertown in Oneida Territory in the 1780s. White settlement of the Western New York frontier forced their final migration to Wisconsin.

Early European traders would have perished in New Netherlands without the assistance of local Indians. Generously sharing their food, shelter, and knowledge of local subsistence techniques, the natives added tobacco, as well as the cereal staple, corn, to the European diet. Many Indian words, such as *succotash, squaw,* and *moccasin* have en-

tered our language. And Long Island place names are rich with the aboriginal presence: Peconic, Manhasset, Patchogue, Hauppauge, Rockaway, Connetquot, Merrick, and others reflect the native heritage.

Although the European settlers took their land, Long Island Indians survived because of their flexibility and traditional skills. The eastern end of Shinnecock territory was "bought" by the Southampton Proprietors in 1640; partial use of the western section was restored in 1703, only after Indian protest. As the Long Island Rail Road inched across the land in the 1840s, the Shinnecock were "given" their current 800-acre peninsula reservation in 1859 in exchange for the 3,000-acre Shinnecock Hills tract wanted for the train line. Indians helped to build the tracks across their land, but local land developers became wealthy through the property sales.

The Shinnecock long had harvested the sea; they showed the settlers how to catch whales along the shore and became early members of Colonial whaling crews. This specialty continued throughout the nineteenth century, with an Indian, often a Shinnecock, the harpooner; many served as mates and "exact sailors." A few became captains.

Indian traditional expertise in hunting made them sought-after guides for the late nineteenth-century gunning trade. Charles S. Bunn, a Shinnecock, produced decoys and led members of the Roosevelt, Herter, and Du Pont families on expeditions. Ancient woodworking talents continued with basketmaking and the production of "scrubs," the first scouring brushes in America. The Shinnecock became the original "Fuller Brush" men by selling

their wares from a wagon traveling the length of Long Island.

When the Shinnecock Fire Island inlet closed and fishing and clamming declined, the Indians worked on local farms, and served as plumbers, mechanics, musicians, caddies, and greenskeepers. The women industriously tended gardens and provided the extra hands that enabled Southampton society to lead an elegant lifestyle.

Long Island Indians today are concentrated in state-recognized reservations at Mastic, where about 100 Unkechaug reside at the Poosepatuck reservation, and Southampton, which roughly 350 Shinnecock call home. Descendants of the Montauk dwell in Sag Harbor and East Hampton; more live in Wisconsin, the last stop of the late eighteenth-century exodus led by Samson Occum. Descendants of the Matinecock still live in Nassau County. Other Long Island Indians are scattered throughout the Island, Manhattan, and various parts of the United States.

Shinnecock and Poosepatuck are presently maraculture specialists, clerks, doctors, factory workers, lawyers, teachers, mechanics, students, administrators, craftsmen, housewives, laborers. They have survived by a combination of exogamy (marriage out of the group) and endogamy (marrying within). Today most Shinnecock are multiply related to each other, descendants of their historic four bands through thirteen or more generations. Their family ties remain deep and supportive; their determination to keep their lands is firm (the last challenge was made only twenty odd years ago); and their quest to recover and nourish their ancient traditions, strong.

# New World, New Amsterdam, New York

Long Island's earliest European visitors came searching for gold, furs, and trade routes to the Orient. Italian Giovanni Verrazano first arrived in 1524 while sailing for the king of France. Nearly a century later, in 1609, Englishman Henry Hudson guided his small ship *Half Moon* through the New York narrows and commenced serious exploration. He was soon followed by Holland's Adrian Block and Hendrick Christiaensen, who initiated a series of trading voyages. On one trip in 1613 Block's vessel burned while anchored in New York harbor. Undaunted, he and his crew built the tiny shallop *Restless* and the next year journeyed up the East River, through Hell's Gate, and then eastward down the length of the Sound. They then discovered that Long Island was indeed an island and not part of the mainland. Block later called the fish-shaped landmass "T Lange Eilandt"; the name has stuck ever since.

Explorers and colonial officials described the area in glowing terms. One labeled Long Island "the crown of the province by reason of its . . . excellent harbors and bays, as well as convenient and fertile lands . . . it is the levelest and finest soil." Another observed, "Oyster Bay . . . has on its borders fine maize lands . . . the land is situated on such a beautiful bay and rivers that it could . . . be converted into good farms fit for the plough."

In 1621 the commerce-minded Netherlands government chartered the Dutch West India Company to oversee New World settlement, and three years later these merchant adventurers established a small outpost of Walloon refugees at the tip of Manhattan island. Their tiny colony of New Amsterdam grew slowly at first. More intrigued with ventures in Brazil, Guiana, and the Caribbean, the

New Amsterdam, originally a
fur trading center, already
had assumed an air of bustle
and prosperity by the time
Peter Minuit became director
general in 1626. This 1670

view shows the earthen fort
which housed the church, the
governor's residence, and the
prison. From Singleton, Dutch
New York, 1909

*Explorers such as Henry Hudson and Adrian Block sparked Europeans' interest in the New World and its commercial possibilities. Many seventeenth-century books described the land's beauty and fruitfulness. This map appeared in* Description of New Netherland *by Adriaen Van der Donck, printed in 1665.*

*This first map of Long Island, made circa 1616 by Dutch explorer Adrian Block, denotes the names and locations of the area's Indian groups. Block presented the map to the states-general upon his return to Holland, and was one of the first to extol the commercial possibilities of the New World. From Flint,* Early Long Island, *1896*

West India Company viewed Manhattan as a fur trading depot, not the seat of a flourishing colony. Luring Dutch settlers to a new and hostile continent also proved difficult. Hollanders at home enjoyed a stable, republican government, religious toleration, and a thriving economy. Well into the 1630s New Amsterdam remained confined to the tip of Manhattan and a few homesteads scattered along the Jersey and Brooklyn shores.

Alarmed at the slow pace of development and the growing menace of neighboring New England, Dutch authorities in the mid-1630s inaugurated a more vigorous settlement program. Officials pur-chased lands in Brooklyn adjoining Gowanus Cove and Wallabout Bay. Resident Director Wouter Van Twiller and several of his counselors also obtained 15,000 acres in Flatlands from the Canarsie Indians, but home authorities later voided the agreement. Twiller was soon recalled and replaced in 1638 by William Kieft who brought instructions to hasten land acquisition and increase the rate of settlement. As part of his program, the new resident director invited disaffected Englishmen to settle within Dutch territory, providing they would swear allegiance to Holland.

Before the fledgling policies exerted any beneficial impact, however, Indian warfare erupted. In 1643 nervous Dutch militiamen attacked and massacred two bands of friendly Indians camped in Manhattan and New Jersey. This outrage sparked widespread fighting, and many isolated homesteads were ravaged. Over 1,200 Indians and settlers died before calm returned in 1645.

With the resumption of peace, settlement of western Long Island began in earnest. Attempting to impose social order on scattered farmsteads, promote education and religion, and provide for defense, Dutch authorities encouraged the formation of organized townships. Lands across the East River were granted in 1645 to Jan Bout, Huyck Rossun, and Gerritt van Couwenhoven. By December the tiny village of Breukelen, named after a town in Holland, existed. Two years later local farmers began holding market fairs. The community soon maintained a separate church, and the first schoolmaster arrived shortly thereafter. Perhaps eighty adult men lived in Breukelen (Brooklyn) by 1664.

Brooklyn was the first settlement, but efforts to populate the Island gained momentum. Flatlands, farmed sporadically since the 1630s, received a town patent in 1647. Four years later Peter Stuyvesant, the aggressive governor of New Amsterdam, approved a land grant for the region south of Prospect Heights. Colonists called this broad, wooded plain "T Vlacke Bosch" (flat forest), and Flatbush was born. A church was organized in 1654 and a school opened four years later.

New Utrecht became the next Dutch village to spring from the Long Island countryside. In the early 1640s Director William Kieft secured Indian lands stretching from Coney Island to Gowanus Bay. A decade later Cornelius van Werkhoven repurchased that portion abutting Fort Hamilton and the Narrows for a payment of shoes, stockings, shirts, combs, knives, scissors, and adzes. He immediately began developing his site. Though van Werkhoven soon died while on a visit to Holland, his American agent, Jacques Cortelyou, petitioned

New Amsterdam officials to divide the land into small farms. Twenty-one patents were quickly awarded and a town grant proffered in 1660.

Bushwyck, last of the five Dutch towns, was first patented in 1638, but not settled for another twenty-three years. Peter Stuyvesant then took pity on a small group of Huguenot families fleeing French persecution and approved a town charter for them. Twenty-five houses were quickly built; several Dutch farmers joined the settlement. About fifty families resided there in 1664.

While the Dutch and a scattering of French Calvinists populated present-day Brooklyn, other pioneers migrated to western Long Island, too. Among them were dissatisfied Englishmen from Massachusetts and Connecticut who had been alienated by the puritan theocracy.

North and west of Brooklyn lay unoccupied territory in present-day Queens and Nassau counties. Early in the 1640s New Amsterdam officials began

*Above: The Dutch Reformed congregation at New Utrecht, formed in 1677 with twenty-seven charter members, erected this church in 1700. Courtesy, The Long Island Historical Society*

*Left: Dutch houses on Long Island, such as this Flatbush residence, were usually built of wood with a low-pitched gambrel roof. Early Dutch rural farmhouses had no exact prototype in the Old World, but were developed to meet the colonies' different climate and material resources. Courtesy, George B. Brainerd Photograph Collection, Brooklyn Public Library*

# LADY DEBORAH MOODY

While no longer referred to by its seventeenth-century name, Gravesend's claim to fame for most people is that it contained within its boundaries Coney Island, the most popular seaside resort of the country at the beginning of the twentieth century. However, its history is also closely tied to that of a remarkable woman. Lady Deborah Moody, seventeenth-century civic and religious leader and the only woman patentee in the new colony, was a unique figure in the drama of early colonial history and can be considered Brooklyn's first city planner. Women's participation in the early economy and social life of the colony was crucial, serving as wives, mothers, homemakers, and often as farmhands working alongside their husbands, but few have managed to appear in the colonial records. During a time when women's traditional sphere was the small but important one of home and hearth, Lady Deborah Moody was among the handful of women who participated in a wider circle.

Born at Avedon in Wiltshire County, England, Deborah Dunch married Sir Henry Moody of Garesdon in Wiltshire circa 1605. Both her father and husband were members of Parliament and her own family had a long tradition of devotion to civil liberty. Lady Deborah was an outspoken critic of religious intolerance and early showed great independence of

*Before settling in Gravesend, Lady Deborah Moody and her group stayed for protection outside the fort at New Amsterdam. The fort was growing from a crude outpost into a bustling commercial center. Photo by Charles H. Coles. Courtesy, American Museum of Natural History*

mind combined with a strong determination. After her husband's death circa 1629 she decided to leave England rather than pay taxes for the support of the established church. Along with others seeking religious and political freedom, she sailed for Massachusetts in 1639 accompanied by her son Henry, and a number of families from her estate in England. First settling in Lynn, she subsequently purchased a large farm called Swampscott on the Essex County coast and settled

there in 1641. However, religious differences were again to determine the course of her life. Attracted to Anabaptism, she was admonished by the Church of Salem in 1643 for her unorthodox views, one of which was her refusal to accept the doctrine of infant baptism. Deciding to resettle in New Netherland with a group of friends and sympathizers who found in her a leader and spokesperson, she and her followers requested and were granted a patent from Governor Kieft to establish the first English settlement in Brooklyn. Gravesend, on the southwest corner of Long Island, became the first colonial enterprise to be headed by a woman.

Surrounded by the Dutch settlements at Flatlands, New Utrecht, Flatbush, and Bushwick, and under Dutch law and governorship, Gravesend was a small English island in a Dutch sea. Dutch was the common language at the time and continued to be long after the Netherlands surrendered their North American possessions to Great Britain in 1664. It is to Lady Moody's credit as an astute and effective leader that she was able to pilot the early settlement of Gravesend through the sometimes strained and uneven English/Dutch relations.

Gravesend did not just "grow" like most other early communities. It was designed according to a coherent plan from its inception as a settlement. Laid out as a sixteen-acre square, it was bisected by two main roads that formed four quadrants. Each of the four squares was divided into equal sections of ten plots, totaling forty, and one section was allotted to each of the initial forty patentees. In the center of each square was a large public yard providing common pasturage for cattle, and eventually space was allotted for a church, a schoolhouse, a town hall, and a burying ground. The village was surrounded by a palisade fence for defense against Indian attacks as well as wild animals. Gravesend Village was laid out using town planning principles that were surprisingly sophisticated for the time, and remnants of this plan are still visible today in the street layout. The farms, or "planter's

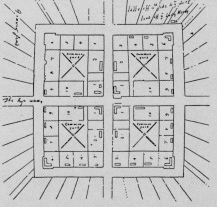

Yᵉ Ancient Plot of yᵉ Towne of s'Gravesende
1645

lots" as they were called, probably consisted of a few acres and were laid out surrounding the village. Lady Deborah Moody was allotted a "bowery" or farm.

Lady Moody took a prominent part in the administration of public affairs. Under her guidance and that of her son and other members of her group, town meetings were instituted and secure titles to the land were obtained from the Indians. The Town Court was established in 1646 and was held at Gravesend for more than forty years before moving to Flatbush. The village grew and prospered and Lady Moody's ability as a town leader won her the respect and friendship of the Dutch governors Kieft and Stuyvesant. In 1654 Governor Stuyvesant appealed to her influence to settle a dispute over his removal of two Gravesend magistrates and finally agreed to let Lady Deborah choose the mag-

*Gravesend was laid out as a sixteen-acre village square consisting of forty house plots surrounded radially by forty farms. From Stiles,* History of Kings County Including the City of Brooklyn, *Munsell, 1884*

istrates for that year, thus avoiding a potential political dispute.

Lady Deborah's interest in and tolerance of new religious ideas was also apparent in the new settlement. Gravesend was to become the site of the first recorded Quaker meeting in America. In 1657 an English vessel landed in New Netherlands containing eleven Quaker preachers, with two eventually coming to preach in Gravesend at her home. While there is no evidence that she became a Quaker herself, Lady Deborah may have been attracted to this new sect because of the place of equality given to women among its members. Although jeopardizing her good relations with the Dutch authorities, Lady Deborah fostered an environment of religious tolerance, open mindedness, and free discussion. Gravesend soon became a center of Quakerism on Long Island.

By the time of her death in 1659, the young colony at Gravesend was firmly established and would go on to prosper and contribute to the development of Brooklyn.

Carol A. Traynor

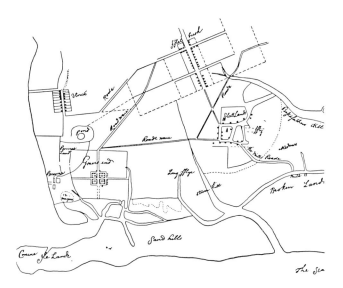

*This 1666 map of Brooklyn locates the original five Dutch towns along with the English settlement of Gravesend. Under British rule in 1665, the towns were incorporated into the West Riding of Yorkshire, renamed Kings County in 1685. From Stiles,* History of Kings County Including the City of Brooklyn, *Munsell, 1884*

populating this area with English immigrants as a barrier to further New England incursions. Among the first residents was Reverend Francis Doughty of Taunton, Massachusetts, who led a flock of dissidents to Maspeth/Newtown. During the Indian warfare which soon engulfed the colony, his settlement was destroyed and the villagers dispersed. Ten years later a second contingent from Greenwich, Stamford, and Fairfield, Connecticut arrived, naming their settlement Middleburgh (later Newtown). They elected town officers in the English manner and often conducted local business in the King's name. Never truly content with Dutch rule, inhabitants reacted to unrest in the 1660s by sending representatives to Connecticut's General Court.

Further east another group of non-conformist Englishmen founded Vlissingen (Flushing) under Dutch auspices in 1645. Earlier they had sought refuge from King Charles I by migrating to Holland, then to New England, and ultimately to New Amsterdam. They soon proved receptive to Quaker missionaries, and many converted. George Fox, the great Quaker leader, visited both Flushing and Gravesend in 1672.

Hempstead became still another substantial settlement on New Amsterdam's eastern frontier. The population traced its origins back to early New England, many having arrived in America with John Winthrop and Sir Richard Saltonstall in 1630. These settlers migrated from Watertown, Massachusetts to Wethersfield, Connecticut. By 1640 the church there had fragmented, and a splinter group moved to Stamford. Several restless souls crossed

Long Island Sound in 1643, purchasing thousands of acres from local Indians. After obtaining a Dutch patent, they returned the following year to erect homes. Nearly seventy freeholders resided in Hempstead by 1647 and a church was established in 1650.

Jamaica, after the Indian name Jameco, was the last (1656) English town established in Dutch territory. Originally called Rusdorp, it began as an offshoot of nearby Hempstead. Jamaica had its own minister by 1662 and a meetinghouse was constructed the following year.

By this time, Holland's Long Island empire extended from the East River to the western borders of Oyster Bay. It included a heterogeneous mix of Dutch farmers, English dissenters, and French and Walloon refugees. Relatively broad religious and ethnic toleration, a keen interest in material possessions, and a thriving commercial spirit characterized the region. Jumbled together in a colonial stew were the customs and traditions of rural Holland, bourgeois Amsterdam, the English countryside, and London.

While Dutchmen and their British guests occupied today's Kings and Queens counties, other colonists from New England arrived in eastern Long Island, about 100 miles away. Central to the settlement process was Sir William Alexander, the Scottish Earl of Sterling and a close friend of King Charles. Through his royal patron's influence, Sterling secured a 1636 Plymouth Company patent for all of Long Island and the adjacent territories. Such a patent naturally conflicted with Dutch claims in the region.

Active English colonization efforts commenced in 1637 when Sterling appointed James Farrett as his American agent. The industrious Mr. Farrett quickly began populating Lord Sterling's domain. Lion Gardiner of Connecticut received his famous property in 1639, and Farrett sold Shelter Island to Stephen Goodyear, a New Haven merchant, iron master, and government leader in the same year. Men from Lynn, Massachusetts then purchased lands near Matinecock (Oyster Bay), but the Dutch chased them away. Undaunted, the travel-weary immigrants next obtained property from Southampton's Shinnecock Indians in December 1640. Their first town meeting assembled in April of the following year. Several other Lynn families soon arrived, agreeing to hold power, distribute land, and admit inhabitants, with such rights remaining " . . . at all times in the hands of us . . . and our heirs forever." Boston minister Abraham Pierson and his previously-established church followers exercised considerable influence over the early community. Within twelve months about fifty adult males had moved in and secured Indian lands in exchange for annual payments of corn. English promises to protect the local tribes against Rhode Island's Narragansetts were also part of the bargain.

Settlement at Southold across Peconic Bay preceded even the Southampton migration. Many pioneer residents were natives of Hingham, England and reached Long Island with their leader, the Reverend John Youngs, by way of New Haven. The Connecticut town's officials aided further immigration efforts, helped negotiate the original 1640 purchase, and for some years exercised distant control over the fledgling colony. Such power did not always rest lightly, however. Captain John Youngs, son of the town minister, later appeared before a New Haven court for denouncing the mother colony

as a "tyrannical government." Charged with attempting rebellion, he soon apologized "for his rash and foolish words."

East Hampton, third of the East End villages, was settled in 1648 when a few Lynn residents purchased 30,000 acres for twenty coats, one hundred axes, and twenty-four hatchets, hoes, knives, and mirrors. Local Indians retained the right to hunt and fish. They also received the tails and fins of any whales cast upon the beach. Many original families hailed from Kent, England and they called the village Maidstone after their native hamlet.

As the North and South forks filled, English settlement rapidly shifted westward. In 1655 a group from around Boston settled in present-day Setauket, naming their tiny village Ashford. They obtained a territory of about thirty square miles, running from the Nissequogue River to Mount Misery. Their cost was the usual assortment of coats, hoes,

*Above: The English ancestry of eastern Long Island's early settlers is clearly reflected in this house in Southold built by John Budd of Rye, England, in 1649. The four-room, timber-framed structure perpetuates the domestic designs of English yeomen's homes. Photo by James Van Alst. Courtesy, Society for the Preservation of Long Island Antiquities (SPLIA)*

*Left: New England's influence on eastern Long Island is discernible in the design and decorative detail of this chest made circa 1650-1700 in Suffolk County. (SPLIA)*

# LION GARDINER

Of all the dreamers and adventurers who settled colonial Long Island, few could match the energy, talents, and accomplishments of Lion Gardiner. Though trained as a soldier, he emerged as a statesman, helping establish the English presence on eastern Long Island while championing amicable relations with the native inhabitants. Along the way he also found time to create a town or two, purchase an island fiefdom, and author a book describing it all.

Gardiner was born in Scotland in 1599, but trained as a soldier and engineer with the Prince of Orange. Gardiner later recalled that both he and Captain John Underhill "had been bred soldiers from their youth." For a time more Dutch than English, he married Mary Willemsan of Waredon, Holland. Later Gardiner served under the English general Fairfax and came to the attention of Lords Say and Brook, who were attempting to establish a colony at the mouth of the Connecticut River. As a result, Gardiner journeyed to America in 1635 to build a fort to protect traders and colonists along the river. The fort was deemed necessary because the region coveted by the English was the traditional realm of the powerful and warlike Pequot tribe.

More a diplomat than a warlord, Gardiner counseled moderation and advised against fighting the Indians. He later wrote that his

*Lion Gardiner, soldier, engineer, and statesman, founded the first English settlement in New York State when he acquired Gardiner's Island in 1639. Courtesy, East Hampton Star*

duties included "only the drawing, ordering, and making of a city, town, or forts of defense." Fighting erupted nonetheless and Gardiner was soon caught up in it. He and his men endured a perilous winter seige by the aroused natives. Gar-

diner later recounted his harrowing experiences in his *Relation of the Pequot Warres.* The following spring, Captain John Mason from Hartford and Captain John Underhill from Massachusetts Bay destroyed the Pequots' power, ending the danger.

While at Saybrook fort, Gardiner had exercised his diplomatic talents by securing the release of two women held captive by the Indians. He also met an important Montauk chieftain named Wyandanch. Impressed with the young soldier who counseled peace, Wyandanch sold Gardiner a large island between the north and south forks of Long Island. The price, according to legend, was one large black dog, a gun, powder and shot, some rum, and a few blankets. The natives called the island Manchonake, land of the dead. Gardiner renamed it the Isle of Wight.

To secure his title, Gardiner also purchased the land from James Farrett, an agent of Lord Sterling who held a patent for the entire region from his patron, King Charles I. From Farrett, Gardiner secured permission to create a separate and independent plantation, with powers to control church and civil government. He moved to the island in 1639 with his family and several laborers from the Saybrook garrison.

Gardiner was an energetic and ambitious man, and not content with his island kingdom alone. He continued to amass property and within a few years became one of East Hampton's founding proprietors. By 1653 he had moved to East Hampton with his wife and daughter, leaving his son David and additional laborers on the island.

Throughout his life Lion Gardiner exercised impressive talents as mediator and peacemaker. On one important occasion he secured the return of Wyandanch's daughter who had been seized by marauding Narragansetts. In gratitude the Montauk sachem granted Gardiner an immense tract of land in central Long Island which he later conveyed to Richard "Bull" Smythe, forming the basis of present-day Smithtown. So favorably was Gardiner regarded by the Indians that they referred to him in one deed as "the most honorable of the English nation here about us."

Gardiner died in 1663, esteemed by his neighbors. He had founded a family dynasty that was destined to play a crucial role in local affairs for generations to come. Gardiner had lived a full life, according to his own lights, and he once confessed that if his comments and actions were occasionally rough-hewn and blunt, it was because he simply could not abide the smoothing plane.

Geoffrey L. Rossano

hatchets, awls, needles, lead, and powder. Nearby Old Field was purchased between 1655 and 1659, and Stony Brook was first inhabited around 1660. Eight families relocated to Wading River ten years later. More southerly Islip, however, was not settled until two or three decades after that.

Neighboring Smithtown was, for most of the seventeenth century, the enormous private preserve of Richard "Bull" Smythe and his family. West of Smithtown and directly across the Sound from Norwalk and Stamford, Connecticut stood Huntington. Its land had been acquired over a decade or more. Governor Theophilus Eaton of New Haven purchased Eaton's Neck in 1646, and seven years later negotiators obtained title to the original town center. Lloyd's Neck (1654), Northport (1656), and Babylon (1657-1659) were soon added.

Oyster Bay, westernmost of the English towns, stood as a sort of no-man's land between Dutch and New England jurisdictions. A 1639 grant from Lord Sterling to Boston seaman Mathew Sunderland was later repudiated. In the late 1640s Robert Williams of Hempstead secured a large tract in present-day Hicksville. Though a formal boundary line between New Amsterdam and New England was established in 1650, a border dispute persisted until 1664. Actual settlement in Oyster Bay began in 1653 with the arrival of families from Hempstead and Sandwich, Massachusetts. Later purchases rounded out the township: Caumsett in 1654, Matinecock in 1658, Musketa (Glen) Cove in 1668, and Glen Head-Jericho in 1685.

The men who founded these English towns were often footloose dreamers and adventurers. A few, like Oyster Bay's Captain John Underhill, were soldiers of fortune, while others, such as East Hampton's Thomas Chatfield, sprang from the minor nobility or gentry. Most, however, were yeoman and artisans, seeking religious freedom, agricultural prosperity, and local autonomy in the face of Tudor/Stuart centralization at home. Having severed ties with families, friends, and communities, and crossed a stormy ocean, they found it very difficult to reestablish roots in the New World.

Typical of these wanderers was the Reverend William Leveredge. A 1625 graduate of Cambridge, he ministered in Dover, New Hampshire; Boston, Duxbury, and Sandwich, Massachusetts; and Oyster Bay, Huntington, and Newtown, Long Island. Joseph Rogers of Huntington lived successively at Plymouth, Duxbury, Wethersfield and Southampton prior to establishing permanent residency. Thurston Raynor first passed through Watertown (1639), Wethersfield (1640), New Haven (1641), Stamford (1642), and Hempstead (1643) before finally settling in Southampton.

With the exception of Brooklyn's small, quiet communities of Dutch farmers, most early Long Islanders arrived from New England, bringing an intense religious preoccupation with them. A few hoped to find freedom of conscience and practice, while others sought to recreate the tiny puritan republics which defined Massachusetts and Connecticut society. Several communities, Hempstead, Southold, Southampton, and Flushing among them, began life as outposts for specific congregations. Protestant divines like John Youngs of Southold, Abraham Pierson of Southampton, Robert Fordham of Hempstead, Thomas Doughty of Newtown, and William Leveredge of Oyster Bay and Huntington were principal actors in this pioneer drama. For these inhabitants, God was a palpable presence, acknowledged in public worship and incorporated into the fabric of daily life.

Settlers were quite explicit about their intentions. Early on, Hempstead's freeholders noted,

*For as much as contempt of God's word and the sabbath is the desolating sin of civil states . . . it is therefore ordered and decreed . . . that all persons inhabiting this town or the limits thereof should duly resort and repair to public meeting's on the Lord's day . . . both on the forenoons and afternoons.*

East Hampton villagers agreed in 1653 to "maintain and preserve the purity of the gospel . . . and also the discipline of the church." Lofty sentiments often translated into action. Town meetings selected the minister and granted him lands, while local taxes paid his salary, built his home, and erected the meetinghouse. In some villages only church members participated in civil affairs. Attendance at religious services was compulsory and violations of the sabbath were punishable crimes. In 1682 Huntington's Robert Kellam received a twenty-shilling fine for carrying bags of meal on Sunday.

Given the colonists' dissenting background, the

*The first Quaker meeting house on Long Island was built in Oyster Bay in 1672; others soon sprang up in Locust Valley, Flushing, and Manhasset. The Manhasset Society of Friends, as the Manhasset Quakers preferred to be called, was founded in 1702 by Thomas Story and William Mott, and this meeting house was erected in 1812. Courtesy, Clarence Purchase Photograph Collection, SPLIA*

Church of England aroused deep suspicion and attracted few adherents. Setauket permitted Anglicans to settle but forbade them public worship. When the New York Assembly in 1693 enacted a tax to support Anglican ministers at Jamaica and Hempstead, Oyster Bay voters responded: "This town met together in order to consider a late act of Assembly for settling two ministers in this county, but nothing was done about it, but made return that it was a thing against their judgement . . ."

The same villagers who felt God's presence so strongly, also believed that the devil lurked nearby. While no witchcraft hysteria wracked the Island, several incidents betrayed the colonists' fears. Accused of witchcraft in 1657, East Hampton's Goody Garlick was ordered to Hartford for trial. Ralph Hall and his wife were seized in Setauket to be examined by a New York court. Similarly, officials arrested Mary Wright of Oyster Bay and sent her to Boston. Though acquitted of devil worship, she was soon convicted of something equally heinous: Quakerism. For her heresy Wright was banished from the colony.

Holding fast to New England dogma, many Long Islanders opposed those who challenged the established religious order; Quakers seemed the worst offenders. Arriving from Britain in the late 1650s, their missionaries soon held meetings in Gravesend, Flushing, and Oyster Bay. By denying the validity

of puritan church government, infant baptism, oath taking, and public support of religion, the Quakers earned widespread enmity. Peter Stuyvesant, normally tolerant of English Calvinists, actively persecuted them, especially in Flushing and Newtown. Several fled to Oyster Bay.

Transplanted New Englanders further east proved equally hostile. Southold Quaker Humphrey Norton was arrested in 1658 and sent to New Haven to be convicted of blasphemy and heresy. His punishment included a fine, whipping, branding on the hand, and banishment. Hempstead forbade its inhabitants to offer Quakers shelter. When two local women absented themselves from public worship and instead attended a Quaker "conventicle," they were each fined twenty guilders.

Despite continuing harassment, the peaceful Quakers endured, especially in Oyster Bay township. Long Island's first meetinghouse was erected there in 1672 and several influential families converted, including the Wright, Townsend, and Underhill clans. By century's end substantial Quaker communities existed at Westbury, Jericho, Oyster Bay, and Bethpage. They went on to form a permanent, if not always appreciated, element of Long Island society.

Regardless of religion or patriotic allegiance, colonial Long Island was a region of small farms; virtually the entire population depended on the soil

# RICHARD SMYTHE

As founder and patentee of Smith-town, Richard Smythe, or Smith as it is now spelled, played an important part in the history of Long Island. Much about Richard Smythe is legendary. Historians are unsure of his ancestry and especially uncertain how he managed to acquire one of the largest proprietary land grants in the New World. Legend has it that Smythe acquired the land that is today Smithtown after making a "deal" with the local Indians to sell to him as much land as he could ride around in one day.

Aside from legends, however, the first record of Smythe on Long Island is in Southampton, where he lived from 1643 to 1656. He was apparently a man of note in this early community; as one of the town's two assessors, he was on the committee to allocate town lands and was appointed constable in 1650. Yet, in 1656 he was suddenly and mysteriously banished from the community. The town records include a charge of "unreverend carriage to the magistrates contrary to the order," and it has been suggested that Smythe converted to Quakerism—an act which his Puritan neighbors apparently could not tolerate.

Smythe sought refuge in Setauket, where he stayed for nine years. He first appears in the town records of Brookhaven as a freeholder in 1661. How he eventually secured title to the lands that make up Smithtown is an interesting part of

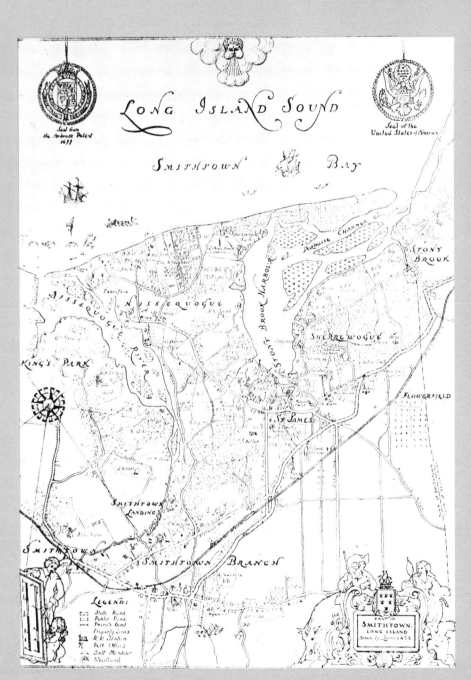

*Richard Smythe acquired extensive lands in 1663, including that around Stony Brook Harbor and the surrounding shoreline, which he settled with his sons. The land was subsequently divided among his descendants, some of whose names still appear on this twentieth-century map of the area. (SPLIA)*

the development of early Long Island communities. Smythe was a witness to the signing of the deed of gift dated 1659 by which Wyandanch, the sachem of the Montauks, made over to his friend, Lion Gardiner, his title to the land now comprising the town of Smithtown. In 1663, Lion Gardiner deeded the property to his friend, Richard Smythe. While this deed does not survive, a subsequent endorsement signed in 1664 by Gardiner's son, David, does survive. However, this was not the end of Smythe's negotiations for the Smithtown lands. He was eventually to wage twelve court battles to obtain clear title by securing deeds from Wyandanch's descendants, from the Nissequogue Indians who traditionally held and occupied the lands between the Nissequogue River and Stony Brook, and from the towns of Huntington and Brookhaven. In addition, he secured land grants from two English governors and a Dutch governor. In 1677 a final patent was issued by Governor Andros.

Finally securing a patent from the colonial government that stipulated that he had to establish ten families upon the land, Smythe settled with his family and built a house in a little cove in what is today the village of Nissequogue. It was a logical place for Smythe to settle because of its proximity to the river, adequate fresh water supply, and its amenities as the probable site of an Indian village. This would mean that paths led to the area, fields had already been cleared for farming, and the Smythes could more easily establish themselves. Smythe had six sons who would eventually build homes in this area and establish a community in the wilderness. This little settlement, far removed from the present-day Main Street, was the beginning of the town of Smithtown, or Smythefield, Smithfield, or Smith's Fields as it has been variously called. Some of these original houses are still standing and have become part of the Smythe legacy.

By the time of Smythe's death in 1692 he presided over a vast agricultural empire whose livelihood was farming and milling. Through determination, perseverance, and shrewd legal negotiations, Smythe had become the owner of an estate which proved to be one of the largest single estates acquired by an early settler of this country.

Brad Harris

*Left: This circa 1675 room in the Jan Martense Schenk house in Flatlands was probably used as the kitchen and all-purpose work and living room. Schenck was a prosperous farmer and miller, and the furnishings reflect his affluence as well as his Dutch ancestry. Courtesy, The Brooklyn Museum*

*Opposite page: The last of the Dutch governors, Peter Stuyvesant encountered ever-growing opposition from his English constituents and considered Long Island the hotbed of his jurisdictional troubles. From Overton,* Long Island's Story, *(1929), 1963*

for its livelihood. Access to land sparked most immigration, and this agricultural preoccupation characterized local society until the dawn of the twentieth century.

Many settlers believed they could not have selected a better spot. Chronicler Daniel Denton observed:

*The island is most of it of very good soil, and very natural for all sorts of English grain . . . as also tobacco, hemp, flax, pumpkins, and melons . . . the island is plentifully stored with all sorts of cattell, horses, hogs, sheep, goats, and no place in the north of America better, which they can both raise and maintain by reason of large and spacious meadows.*

Denton was especially impressed with the wild strawberry crop,

*. . . of which last is in such abundance in June that the fields and woods are dyed red, which the country people perceiving, instantly arm themselves with bottles of wine, cream, and sugar . . . everyone takes a female on his horse behind him, and so rushing violently into the fields, never leave until they have disrobed them of their red colors.*

Early farms were necessarily small and crude by modern standards, though Dutch "bouweries" re-

ceived universal admiration for their thrift, cleanliness, and bounty. Production was usually limited to the amount of land a man and ox team could cultivate, plus the level of surplus the farmer could market. Common agricultural products included wheat, corn, butter, cheese, apples, ham, bacon, lard, and beef.

Typical of the broad range of yeoman was East Hampton's Samuel Mulford whose small farm, valued at eighty-three pounds, supported two oxen, seventeen cows, two horses, three pigs, and fifteen sheep. A few men fared much better and acquired substantial estates. Peter Wyckoff's one hundred acres, five horses, two oxen, and twenty-eight cows were worth £304 and ranked him as the second wealthiest man in Flatlands. The much-tormented Quaker John Bowne of Flushing, who was the third richest individual in that village, owned sixty acres, nine horses, four oxen, eighteen cows, and fifty sheep, and was assessed £245. Others were less lucky, or less industrious, and achieved meager results. William Chatterton of Flushing cultivated only nine acres, owned just one cow and two yearlings, and his property was rated at only thirty-five pounds.

Though markets for surpluses were small and the state of technology rather primitive, local settlers refused to endure as hardscrabble rustics. Long Island farms, therefore, were never isolated from larg-

er economic society. Despite the importance of home consumption and self-sufficiency, the profit motive invariably obtained surprising heights. Agricultural fairs became important events in Dutch Brooklyn only a decade after settlement commenced. The eastern towns, too, conducted extensive trade with Boston, Newport, New York, Barbados, and the West Indies. Throughout the late seventeenth century villagers voiced extreme displeasure with the prices of imported goods, actively opposed efforts to control their commerce, and engaged in persistent smuggling—all evidence of their entrepreneurial orientation.

Though economically prosperous, Long Island could not maintain its precarious political balance in the face of larger world events, and tensions generated by the global Anglo-Dutch rivalry were quickly communicated to American shores. Several eastern towns requested aid from across the Sound. Anxious to annex English Long Island, Connecticut proved eager to help, and Southampton joined the mainland colony in 1644-1645. East Hampton followed in 1658, Brookhaven in 1661, Huntington in 1663. Perched on the frontier, Oyster Bay trod a more tortuous path. Settlers first voted in 1654 to unite with New Haven colony. Angry Dutch officials then insisted the land belonged to them and ordered the Englishmen out. Again, Oyster Bay appealed to New Haven. A visit by Peter Stuyvesant

persuaded town fathers to join the Dutch sphere, but nothing concrete developed; in 1660 a town meeting prohibited anyone from negotiating with either political bloc. Two years later Oyster Bay finally swore allegiance to Great Britain. When international tensions reached a critical stage in 1663-1664, East Hampton, Southampton, Southold, Brookhaven, Huntington, Hempstead, and Newtown all sent deputies to Connecticut for support.

The colonial pot finally boiled over in 1664 after King Charles II turned the entire region over to his brother James, Duke of York. James quickly dispatched an armed force under Colonel Richard Nicolls, who landed troops at Gravesend in late August. Six days later he accepted Peter Stuyvesant's reluctant surrender and New Amsterdam became New York. All of Long Island was annexed to the fledgling colony, much to the chagrin of expansionist Connecticut and the East End towns.

Most residents viewed the shift to unified rule with relief, and they began to press for their version of local rights modeled after the familiar New England pattern: popular election of town and militia officers, no taxation without a representative assembly, free enjoyment of lands without annual quit rents or patent fees. Colonel Nicolls responded to popular ferment with the Duke's Laws, which he read to a gathering in Hempstead on March 1, 1665. Long Island would henceforth be known as Yorkshire and divided into East Riding (Suffolk), West Riding (Brooklyn and Queens), and North Riding (Queens and Nassau). Towns would be ruled by locally elected constables and overseers. Militia units would be drawn into a colony-wide organization, and the royal governor would appoint sheriffs and justices. Though the Duke's Laws incorporated many common New England and British colonial practices, they did not sanction a representative assembly. As a further irritant, new (meaning replacement) land and town patents were required.

Many resisted such demands, viewing the laws as infringements on their cherished autonomy. As late as 1669, Southold, Southampton, and Oyster Bay had not secured the necessary documents. Southold waited until 1676, Oyster Bay until 1677. Further expressing their displeasure, the three East End towns petitioned the king in 1672 for a return to Connecticut's jurisdiction. A few years later an exasperated Governor Edmund Andros dispatched the

# CAPTAIN JOHN UNDERHILL

Boston's Puritan saints labelled him a rogue and an adulterer. To the Indians of New England and New York he was a warrior chieftain. Still others viewed him as a champion of religious freedom, a respected political leader, a town builder, or a chronic malcontent. Undoubtedly Captain John Underhill was, as an early chronicler claimed, the most "dramatic person" in the history of colonial Long Island.

Though his family originally hailed from Staffordshire, England, Underhill was born circa 1597 at Kenilworth Castle in Warwickshire, where his father served as a trusted retainer for Robert Dudley, the Earl of Leicester. When Dudley departed for the Netherlands in 1605, the Underhill family accompanied him, and young John grew up in war-torn Holland. He soon entered military service with the Prince of Orange and later married a Dutch woman, Heylken deHooch (1608-1658). On a trip back to England in the late 1620s he met John Winthrop, a leader of the restive Puritan faction, and in 1630 departed for Massachusetts Bay as the fledgling colony's military commander.

A distinguished soldier and friend of the powerful Winthrop, Underhill quickly achieved great local prominence. He became a freeman, joined Boston's First Church, and served as a town selectman and a provincial deputy. As Massachusetts Bay's militia leader, he often acted as the strong arm of the Puritan theocracy, leading expeditions to supress Sir Christopher Gardiner, a local Catholic, and free-spirited Thomas Morton of Merrymount, famed for his Maypole frolicking.

Until 1636 Underhill's career proceeded in orderly fashion, but his settled life was soon disrupted, and he rapidly earned both extravagant praise and heated censure. The praise came first. In August 1636 Underhill led an attack against Block Island's Indians, and during the fighting he was hit in the head with an arrow. His life was saved only by the helmet his wife insisted he wear. The following year Underhill and Captain John Mason of Hartford, Connecticut, commanded an expedition against the warlike Pequots. They stormed the largest Indian settlement, burning it to the ground.

Unfortunately, Underhill's military successes did not protect him from a storm that was brewing back in Boston. Mistress Anne Hutchinson and the Reverend Thomas Wheelwright were challenging the authority of the Puritan ministry, and Underhill had earlier offered his support. Now he was denounced by officials as "one of the most forward of the Boston enthusiasts," disfranchised, and stripped of his military rank. Humiliated, he was also tried for adultery, and soon quit Boston to visit England where he wrote a book describing his adventures.

The New World was in Underhill's blood, however, and he returned to Boston in 1638, where he was again tried for adultery and banished to New Hampshire to serve as "governor" of the Dover and Exeter settlements. Underhill's subsequent return to Boston generated still further turmoil as

*In 1638 John Underhill published in London his* Nevves From America, *which contained an account of his military exploits against New England Indians. It included this depiction of an Indian fort, or "palizado." Courtesy, The Underhill Society of America, Inc.*

*This bronze commemorative plaque erected in 1908 depicts Captain John Underhill receiving peace entreaties from the Indians. During his eventful life Underhill both fought and befriended Indian groups on Long Island. Courtesy, The Underhill Society of America, Inc.*

he was twice more charged with adultery. Severely chastened, he was forced to publicly confess his sins and bow to the magistrates' authority.

Underhill and Boston had now tired of each other and in the early 1640s he moved on to Stamford, Connecticut, in a successful effort to recoup his fortune and reputation. There he was selected a deputy to the New Haven assembly. When in 1643 warfare erupted between the Indians and the nearby Dutch, Underhill raised a troop of mercenaries and fought against the Canarsies on Long Island and the Wappingers and Wequasegeeks near Greenwich, Connecticut. The triumphant soldier was rewarded by the grateful Dutch with land on Manhattan, an island in Jamaica Bay, and a seat on the council of New Amsterdam. A few years later he was named Sheriff of Flushing.

But Captain Underhill's allegiance to his new masters only went so deep, and during the 1653 war between England and Holland he was jailed for opposition to Dutch rule. Upon release he journeyed to Newport, Rhode Island, and later to Southold, Setauket, and finally in 1661 to Oyster Bay. Despite his controversial past, Underhill retained popular and official respect, and was selected to attend the famous Hempstead assemblage of 1665. He also served as sheriff of North Riding and sur-veyor general of customs. In 1666 the former Indian fighter represented the Matinecock tribe in a dispute with Hempstead town. His clients rewarded him with a plot of land which he named Killingworth after his childhood home.

By now an elder statesman known for his Quaker sympathies rather than warlike disposition, Captain John Underhill lived out the remainder of his life on his new estate with his second wife, Elizabeth Feake. His last child was born just five months before Underhill's death in 1671 at the age of seventy-four.

Geoffrey L. Rossano

*Responding to demands for self-government on Long Island, Governor Richard Nicolls called a meeting of town deputies in Hempstead on March 1, 1665. The meeting established the basic laws of the province, called the "Duke's Laws," which were based on the codes of older New England colonies. From Bailey,* Early Long Island, *1962*

high sheriff to quash such notions.

On several occasions disgruntled colonists sought changes in the legal system, demanding creation of a representative assembly, designation of local free ports, and imposition of fixed prices on imported goods. Colonial governors denied every one of those requests. A special levy for the repair of Fort James in Manhattan and the 1671 decree ordering all trade through New York harbor added to the colonists' resentment. By 1681 some townsmen were dissatisfied enough to gather at Huntington, where they petitioned redress. Colonial leaders were promptly arrested and thrown into jail.

Protest also assumed less political forms—smuggling being among the most popular. Oyster Bay traders ran afoul of both English and Dutch authorities in the 1660s. Governor Thomas Dongan angrily reported in 1687 that "What is produced of their industry is frequently carried to Boston, notwithstanding the many strict rules and laws made to confine them to this place." A decade later another governor singled out Setauket, Southold, Oyster Bay, and Musketa Cove for their illegal activities. The appointment of Oyster Bay's John Townsend as customs officer was quickly withdrawn, however, after neighbors and relatives threatened him with physical harm.

Political tensions had abated temporarily in 1683 when the Duke of York appointed Thomas Dongan governor. Soon after his arrival in New York, Dongan called a convention which then enacted a Charter of Liberties. This proclamation guaranteed freedom of worship and trial by jury, while also creating an elected assembly. Unfortunately for advocates of colonial self-determination, when Duke James became King James II in 1685, he disavowed the charter. Local disaffection intensified as Dongan demanded that the towns again apply for charters and patents. Many refused, characterizing the entire affair as a transparent scheme to extort money and crush local independence.

Rumors then began to circulate among the suspicious puritan population that Dongan and the King were plotting to impose Catholicism on the colony. Islanders also opposed James' plan to merge them into the recently-formed Dominion of New England under Governor Edmund Andros, who was already heartily detested for his earlier service in New York. Such an explosive situation lacked just one final spark, and it appeared in 1688. The Dutch Protestant monarch, William of Orange, invaded England and overthrew King James. After the news reached the colony in April 1689, a Committee of Safety coalesced in Manhattan to guard against a possible French invasion and prevent any Catholic treachery. Captain Jacob Leisler, a wealthy merchant, emerged as the revolutionary leader. With the assistance of Long Island militia, he captured Fort James and raised the banner of William and Mary.

Leisler's revolt and subsequent assumption of power plunged the entire colony into turmoil. Order was not fully restored until 1693, after Leisler's arrest and summary execution for treason. Despite the disorder, some progress occurred, including creation of the New York Assembly in 1691.

By century's end the economic, social, and political patterns that would dominate Long Island life for the next seventy-five years had been estab-

lished. In addition, three rather distinct zones of settlement existed. Brooklyn's small Dutch communities stubbornly clung to their language, faith, and customs; local inhabitants resisted the use of a foreign tongue in official documents and few Englishmen opted to settle there. With the flow of European immigrants cut off by the British conquest, the Dutch towns grew slowly. Emerging labor shortages were usually filled by black slaves. Given its distinctive origins, established patterns of trade, and proximity to New York City, Dutch Brooklyn played little role in the affairs of eastern Long Island.

Stretching across present-day Queens and Nassau counties lay a string of villages generally characterized by religious toleration and ethnic diversity. Several were founded by New England dissenters and offered havens for outcast Quakers and Baptists. Limited Dutch migration into Flushing, Newtown, Jamaica, and Oyster Bay insured that no unified social structure or political view would dominate. Many towns also developed strong links with New York's cultural and economic institutions because they were so close to Manhattan. Both Jamaica and Hempstead became Anglican outposts and home to several royal favorites.

East End communities constituted another world entirely. One governor complained in 1703: "Indeed the people of the East End of Long Island are not very willing to be persuaded to believe that they belong to this province; they are full of New England principles." First populated by Massachusetts and Connecticut migrants searching for land and autonomy, they maintained strong ties of kinship, commerce, and religion with their ancestral communities and perpetually chafed under New York rule. They also attempted to enmesh themselves in virtue and piety, recreating the orthodox New England town, a closed community designed to protect their distinctive church government and unique social vision. That they did not ultimately succeed was not for want of trying.

In all cases the first migration of adventurers, dreamers, and builders had given way to succeeding generations of farmers who cultivated their parents' fields and inherited their gray-shingled homesteads. The meadows, walls, and paths which now defined the landscape gave tangible evidence of sixty years' unceasing struggle with the elements.

# CHAPTER THREE

# Colonial Life and Revolutionary Politics

Eighteenth-century Long Island was a world of small farming villages, large families, solemn religious observance, and oligarchic politics. Scattered sawmills, gristmills, and the elegant manor estates of the politically and socially-prominent gentry dotted the bucolic landscape. A few of the Island's coastal villages supported busy shipyards throughout the century, and trade with New York, New England, and the Caribbean grew steadily. To the casual visitor it must have seemed as if local residents enjoyed all the blessings their ancestors had journeyed so far to find.

But despite the seeming calm and stability, Long Island society was soon plunged into that great cauldron called the American Revolution. The ensuing upheaval divided towns and families, generated hardship and strife, and inspired much of the political and social change which ushered Long Island into the nineteenth century.

Family farms and small farming hamlets lay at the center of colonial Long Island life, much as they had since the first days of settlement. A rapidly expanding population continued clearing the remaining coastal acres and then pressed inland in search of new lands. While citizens might visit the town center for annual meetings, militia musters, occasional shopping, or religious services, most hours were spent on the homestead tending crops and livestock. This was a quiet world where patterns of temperature, tide, and rainfall far outweighed the impact of international political crises or the latest currents in fashion and literature. Even at the end of the century, a visitor could write of many Long Island residents: "Living by themselves, attentive to whatever is their own . . . their views, affections, and pursuits always exist on a small scale . . ."

Colonel Marinus Willett of Jamaica, Long Island, halted a British troop shipment of arms. This act and Willett's other exploits during the Revolution earned him the esteem of his country, and he was appointed sheriff and then mayor of New York City. From Hazelton, The Boroughs of Brooklyn and Queens, Counties of Nassau and Suffolk, N.Y., 1609-1924, Lewis, 1925

In so circumscribed a world the institution of the farm family prevailed. It provided education, entertainment, and economic support, forming the web which held society together. The Englishmen who first settled Long Island retained many Old World family customs. Land in Europe was scarce and large families a burden. As a result, delayed marriages and relatively low birthrates were common. Long Island's early settlers perpetuated these habits. Men usually postponed marriage until their late twenties, and the number of children rarely exceeded six per family.

But as New World opportunities unfolded and the need for more hands to tame the wilderness became imperative, marriage and child-rearing practices shifted dramatically. Men and women began marrying much earlier and the number of their offspring increased markedly. In both Huntington and Oyster Bay the customary age of marriage for men dropped from about twenty-eight to only twenty-four in just two generations. Brides were younger, too, by nearly two years. Births rose to an average of nearly eight per family. With increased childbearing, however, came sharply increased female mortality, and by 1725 nearly four women in ten died before the age of forty. Anna Floyd of Setauket succumbed at thirty-eight, on the same day her daughter Nancy was born, while Smithtown's Susannah Gelson was thirty-two when she died, eighteen days after the birth of baby Hannah. Though not usually as high as some myths would indicate, child mortality also reached shocking levels, at least by modern standards. Isaac and Mary Hedges of

East Hampton lost five of eleven children, and their neighbors, Jonathan and Mehetable Stratton, buried five of seven. By contrast, David and Phebe Miller had eleven children and all survived to maturity.

Around mid-century demographic patterns began shifting once more. The increasing population and frequent subdivision of family lands meant rural overcrowding and reduced opportunities for future offspring. The age of marriage rose, while birth rates dropped nearly 35 percent. After a century of exuberant growth, local society began to replicate the more static Old World patterns.

Although individual farms and families often produced food, clothing, tools, and furniture, artisans occupied essential positions in the local economy. By mid-century a network of craftsmen supplied most villagers with simple manufactured goods. Huntington's 1778 population included numerous

*Above: Mourning pictures done in embroidery, such as the one shown here, were made by young women to commemorate the departure of a loved one. Courtesy, The Museums at Stony Brook, Museums Collection*

*Left: Settled in 1640, Southold's village center grew slowly, as this nineteenth-century illustration reveals. The Presbyterian Church stands on the right, the Academy is in the center, and the brick schoolhouse is on the left. From Pelletreau, A History of Long Island, Lewis, 1903*

*The importance of mills to the new colony is attested to by the fact that millers were granted free land and guaranteed water rights. Grist mills for flour and animal feed, such as this one built on the Cold Spring Harbor in 1791, were numerous throughout Long Island until the introduction of steam-powered mills in the latter part of the nineteenth century. Courtesy, George B. Brainerd Photograph Collection, Brooklyn Public Library*

weavers, cordwainers, coopers, carpenters, smiths, tailors, and papermakers. Blacksmith George Weeks of nearby Oyster Bay was able to open both a general store and tavern, having accrued savings by "shueing a mare," "sherpening sheres," and manufacturing fittings for the local shipyard.

Typical of many artisans were the Hedges of East Hampton, three generations of shoemakers. In 1683 patriarch Stephen Hedges owned the village's largest herd of cattle, and around 1700 the family opened a tanning yard. John Hedges, Stephen's grandson, started shoemaking in the 1720s, mostly in the winter when farm chores were less pressing. Around mid-century his son, Daniel, joined him. A separate shop was erected to house their growing business. Like other nascent merchant/artisans, the Hedges serviced both local and distant markets, including New York, Rhode Island, and Nantucket. Relatives often acted as sales agents, and a brother-in-law, Thomas Chatfield, once advised, "In the future make half pumps and half women's shoes . . . and make them long." Not until the rise of factory production a half century later would local craftsmen retire from the village scene.

Despite generally poor transportation and considerable local self-sufficiency, colonial society occasionally developed ties with nearby cities and the world beyond. Mariners, travellers, craftsmen, and itinerant preachers all played a part in the process. But the most important actors were the country merchants who exported raw materials and farm produce while importing the manufactured goods and tropical Caribbean crops so desired by households of the day.

Throughout the seventeenth century, North Shore settlers exported beef and grain across the Sound to Connecticut. East End villagers, on the other hand, traded with Newport, New Haven, Cape Cod, and Boston. As early as 1668, a group of Rhode Island and Oyster Bay investors erected a sawmill at Musketa Cove so that they could tap the New York City market. Among their Manhattan customers was merchant Jacob Leisler, later leader of the 1689 revolt against the Stuarts. With population and commerce expanding throughout the eighteenth century, country merchants developed extensive trading networks.

Not every Long Islander, however, was a sturdy yeoman, artisan/craftsman, or even merchant/entrepreneur. Scattered across the landscape in Hempstead, Lloyd's Neck, Massapequa, Islip, and Gardiner's Island, lay the manor estates of prominent and powerful families. Here, on private preserves, they built elegant mansions and managed large commercial farms worked by tenants and slaves. Adopting the lifestyle of the English gentry, these aristocrats imported fine clothes and furniture and corresponded with the empire's economic, social, and political leaders. Moreover, they often proved strong supporters of both the Anglican Church and the British throne.

Local magnates included wealthy merchants like

# WILLIAM FLOYD

William Floyd, Long Islander, country gentleman, revolutionary, and public figure, typifies a prominent man at the center of local and national events during the hectic and formative years of the young republic. Floyd was an important member of his community, both economically and politically, a major-general in the militia, a representative to the first Continental Congress, a state senator, and the first, as well as the youngest, member of the New York delegation to sign the Declaration of Independence.

The progenitor of the Floyd family on Long Island was Richard Floyd (1620-1690), who came to New England from Wales in 1654. He settled in Setauket shortly after its founding in 1655 and purchased large holdings of land on Mastic Neck, directly across the Island on the south shore. Richard's grandson, Nicoll Floyd (1705-1753), the father of William, was a prosperous farmer on Mastic Neck. William Floyd was born there in 1734 and was only twenty years old at the time of his father's death, when he assumed the responsibility of running the large family farm. Like many of the pioneering South Shore estates it was a "long lots" property, running about six miles north-to-south and about one mile east-to-west. Only the portion closest to Moriches Bay was agriculturally useful. When William Floyd took over the

*Above: William Floyd supported American independence and was forced to flee his home at Mastic during the Revolution. Courtesy, Independence Historical Park, Philadelphia*

*Below: William Floyd was one of three New Yorkers to sign the Declaration of Independence. From Pelletreau, A History of Long Island, Lewis, 1903*

estate it was already a large-scale enterprise in commerical agriculture, operated by slave labor, and producing goods—primarily cattle, sheep, grain, flax, and wood—for export to New York City.

Through his aunts and uncles, Floyd had blood and marital connections to the provincial elite, a network that expanded as his seven siblings, whose charge he had inherited, married and moved out. His father had also left a substantial fortune in notes and obligations due on loans made to local residents of all classes. William Floyd's "estate," therefore, con-

sisted of not only the land at Mastic, but social and economic ties to a large segment of the regional population as well.

William Floyd used these ties and expanded them, emerging as a leader in the major social institutions of the area—church, town government, and county militia—in the years leading up to the Revolution. With his brothers-in-law, General Nathaniel Woodhull and Ezra L'Hommedieu, he led the patriot cause in Suffolk County and was sent to represent New York at the Continental Congresses in Philadelphia. After the British won the Battle of Long Island in August 1776, Floyd remained an exile from his home until 1783.

Except for one year, Floyd continued to serve in the Continental Congress and, beginning in 1777, in the new state senate as well, thereby retaining a handle on government at both the national and the local level at a time when it was uncertain which level would attain primacy. The similarity of economic and political interest between William Floyd, the Long Island planter, and his friends Thomas Jefferson and James Madison caused one foreign observer to identify Floyd as a member of the "Southern interest" in Congress. In fact, Floyd sealed the political ties with personal ones, betrothing one daughter to Madison (it was later broken off), marrying another to George Clinton's son, and marrying his son to the daughter of a Jefferson ally in New York City, David Gelston. In 1791, when Jefferson and Madison took the trip that helped create the Democratic-Republican Party, they stopped at William Floyd's estate and solidified their political ties on Long Island. Floyd's personal political career ended in 1795, when he lost the election for lieutenant governor of New York, but he remained a Jeffersonian for the rest of his life.

Floyd's activities went beyond politics and he took part in the general expansion of business enterprise after the Revolutionary War. Like many of the Founding Fathers and other wealthy Long Islanders, Floyd became actively involved in western land speculations. In 1803, he moved to Westernville, New York, on the Mohawk River, where he had amassed large landholdings. Relying more on rents than on personal farm management, Floyd and others like him expanded the sources and nature of their wealth while at the same time forwarding the expansion of the nation itself.

With William Floyd residing permanently on his upstate lands until his death in 1821, the management of the Mastic estate fell to his son, who began the process of shifting the family's interests away from dependence on the land and local lending and into the expanding commercial life of New York City. The Floyds represent a Long Island example of the flowering of major trends in America's future: the combination of wealth based on generations of agricultural pursuits with an entrepreneurial involvement in the growing mercantile and industrial developments during the eighteenth and early nineteenth centuries.

Steven Kesselman

*This contemporary view of William Floyd's estate at Mastic shows later additions to the original house built circa 1724. The estate is now a museum operated by the National Park Service. Photo by Joseph Adams. (SPLIA)*

Hempstead's Colonel Josiah Martin (1699-1778) who built Rock Hall, a splendid Georgian home. Further west in Islip town resided the Nicoll and Floyd families. The Nicolls were descended from Mathias Nicoll, first secretary of the colony, mayor of New York in 1674, and a judge of the Supreme Court. His son, William, became Queens County clerk in 1683, acquired a ten-mile square domain in Suffolk County, and married an heiress to the great Rensselaerwyck manor. After a stormy political career, the younger Nicoll was elected speaker of the Assembly in 1702. William's grandson, also William (1702-1768), was similarly voted speaker in 1758.

Closely related to the Nicolls were the Floyds. An original Setauket proprietor, Welshman Richard Floyd also purchased extensive lands in Mastic. His son, Richard, married Margaret Nicoll, Mathias' daughter, while granddaughter Charity Floyd later wed Benjamin Nicoll, one of Mathias' grandchildren. Among the proprietor's notable descendants were Richard Floyd, Suffolk's most infamous tory, and William Floyd, a signer of the Declaration of Independence. Other influential Suffolk clans included the Sylvesters of Shelter Island and the Gardiners, East Hampton's wealthiest family, who ruled a semi-independent island fiefdom.

Also representative of many manor families were the Lloyds of Horse Neck (Huntington). Grizzell Sylvester of Shelter Island inherited the Neck from both her father and a fiance who died. In 1676 she married James Lloyd, a wealthy Boston merchant,

and a decade later he received a royal patent for his new estate, now titled the "Lordship and Manor of Queens Village." Annual quit rent was set at four bushels of wheat. James' son, Henry, also a merchant, was the first Lloyd to actually live on the Neck (1711) where he built an imposing mansion, a granary, schoolhouse, smithy, and barns. Henry later passed the estate to his four sons, Henry II, John, Joseph, and James. Their farms exported large quantities of meat, grain, fruit, and cordwood. Among the family slaves was Jupiter Hammon, who composed religious poetry, an example of which was published in 1760.

*Henry Lloyd I (1685-1763), built a mansion in 1711 at Lloyd's Neck, Huntington. His son Joseph Lloyd (1716-1780), erected the handsome Manor House in 1766. Both are still standing. Courtesy, Mrs. Orme Wilson*

ton, and 56 percent in Bushwyck. No seventeenth-century town seemed to allow the bottom half of taxpayers to possess more than a quarter of local wealth, and the lower classes usually claimed much less than that.

The passage of time only exacerbated the situation. Forty-seven percent of Huntington's wealth was controlled by the top fifth of ratepayers in 1673. Within a century the figure rose to 56 percent. Powerful clans consolidated their positions through a second and third generation. In Oyster Bay six families amassed 41 percent of all real estate. Four Southampton clans held 25 percent of that jurisdiction's property, and in neighboring East Hampton six families owned one-third of all land and livestock. Extended tenure in office, plural office holding, and dynastic inheritance of offices also characterized oligarchic politics. Between 1690 and 1765 six Huntington clans held nearly 80 percent of all top village posts. Men like Eliphelet Wickes or Epenetus Platt were often elected to five, six, or even seven separate offices, and then re-elected for twenty, thirty, or more terms. Until the American Revolution altered social and political habits, descendents of the original ruling elite dominated the town governments and economies founded by their fathers.

Commencing in 1775, the revolution against Great Britain proved a bitterly divisive struggle. Nowhere was the conflict more intense than on

Although villagers observed many democratic practices and strove to preserve local autonomy, they were not democrats in the modern sense. Rather, between 1690 and 1770 a clannish oligarchy dominated town affairs. Men of merit (generally the wealthy and socially prominent) led, and deference to this elite was an implicit duty for the remainder of society, which accepted the concept of a natural division between the rulers and ruled. Almost all males voted, but restricted their choices to "natural" leaders.

Land distribution patterns reinforced the process. Through luck, hard work, or previous financial status, a few families acquired more and more property, while others made do with smaller portions. Concentrations of wealth developed quite early. By 1683 the top 20 percent of taxpayers controlled 38 percent of all wealth in Flatbush and Brooklyn, 43 percent in East Hampton, 48 percent in Southamp-

AN

# Evening THOUGHT.

SALVATION BY *CHRIST*,

WITH

# PENETENTIAL CRIES:

Compofed by Jupiter Hammon, a Negro belonging to Mr Lloyd, of Queen's-Village, on Long-Ifland, the 25th of December, 1760.

*Religious poet Jupiter Hammon was a slave of the Lloyd family and probably received some education in the schoolhouse established near the Manor House. His first poem, "An Evening Thought," appeared on December 25, 1760. (SPLIA)*

Long Island. Families, congregations, and villages splintered as civil war reared its ugly head. Adding to the bitterness were the social, geographic, religious, and political divisions which had first appeared in the seventeenth century and persisted into the eighteenth. Suffolk's parochial villages had inherited the ancient Puritan suspicion of Anglican missionaries and central governments, and feared the establishment of an American bishopric. These East Enders constituted a rather homogeneous society of dissenters, united by their distrust of the outside world.

Far to the west and cut off from the empire's political and social currents, lay overwhelmingly Dutch Brooklyn. Residents remained strangers in an English domain; they proved loyal to their native tongue and employed ministers from their mother country. Long Island's Dutchmen sought no confrontation with their British masters and ignored the revolution as best they could.

Queens County residents followed a middle course. Originally part of New Amsterdam, their area attracted a significant Dutch minority, as well as many Baptists and pacifist Quakers. Close commercial, social, and political ties with New York, rather than New England, predominated. Jamaica and Hempstead were outposts of the established Anglican Church and home to many royal favorites. A rather polyglot society, Queens functioned by championing no one ideology to the exclusion of others.

Long Islanders reacted to the unfolding revolutionary drama in many ways. Oyster Bay patriots protested the Stamp Act in 1766, and the following year Queens voters petitioned their assemblymen to oppose British trade measures. In the aftermath of the Boston Tea Party, Huntington, East Hampton, and Smithtown agreed to cease trade with England.

Queens' residents, reflecting their mixed heritage and outlook, responded ambiguously. While some Jamaica voters protested British actions in Boston and promised to support the new Continental Congress, others argued against any disloyal actions, calling congresses "tyrranical and unlawful." Shortly thereafter, in December 1774, Newtown patriots created a revolutionary Committee of Correspondence, but the entire town soon disassociated itself from rebel measures. Similarly, Oyster Bay voted 205-42 against "having anything to do with deputies and congresses." In April 1775 Hempstead issued a ringing denunciation of all rebel activity, condemning those "threatening this once peaceful and happy land." Instead, villagers wished the union with England to persist "until time shall be no more."

Long Island, however, now was ensnared in events beyond its control. When news of Lexington and Concord reached New York City, patriots paraded through the streets, seized weapons, and occupied the customs house. Suffolk towns responded with nearly unanimous support for the rebel cause, but many citizens of Kings and Queens counties recoiled with outright horror. A loyal militia led by the Ludlow and Hewlett families drilled at Hempstead in expectation of trouble. Only after emissaries were informed that "they (loyalists) would blow out any man's brains who should attempt to take them" did patriot leaders abandon efforts to confiscate their weapons.

In neighboring North Hempstead the Sands and Onderdonk clans opposed the loyalist trend and formed rebel militia companies. Reaction from their southern compatriots proved hostile, and in late September they seceded from Hempstead town because "the behaviour of the majority was inimical to freedom."

As rebel and loyal factions contended for power, Queens freemen gathered at Jamaica in October 1775 and voted 778-221 *against* supporting the revolutionary Congress. New York's patriot leaders were furious, labelling such conduct "inimicable to the common cause of the United colonies and not to be suffered." The Continental Congress, which met in Philadelphia, responded more directly: in January 1776 the assembly ordered Colonel Nathaniel Heard and his New Jersey troops to occupy Queens County, disarm the loyalists, and arrest opposition leaders.

Heard's men advanced quickly through Jamaica, Hempstead, Jericho, and Oyster Bay, forcing 500 tories to sign a loyalty oath. Many others hid in the swamps, and all ridiculed the colonel in song:

*Colonel Heard has come to town*
*In all his pride and glory.*
*And when he dies he'll go to hell*
*For robbing of the tory.*

Loyalist opposition continued, however, and in

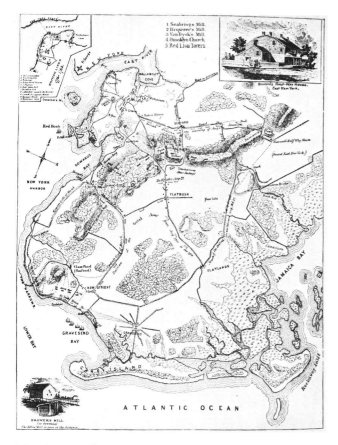

*Left: In early March 1776, General George Washington ordered the fortification of Brooklyn against the British forces under General William Howe. The American forces in and about New York has been estimated at about 19,000. From Stiles,* History of Kings County Including the City of Brooklyn, *Munsell, 1884*

*Below: In this rendering of the Battle of Long Island on August 27, 1776, American forces retreat across Gowanus Creek in the face of a heavy British onslaught. The British landed with 32,000 troops and routed the Americans, who suffered over 1,000 casualties. From Grafton,* The American Revolution: A Picture Sourcebook, *Dover, 1975*

March 1776 General Charles Lee, commander of the New York City garrison, dispatched Colonel Isaac Sears to Queens. A patriot zealot, Sears gleefully recalled, "I arrived at Newtown and tendered the oath to four of the greater tories which they swallowed as hard as if it were four pound shot." When George Washington assumed the New York command in April, he became so distressed at tory opposition that he threatened to depopulate Kings and Queens counties. The general quickly ordered Captain Benjamin Birdsall of Massapequa to seize boats suspected of trading with the British fleet.

By late spring a British invasion appeared imminent and Congress took additional steps to shore up local defenses. Militia units were mustered, but only a handful of men from Brooklyn and Queens appeared. Dutch farmers also refused to sell their cattle to the Continental Army or drive livestock away from the coast for safekeeping. Congress retaliated by ordering the animals seized and advising destruction of any grain or forage that could not be relocated.

New York City and its vast agricultural hinterland offered a rich prize to English strategists, but the key to Manhattan was Long Island; extensive American fortifications appeared on Brooklyn Heights during the summer of 1776. Enemy forces began gathering off New York in late June. By early August an armada of 400 ships and 31,000 troops was poised to strike.

The long awaited invasion commenced on August 22 when British and German soldiers came ashore near Gravesend. Though their movements were clearly visible from American lines, little was done to stop them. A Continental officer lamented: "As there were so many landing places, and the people of the Island so treacherous, we never expected to prevent the landing." Unimpeded, enemy troops quickly occupied Flatbush, Flatlands, and New Utrecht.

Britain's hammer blow fell on August 27, 1776, when General William Howe's legions outflanked George Washington's regulars and militia levies, driving them back into their last fortifications on Brooklyn Heights. Under cover of rain and fog, the beleaguered Americans barely escaped across the East River to Manhattan, leaving the rest of Long Island defenseless.

The English General William Erskine, leading nearly 5,000 soldiers, turned eastward on August 29. He called on Suffolk rebels to return to their homes, promising to destroy the property of the disobedient. Two days later General Oliver DeLancey again urged Suffolk to surrender and accept the King's peace. Commissary agents then were directed to seize "all the grain, forage, and creatures you can find" of those remaining in rebellion. Both Smithtown and Huntington capitulated on the fifth of September. For some patriot leaders like John Sands of Cow Neck and John Kirk of Norwich, the British conquest meant arrest and imprisonment. Hundreds of others fled across the Sound to exile in Connecticut. In a mass October display, 1,293 Queens residents took a new loyalty oath to King George III.

By December 1776 royal authorities believed the region calm enough to muster a loyal militia. Governor William Tryon reviewed 820 men at Jamaica and 800 more in Smithtown. Britain's victory appeared complete and the governor informed his superiors, "There is not the least apprehension of any further commotions." But Tryon could not have been more mistaken, and for the next seven years, Long Island was to endure continual strife, conflict, and bloodshed.

With New York now headquarters of Britain's North American war effort, large forces camped in and around the city. General Oliver DeLancey's loyalist brigades were stationed at Lloyd's Neck, Herricks, Hempstead, Flatbush, Jamaica, and Brookhaven. The Queen's Rangers unit of Connecticut tories led by Lieutenant Colonel John Graves Simcoe encamped at Oyster Bay, while Hessian troops bivouacked at Wolver Hollow.

This vast military post required huge quantities of food, forage, and wood, and much of this burden fell on Long Island. In the summer of 1777 General William Howe ordered villagers to provide hay, straw, corn, and oats. Little forage appeared, and in September Howe repeated his orders, adding the threat of confiscation and imprisonment. Colonel Simcoe noted in his diary "I did not give receipts to a great number of people on account of their rebellious principles or absolute disobedience of the general order."

Military occupation spawned continuous outrages against the civilian population, especially in rebel towns. Presbyterian churches were often converted into granaries, stables, or barracks, or simply torn down to provide firewood and building materials. British troops constructed a fort in the middle of Huntington's cemetery, using tombstones for firebacks and bake ovens.

Conflict between civilians escalated, too. In 1779

*Opposite page: George Washington directs the retreat from Brooklyn Heights to New York. The successful, massive retreat under desperate conditions is considered one of the most remarkable achievements in the history of warfare. From Grafton,* The American Revolution: A Picture Sourcebook, *Dover, 1975*

*Left: The British victory at Long Island was announced in London on October 10, 1776, and this cartoon appeared shortly thereafter. It portrays a pleased King George III and other noblemen on the right, scowling commoners who opposed the war on the left, and a tawdry woman with liberty cap and staff weeping in the center. Courtesy, Library of Congress*

*Below: After the British occupied Long Island, citizens were forced to sign loyalty oaths. From Pelletreau,* A History of Long Island, *Lewis, 1903*

I Do hereby certify, that *Elihu Rayner* Aged 26 of Southampton Townfhip, has voluntarily fwore before me, to bear Faith and true Allegiance to his Majefty King George the Third; and that he will not, directly or indirectly, openly or fecretly, aid, abet, counfel, fhelter or conceal, any of his Majefty's Enemies, and thofe of his Government, or moleft or betray the Friends of Government; but that he will behave himfelf peaceably and quietly, as a faithful Subject of his Majefty and his Government. Given under my Hand on Long-Ifland this 22 *Sept,* 1778.

*Wm Tryon Govr*

fearful tories cautioned travellers about a rebel lair at Bread and Cheese Hollow (Smithtown) where "unfortunate loyalists are greatly exposed to the cruelty of these assassins." On another occasion exiled Major Jesse Brush sent word to a tory farmer occupying his Huntington property. "I have repeatedly ordered you to leave my farm," he wrote. "This is my last invitation. If you do not your next landfall will be in a warmer climate than you have ever lived in yet."

Kidnappings also became popular. General DeLancey warned loyal townsmen to look out for those taking "a leading part in committing scandalous robberies and secretly in the night carrying off peaceable and inoffensive citizens." A spectacular example occurred in May 1779, when the ardent royalist, Judge David Jones of Massapequa, was abducted and spirited across Long Island Sound. He was not exchanged for an American officer until 1780.

With rebel Connecticut so close, cross-water warfare erupted frequently. Privateers, smugglers, and pirates also roamed the Sound, attacking provision ships bound for New York City. Lightning-quick whaleboat raids were common, too. In 1777, 170 men in thirteen boats crossed the Sound to Greenport, portaged to Peconic Bay, and in a fierce assault on Sag Harbor, killed six British soldiers, captured ninety, and burned ten ships. Connecticut-based whaleboatmen also captured Fort St. George, an English outpost overlooking Bellport Bay, and Fort Slongo (Salonga), located between Huntington and Smithtown.

Sometimes the war effort took a more secretive turn. General Washington's acute need to discover British troop movements fostered the creation of an extensive Long Island spy ring. Among its prominent members were exiled Colonel Benjamin Talmage of Brookhaven, Abraham Woodhull of Setauket, and

# SAMUEL TOWNSEND

For most of the eighteenth century, country merchants dominated Long Island's economy. Acting as traders, bankers, shipbuilders, and storekeepers, they linked isolated rural farmers with the rising urban centers of London, New York, and Boston. Prominent among local merchants was the Townsend family of Oyster Bay, led by patriarch Samuel Townsend, a fifth-generation Long Islander. Born in Jericho in 1717, he moved to coastal Oyster Bay in 1738 and married shortly thereafter. In partnership with his younger brother Jacob, he built his first trading sloop, aptly named *Prosperity,* in 1747 at a cost of £1,100. From this initial successful investment, Townsend created a small mercantile empire, with ships and cargoes venturing to the Caribbean, Central America, Portugal, and England. With a growing fleet he marketed Long Island's beef, pork, grain, and lumber, and imported molasses, sugar, and rum, which he then exchanged in London or New York City for imported goods to satisfy local customers. His account books bulged with orders for cloth, buttons, nails, coffin boards, paper, rum, and even slaves.

The impact of Townsend's mercantile activities on Oyster Bay was dramatic. Construction and repair of ships and the exchange of varied cargoes employed carpenters, shipwrights, smiths, and

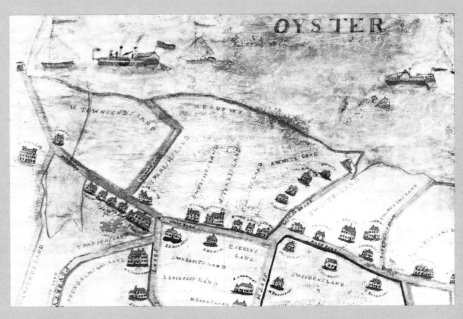

*Because of its deep, excellent harbor, Oyster Bay was involved in many aspects of the burgeoning eighteenth-century maritime industry. This 1834 map depicts the wharves, warehouses, and residences surrounding the harbor, including the Townsend family property on the left. Courtesy, Raynham Hall Museum*

teamsters. Townspeople not directly employed by Townsend undoubtedly knew him as shopkeeper and retailer, for by the late 1750s he maintained over 275 credit accounts, the majority of the village population.

Much of Townsend's commercial success depended on a talented network of family, in-laws, and business agents. Their discretion in

buying, selling, navigating, and negotiating was crucial. Of Townsend's five sons, one labored as a ship's captain and two more acted as business agents. Neighbors like the Lloyd family of Huntington provided valuable banking services and one Lloyd son served as a Townsend commission agent in Jamaica.

The momentous year 1775 found Samuel Townsend a wealthy and respected merchant. He owned extensive real estate, held nine slaves, and served as town clerk. For more than a quarter century his ships had supplied Long Islanders with tropical produce and European imports. Unfortunately his carefully wrought commercial empire could not withstand the damage inflicted by the American Revolution. An important town figure and an active patriot, Townsend was drawn to the center of the military and political storm. His family was separated and his home in Oyster Bay occupied by Loyalist troops. One son became a patriot spy while another sailed under the English flag. British regulations sharply restricted commerce, local business dwindled, and the triangular trade between the colonies, England, and the Caribbean—so integral to Townsend's success—collapsed.

With the triumph of the revolutionary cause in 1783, Townsend regained public respect and political influence. He was elected to the state senate and named a member of the Governor's Council. But his business interests were not so easily revived, and Townsend's advancing age meant that the task of resurrecting the family empire fell to his son Robert. The task proved a daunting one, for Robert Townsend confronted all the debilitating conditions that plagued post-Revolutionary America. Many wealthy merchants and former business associates had fled the country. Trade with Britain's Caribbean colonies was forbidden. No unified American currency existed, severely hampering the task of collecting prewar debts.

Ultimately Samuel Townsend's mercantile business could not be revived. Oyster Bay's small harbor and limited facilities could not hope to compete with the large ports and mercantile elites of Boston, New York, and Philadelphia. Instead, his sons, like so many ambitious young men of their generation, moved to New York to strike out on their own. When Townsend died in 1790, his commercial empire was only a memory, and the age of the independent country merchant died with him.

Geoffrey L. Rossano

*Samuel Townsend's 1761 account book records some of his business activities. Courtesy, Raynham Hall Museum*

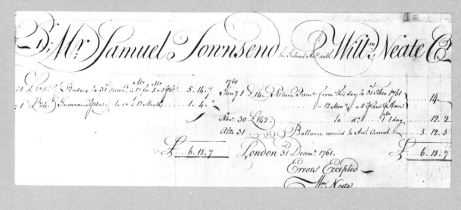

*Above: General William Howe achieved a brilliant victory in the Battle of Long Island, but has been criticized for missing the opportunity to bottle up Washington's troops on Manhattan. From Cirker,* Dictionary of American Portraits, *Dover, 1967*

Robert Townsend of Oyster Bay. When enemy troops marched eastward in 1779, agents advised: "Redoubts have been built at Southampton, East Hampton, and are being constructed at Canoe Place." In July 1779 Robert Townsend reported: "The British fleet is arrived and off New York with 7,000 troops . . . the 54th Regiment, the Queen's Rangers, and Lord Rawdon's Corps may also be preparing to embark on ships for Carolina."

But the war could not last forever. After repeated delays, diplomats signed a peace treaty in April 1783; Britain began evacuating Long Island shortly thereafter. Local patriots immediately turned on their loyalist tormenters, and a New York newspaper warned "that the calm the enemies of Columbia have heretofore enjoyed will ere long be succeeded by a bitter and neck-breaking hurricane."

These were not idle threats. In 1779 the state legislature had passed acts of attainder against leading tories, and after the war at least fifty-two loyalist estates were seized in Queens County, as were the Suffolk lands of Richard Floyd, George Muirson, and Parker Wickham. Town officials serving the occupation government also felt their neighbors' wrath. Hempstead and Oyster Bay, for example, turned out all their royalist rulers. Other friends of the King were dragged into court. Oyster Bay's John Luister accused Squire Van Wyck of helping the British seize his horse and wagon. Van Wyck

was convicted, fined, and later left the town.

In 1784 the legislature took further revenge when it disfranchised loyalists, cancelled patriot debts to them, and disbarred tory lawyers. Representatives also laid a tax of $100,000 on Long Island "as compensation to the other parts of the state for not having been in a condition to take an active part in the war against the enemy."

Not surprisingly, many loyalists found the local environment extremely uncomfortable, and approximately 6,000 departed for new settlements in Atlantic Canada. Colonel Gabriel Ludlow of Hempstead and DeLancey's Brigade emigrated to New Brunswick in 1783. DeLancey successively became mayor of St. John, judge of the Vice Admiralty Court, a member of the Council, and finally, colonial governor. Others, like Hempstead's Anglican rector Leonard Cutting, quietly moved to Maryland. As American as their neighbors, these unfortunate citizens had chosen the wrong side. One man's liberty was another's mob rule, and for many the blessings of liberty proved very hard to bear.

The Revolution and its aftermath also affected numerous social institutions which had previously defined Long Island life. Local citizens took the ideology of the war to heart and quietly transformed long-established political habits. Most notably, Hempstead and Huntington witnessed an increasingly rapid turnover of elected officials and the practice of plural office holding came to an end. The post-Revolutionary generation feared the concentration of power as corrupting and moved to check the now perceived excesses of oligarchy and privilege. Furthermore, the emerging republican ethos placed less emphasis on family history or economic status. A struggle to defy privilege and overthrow a foreign authority could not help but raise similar questions about political institutions at home.

Religion, a cornerstone of colonial society, was

*Sarah Townsend gathered information on British troop movements from her home in Oyster Bay. She passed the information to her brother, Robert Townsend, one of Wash-ington's spies on Long Island. From Pennypacker,* General Washington's Spies, *LIHS, 1939. Courtesy, Raynham Hall Museum*

similarly affected by the Revolution. In some places the Anglican Church, tainted with toryism, went into sharp decline as state support vanished and loyalist stalwarts emigrated. Even more important was the war's liberating effect on previous patterns of behavior and belief. The prevalence of one or two denominations was broken, and pluralism became the order of the day. Appealing to the humblest of citizens, Methodists and Baptists attracted the greatest number of converts.

Methodist missionaries were the most active. Circuit riders made fervent exhortations to the common man, who responded with animated hymn singing and extravagant rejoicing. Missionary Phillip Cox described a 1784 meeting held in Searingtown. "Very many attended," he exulted, "until the alarm was sounded that the false prophets

*Opposite page: Patchogue was one of the most flourishing villages in Brookhaven during the eighteenth and nineteenth centuries. It served as an overnight stopping place for the stages, which ran from East Hampton to Brooklyn carrying passengers and mail. From Pelletreau,* A History of Long Island, *Lewis, 1903*

*This tombstone erected in memory of Anthony Hannibal Clapp, an indentured servant who died in Setauket in 1816, bears silent testimony to his character and value to his master, as well as to the pleasure he gave to others with his fiddle playing. Courtesy, The Museums at Stony Brook, bequest of Ward Melville, 1977*

Rachel Seaman Hicks became a dedicated minister in the Society of Friends. Born in Westbury, she traveled and preached as far west as Ohio and Indiana. From Memoir of Rachel Hicks, G.P. Putnam's Sons, 1880. Courtesy, Haviland Records Room, Religious Society of Friends

Throughout the Dutch period, Brooklyn boweries provided a small but steady market for scores of slaves.

England's conquest in 1664 did not materially alter the institution. Setauket town records mention slave sales in the 1670s, and by century's end slaves resided throughout Long Island. More than one-third of Brooklyn and Bushwyck households contained servants, while half the farms in Flushing, Flatbush, and Flatlands utilized slave labor. Black bondsmen comprised 10 percent of Southampton's population.

Slavery expanded steadily throughout the eighteenth century. There were 1,100 Long Island bondsmen in 1698; 3,400 in 1749; and nearly 5,000 by 1775, when demand and sale prices peaked. During the revolutionary turmoil local whigs worried lest loyalist neighbors induce their servants to flee. When patriot refugees departed for Connecticut in 1776, many took their chattels with them.

Political and social pressures generated by the war dramatically altered local attitudes, and soon conscience-stricken Quakers and New York philanthropists initiated an anti-slavery movement. A society advocating manumission was established in 1785; voluntary emancipations began soon thereafter.

The 1790 census reveals large numbers of freed blacks in several East End towns, and the release of servants accelerated in central Long Island after 1793. Brooklyn, with the highest concentration of slaves (65 percent of all households, compared with 35 percent in Queens, and 15 to 20 percent in Suffolk), recorded its first manumission in 1797, as Quaker John Doughty freed his bondsman, Caesar Foster. But anti-slave agitation really triumphed in 1799, when the state legislature finally passed a gradual emancipation act. By 1827 virtually all slaves had been freed, ending two centuries of bondage.

With the election of presidents Washington, Adams, and Jefferson, Long Island turned away from its colonial and revolutionary path and assumed a place in the new nation. A distance more profound than time separated local society from its recent past. Established allegiances and institutions had been altered, the old orthodoxies challenged. Long Island had taken its first uncertain steps into the modern world.

foretold in scripture had come. The word of truth, however, did not fall to the ground. Souls were awakened." Inspired by the message, Methodist converts gathered at Roslyn and Glen Cove in 1785, Rockville Center in 1790, Patchogue and Brookhaven in 1791. By the mid-nineteenth century, they were Long Island's largest denomination. Having led men to question the old verities, the war also caused them to examine their spiritual lives, which they did with great vigor, casting aside past orthodoxies and embracing new faiths.

The liberating sentiments unleashed in the war years affected local black inhabitants, too, culminating in the Manumission Act of 1799 which set several thousand slaves on the road to eventual freedom. This liberation was a long time coming, for slavery possessed an extensive history on Long Island. Dutch colonists first imported bondsmen around 1626 and shortly thereafter the West India Company promised to "use their endeavors to supply . . . as many blacks as they conveniently can."

# City and Country Solidified

As he travelled through post-Revolutionary Suffolk County in the early years of the new century, Yale President Timothy Dwight described the insularity which pervaded rural Long Island society. "Almost all their concerns," he noted, "are absolutely confined to a house or a neighborhood, and their neighborhood rarely extends beyond the confines of a small hamlet." But as he journeyed westward towards New York City, he watched the quality of life change. Religious observance appeared less strict, agriculture was more commercially oriented, transportation facilities improved, and city manners grew more pronounced. Something exciting was in the air.

A generation earlier the struggle with Great Britain had precipitated a political revolution. Now Long Island stood poised on the brink of a social and economic revolution, as well. Between 1790 and 1850 the population of Queens and Suffolk counties leaped from 32,000 to over 70,000. Farming grew increasingly commercial and city-oriented. Industry, banks, and insurance companies sprouted up, as did dozens of country newspapers. Fleets of whaling ships scoured the seas. Visitors and summer residents swelled from a trickle to a flood. Everywhere rural society felt the approaching hand of its urban neighbor.

It was no wonder. Nearby Brooklyn and New York were mushrooming into a great metropolis, generating demands for agricultural produce, financing industrial development, stoking intellectual ferment, setting the tone in fashion and literature. New York City affected and changed everything it touched. Dramatic transportation improvements facilitated the process. In only thirty years Long Island's oxcarts, sandy paths, and sailing sloops

*Just twelve miles from New York City, Jamaica was a thriving and populous Long Island town with a population of over 4,000 in 1850. Its* growth was greatly facilitated by the railroad line from Brooklyn, opened in 1836. *From Pelletreau,* A History of Long Island, *Lewis, 1903*

# RUFUS KING

Names such as Gardiner, Floyd, and Lloyd are sooner associated with Long Island history, but perhaps no family was more accomplished than the Kings of Jamaica. They were dominant figures in New York political life for a century, holding such offices as governor and senator.

Rufus King (1755-1827) had represented his native Massachusetts at the Constitutional Convention and had already earned a reputation as a gifted orator before his marriage to Mary Alsop, daughter of a prominent Manhattan merchant, led to his relocation to New York in the late 1780s. King quickly reestablished his political career, first being elected to the New York State Assembly and then in 1789 to the U.S. Senate, where he was to serve a total of four terms spanning three and a half decades. An effective public speaker and an ardent abolitionist, he opposed the extension of slavery to the Northwest Territory and resisted the admission of Missouri as a slave state. A leading Federalist, King was his party's candidate for Vice President in 1804 and again in 1808. In 1816 he ran for the Presidency, losing to James Monroe.

The statesman from Jamaica is probably best remembered, however, as the new republic's ambassador to Great Britain. In a letter to President Washington at the time of his appointment, Alexander Hamilton praised King as a "re-

Rufus King was a prominent American statesman during the nation's early years, and his sons and grandson would continue to play important roles in New York State politics throughout the nineteenth century. From Pelletreau, A History of Long Island, *Lewis, 1903*

markably well-informed man, a judicious one, a man of address, of fortune and economy." King assumed the post in 1796, succeeding Thomas Pinckney, and quickly became a popular figure in London's social and political circles. With quiet diplomacy, King worked to end impressment of American seamen and to quiet crises while supplying Washington with model correspondence on Great Britain's foreign policy. On learning that the American ambassador (while on a trip to the continent) had passed up an opportunity to be presented to Napoleon Bonaparte to avoid angering the British government, George III is said to have remarked, "Mr. King, you have treated me like a gentleman, which is more than I can say for all of my subjects."

King returned to America in 1803 only to see Anglo-American relations deteriorate. He opposed U.S. entry into the War of 1812, although he supported the government after hostilities had commenced. Perhaps his most famous Senate speech occurred after the burning of Washington, D.C., by the British, when he rose to oppose moving the capitol inland and asked that the outrage be avenged. John Quincy Adams sent King back to London as ambassador in 1825, but illness soon forced him to return, bringing to an end his long career in public service.

On his return from England in 1803, King purchased a farm in Jamaica, which he transformed into his country seat, enlarging the large gambrel-roof house now known as King Manor. City-bound LIRR riders catch a glimpse of this estate every day, just before they pull into the Jamaica station. On his Queens farm, King pursued his deep interest in agriculture and husbandry, developing a model farm that boasted an imported herd of Devon cattle.

Left behind in England in 1803 to complete their education at Harrow, King's eldest sons, John Alsop (1788-1867) and Charles (1789-1867), returned to New York to lead distinguished careers. Charles served in the state legislature and as editor of the *New York American* before becoming president of Columbia College (1849-1864). John Alsop King, who had been a classmate of Lord Byron at Harrow, followed his father into politics, first serving in the state assembly and senate. He accompanied his father to England in 1825 as secretary to the legation and remained as Charge D'Affairs, when illness forced his father's return. In 1849 the people of Queens elected him to Congress and subsequently he became governor of New York in 1856. For many years Governor King, who shared his father's interest in farming, also served as president of the state agricultural society, and from 1827 until his death in 1867 resided at King Manor.

For a century the Kings of Jamaica represented agrarian Queens in Albany and Washington, D.C. They were among the best educated and most able public servants of their age. John A. King, Jr. (1817-1900), the third generation and the fourth member of his family to serve in the state legislature, bought the land on the tip of one of the North Shore's peninsulas in 1854, which is still known as King's Point.

Robert B. MacKay

were pushed aside by turnpikes, steamboats, and railroads that tied city and country together, broadening the lives and expanding the opportunities of all who used them.

Demands for improved roads dated back to the colonial era, when in 1704 the Assembly authorized a route from Brooklyn Ferry to East Hampton named Kings Highway. Later in the century bimonthly post riders carried the mail eastward, but a stage journey from Brooklyn to Southampton lasted four days, including overnight stops at Hempstead, Smithtown, and St. George's Manor. Such time consuming arrangements proved unsatisfactory, and privately funded turnpikes appeared soon after the Revolution. The first ran from Brooklyn to Jamaica, later extending to Jericho and Smithtown. Other routes fanned out to Williamsburg, Oyster Bay, and Babylon. Wooden plank roads built in heavily trafficked portions of Brooklyn and Queens supplemented the turnpike system. By 1845 a network of roads and stage routes crisscrossed western Long Island, speeding the flow of commerce and passengers. A pleased traveller commented, "Numerous turnpikes present as pleasant journeying for man, and as comfortable travelling for beast ... in all seasons of the year, as any other equal district in the state."

Improved roads reached eastern Suffolk County much more slowly. As late as 1840 the stage trip from Brooklyn to Orient consumed three days. A weary passenger lamented: "No one was in a hurry to get to his journey's end, and if he was ... he soon became effectively cured of it." Another be-

moaned that "the roads of (eastern) Long Island are exceedingly numerous and difficult for strangers ... It is impossible to convey an adequate idea of the inconvenience and obstruction to locomotion which are represented." Not until the railroad arrived would East Enders enjoy truly rapid and reliable transportation.

Advances in waterborne commerce, especially the introduction of the steamboat, also helped unite city and country. Inventor Robert Fulton improved this crude and unreliable conveyance early in the nineteenth century and Long Island Sound's first steamer, appropriately named the *Fulton,* began its New York-to-New Haven run in 1815. Within a few years steam traffic of all descriptions plied the coastal waters, visiting every suitable port, efficiently and speedily carrying freight and passengers. Competition between rival lines grew intense. Races

## New Arrangement.
### Huntington
### STAGE.

THE SUBSCRIBER will hereafter drive his Stage between Brooklyn and Huntington, once a week: Leave Huntington on Mondays at 8 o'clock, A. M., and leave Brooklyn on Wednesdays at 9 o'clock, A. M. *Fare,* for Passengers, One Dollar. Seats taken at *Richard S. Williams'* store, corner of Fulton and South streets, New York, and at *Isaac Snedicor's,* in Brooklyn.
NATHANIEL RUSCO, *Proprietor.*
Huntington, Sept. 21, 1826.

*Above: In addition to transporting passengers, stage coaches were an important avenue of commerce, carrying mail, newspapers, and small packages. From* The Portico, *Huntington, September 21, 1826*

*Left: Steamboats provided a rapid and often luxurious mode of transportation. Nearly every North Shore village was served by these boats, some of which were fitted with the finest furniture, carpets, and glassware. (SPLIA)*

## WINTER ARRANGEMENT.
For New Rochelle, Glen Cove, Peacock's Point, Oysterbay and Cold Spring.
*On and after Wednesday, November 20th.*

*The Steamboat American Eagle,*
CAPT. CHAS. B. PECK,
WILL leave New York, every Wednesday and Saturday, at 11 o'clock, A. M. Returning, will leave Cold Spring every Monday and Thursday morning at 8 o'clock, Oyster Bay, 20 minutes past 8, Peacock's Point, quarter past 9, Glen Cove, 10, and New Rochelle, quarter before 11.          November 15, 1839.

THE OLD STONE HOUSE. L.I., 1699.

*The earliest Dutch houses on Long Island were relatively crude, but by the end of the seventeenth century they attained greater size and comfort. The Nicholas Vechte house, a Brooklyn landmark, was the only stone house in Gowanus at the time of its construction in 1699 and for a long time thereafter. (SPLIA)*

*Above: At the beginning of the nineteenth century Long Island Sound was considered to have one of the most well-illuminated coastlines in the U.S., a result of shipping's increasing importance to the Island's economy. This watercolor depicts the 1809 Sands Point lighthouse, which remained in service until 1924. (SPLIA)*

*Right: In this 1776 view of Brooklyn, the steeple of the Dutch Reformed Church on Fulton Street dominates the surrounding countryside. This peaceful scene would soon be interrupted by British troops, who occupied Long Island during the Revolution. Courtesy, The Long Island Historical Society*

*Below: British artist Francis Guy painted this Brooklyn winter scene in 1816, looking from the second floor of his home at 11 Front Street. He was particularly intrigued by this intersection at Fulton Street, painting six known versions of it during his stay in America. Courtesy, The Brooklyn Museum*

*Left: Alden Spooner (1783-1848) published the Suffolk Gazette from 1804 to 1811 and then purchased the Long Island Star, which he supervised until 1840. Spooner also published books on the work of many of Brooklyn's poets, founded his own circulating library, and helped establish the Female Seminary of Brooklyn. Courtesy, The Long Island Historical Society*

*Above: Born in Setauket, William Sidney Mount spent most of his life on Long Island faithfully recording his observations in portraits, genre scenes, and landscapes like "Flax Pond, Old Field, Long Island." (SPLIA)*

*Right: An unknown artist captured this view of sperm whaling in the bark* Washington *of Sag Harbor. The Sag Harbor whaling fleet totaled sixty-three vessels at its peak in 1845. Courtesy, The George Latham Collection, Oysterponds Historical Society*

*Around 1840 Montgomery Queen established Brooklyn's first effective line of stage coaches, or omnibuses, which spurred the growth of the city's residential neighborhoods. He commissioned painter Henry Boese to depict his new stage, the* Sewanhackey, *in front of the new City Hall building in 1852. Courtesy, The Long Island Historical Society*

*"Farmers Nooning," painted in 1836, exemplifies William Sidney Mount's concentration on the daily life of his Long Island friends and neighbors as a theme. Courtesy, The Museums at Stony Brook, gift of Mr. Frederick Sturges, Jr., 1954*

*Left: Brooklyn before the bridge was to a great extent a creature of the ferries—they were the heart of its transportation system until the late nineteenth century. Walt Whitman celebrated their importance in his 1860 poem, "Crossing Brooklyn Ferry." Courtesy, The Long Island Historical Society*

*Right: In this circa 1840 view from Gowanus Heights, Brooklyn, French painter Victor de Grailly depicted the John F. Delaplaine house (right), noted for its lavish interiors that included frescoes and marble halls. The house stood at the present-day intersection of Second Avenue and 40th Street. Courtesy, The Long Island Historical Society*

*For Long Island, as well as the rest of the nation, the nineteenth century represented change and growth. However, this 1839 view of Elmhurst shows that some areas developed more slowly than others, retaining a rural character typical of the bygone colonial era. Courtesy, SPLIA*

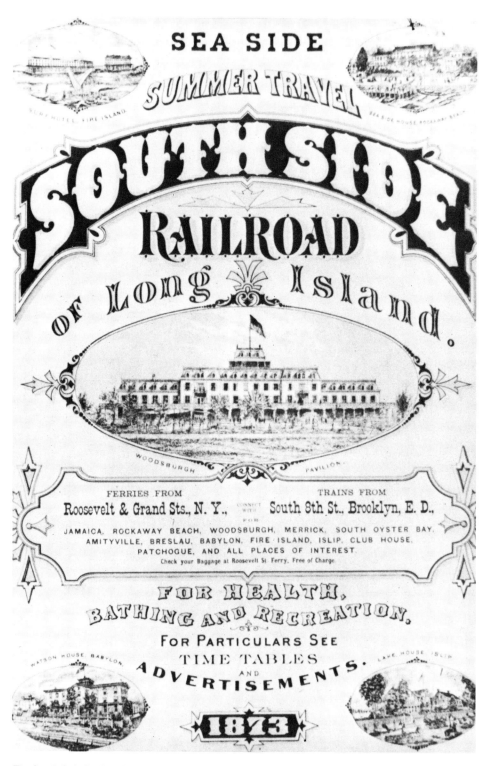

*The South Side Railroad was one of the Long Island Rail Road's first competitors, operating as an independent line from 1867 to 1876. The promotional advertisements of both railroads lured thousands to Long Island's summer resorts. Courtesy, New-York Historical Society, Landauer Collection*

were common, as were collisions and boiler explosions. One of the worst maritime disasters involved the swift and elegant steam packet *Lexington.* On January 13, 1840, while cruising off Eaton's Point, the *Lexington's* red-hot smokestacks ignited cotton bales stored on deck. Flames quickly engulfed the vessel; panicked passengers swamped the lifeboats, and 120 perished in the icy waters.

Despite periodic mishaps, steamboats forged rapid links to New York and New England's ports. They also proved ideal for conveying city excursioners to country inns, beaches, and picnic groves, remaining an important feature of Long Island life until the twentieth century.

Railroads provided the final component of Long Island's transportation revolution. The flat, sandy landscape proved ideal for railroad construction, and planning began in 1832 for a line from Brooklyn to Greenport. From there, steamers would carry passengers to Connecticut or Rhode Island. Conceived as a through-route to Boston, little heed was paid initially to local needs or sensitivities. Construction commenced in 1833 and the new line reached Jamaica shortly thereafter, pushing on to Hicksville by 1837. That same year Long Island's only two engines, the *Ariel* and *Postboy,* collided near the Hicksville station.

Despite the banking panic of 1837, the line reached Farmingdale in 1841 and Greenport in 1844. There, a great and uproarious celebration commemorated the event. Nathaniel Prime, a prescient local observer, noted: "To a people thus situated, in almost entire seclusion from the rest of the world, a railroad must open new and unconceived facilities . . . producing an amazing revolution in manners and habits of the country." Such changes, especially the Sunday trains which disturbed traditional sabbath observance, were not always welcomed, however. Fire posed another problem, since engine sparks ignited vast tracts of Suffolk's Pine Barrens, destroying much valuable cordwood.

Despite the promoters' initial hopes, plans to speed travellers from New York to Boston quickly collapsed after completion of the rival Connecticut Shore Line in 1849. Traffic on Long Island declined precipitously, and by 1850 the railroad was bankrupt. In the reorganization that followed, management decided to encourage local traffic. But while the Long Island Rail Road hesitated, rival lines

known as the North and South Side systems initiated their own construction programs. Rails soon spread in every direction, reaching out to Hunter's Point, Glen Cove, Garden City, Port Jefferson, and Sag Harbor, all by 1872. Three systems vying for limited traffic was a sure prescription for financial disaster, and in 1874 the South Side lines defaulted. A rate war between the surviving companies led to final consolidation of the entire system in 1876.

Although the railroad provided an important tool for hauling farm produce to urban markets, and manure and ashes back out again, the lines' most frequent patrons were the thousands of summer travellers who sought temporary respite from the city's heat and congestion. During the winter, however, management was forced to slash train schedules in an effort to reduce operating losses. Nevertheless, the railroad offered both Island and city residents convenient and speedy access to distant markets, jobs, and resorts. It was the iron pin which united the two halves of nineteenth-century America.

Throughout the first half of the century, Long Island's pleasant weather and attractive scenery tantalized many New Yorkers. Improved transportation also enticed ever increasing numbers to visit and settle there. The precedent was established as early as 1684, when Governor Thomas Dongan purchased a country estate at Hyde Park. Mathias Nicoll, first Secretary of the Province, resided at nearby Cow Neck. Throughout the eighteenth century, traders and royal favorites established Island homes. Antigua merchant Josiah Martin built his Rock Hall mansion in 1767 and Lieutenant Governor Cadwallader Colden lived in Flushing. A visitor to Queens County wrote in 1759, "I took a ride upon Long Island, the richest spot in the opinion of New Yorkers of all America, and where they generally have their villas or country houses."

The post-Revolutionary era witnessed a sharp expansion of this long-established practice. Many, like Newtown's Doctor Isaac Ledyard, "possessed a keen relish for country life . . . and was anxious to escape the noise and bustle of the city." Noted politician Rufus King moved to Jamaica in 1805, and five years later it was noted that the village displayed "a polish not visible in towns further eastward, due to its neighborhood to New York and from long having been a resort for the inhabitants of that city."

Transportation improvements further encouraged the flow of suburbanites and by 1840 Hempstead sported a reputation as "one of the most convenient and desirable residences on Long Island." Nearby Jamaica contained "splendid private residences, erected by gentlemen of the city." Blessed with the "great facility of communications with New York," neighboring Flushing boasted some of the "most imposing and splendid residences in that state."

Many other New Yorkers came simply to vacation. Already at the beginning of the nineteenth century, thousands sojourned at Rockaway Beach "in pursuit of pure air and the luxury of sea bathing." City dwellers also visited Long Island to hunt and fish. Timothy Dwight's extensive travels were occasionally interrupted by "sportsmen who come hither to catch trout."

Horse racing attracted additional thousands. Established on Salisbury (Hempstead) Plain in 1665, by the late 1700s racing drew competitors from New

*The flat Hempstead Plain made Long Island the home of horse racing from the moment the English settlers had horses to race. In 1821 the Union Race Course was organized; this lithograph shows a trotting match there between Flora Temple and George M. Patchen. Courtesy, The Long Island Historical Society*

Jersey, Boston, and Virginia. Legislation permitting "speed trials" was enacted in 1821, and meets were held each May and October thereafter. So heavy did the crush of spectators become that on one day in May 1823, the Fulton Ferry Company collected more than $5,000 in fares. Not everyone, however, waxed enthusiastic about the sport of kings, believing instead that racing was a "principle means of demoralization," fostering gambling, drinking, and swearing.

# WALTER R. JONES

Left: Walter R. Jones (pictured circa 1853) and his four brothers were important local businessmen in Cold Spring Harbor. (SPLIA)

Right: Walter R. Jones and Lambert Suydam witness the first experiment made by Captain Douglas Ottinger for throwing a line and sending a "Life Car" to a stranded vessel off the South Shore of Long Island in April 1849. From Overton, Long Island's Story, (1929), 1963

Among the many Long Islanders contributing to New York's development as an artery for maritime commerce, Walter Restored Jones (1793-1855) ranks as a major figure. As an entrepreneur Jones was responsible for the success of such ventures as Atlantic Mutual Insurance, still a major force in marine insurance. Although he spent most of his adult life in Manhattan guiding the fortunes of Atlantic Mutual, Jones also left his mark on his native Long Island. In 1836 Walter, with his brother John and a small group of associates, founded the Cold Spring Whaling Company. Over the next twenty-five years Cold Spring Harbor was the home port of a nine-ship whaling fleet, the third largest aggregation of such vessels on Long Island.

The role played by the Joneses in this endeavor is hardly surprising given their prominence in other aspects of village affairs. The Jones family dominated life in Cold Spring Harbor during the first half of the nineteenth century, operating such businesses as a steamboat company, textile mills, and general store. For the Joneses the decision to enter the whaling trade was based on both local and national trends. The 1830s witnessed severe inroads by foreign woolens into domestic textile markets. Whaling, on the other hand, offered the chance of huge profits and was already dominated by American interests. While the 1830s brought troubles for some domestic manufactures, it also brought burgeoning markets for the oil, candles, and whalebone

was necessary to buy ships and secure insurance. With an active shipbuilding industry and market for used vessels, New York offered Jones and his fellow owners the best opportunity for adding new vessels to the Cold Spring fleet. Walter's position at the helm of Atlantic Mutual put him in an advantageous spot when insurance was required.

The Cold Spring fleet was modestly successful through the 1840s. By the 1850s, however, long voyages and dwindling profits were hurting marginal ports like Cold Spring Harbor. Equally damaging to the local fleet was the loss of both Walter and John Jones within a few years of each other. Walter died in 1855, while John died in 1859. Deprived of their guidance, the whaling fleet slowly broke as vessels were sold and lost to accidents.

The last whaleship departed Cold Spring Harbor in 1858, and was sold nearly four years later. In all likelihood the Joneses and other investors in the Cold Spring fleet realized a modest profit from their investment. For Walter Jones whaling was a venture that fit the pattern of control which his family exerted over the economy of Cold Spring Harbor. That control, like the fortunes of the whaling industry, slowly ebbed and by the 1860s was on its way to disappearing.

Robert Farwell

produced by the whaling industry. When attempts to protect American goods from foreign competition failed, Walter Jones and his kin turned to whaling.

While his brother John served as managing agent of the nine whaling vessels, Walter played an important part in purchasing and insuring these vessels. Although his work at Atlantic Mutual kept him away from Cold Spring Harbor for long periods of time, Walter's position in New York was of considerable advantage when it

Railroads and steamboats further spurred the tourist trade, especially in the summer, speeding visitors to towns and villages scattered across the Island. Distant Oyster Ponds (Orient) maintained a fine hotel, while Patchogue was renowned for its fishing and fowling. Nearby Babylon was a place "much resorted to by travellers and sportsmen." All came searching for a pleasant, rustic diversion from city life.

These suburban residents and throngs of visitors inevitably affected local society. By the early 1800s, Jamaica possessed a noticeable "city air." Straightlaced chroniclers complained that in much of Kings and Queens counties, the sabbath was corrupted by hunting and fishing, visiting and amusement. "Proximity to the city has doubtless increased these evils." Slowly but steadily rural Long Island was being drawn into the urban orbit.

Diversification of Long Island's economy followed quickly upon the heels of improved transportation and increased contact with the city. Though lacking abundant water power or rich mineral resources, the Island was not immune to the stirrings of the Industrial Revolution. Rapidly growing urban markets created new opportunities for rural entrepreneurs, and traditional mills did a booming business. A Cold Spring grist mill ground over 1,000 bushels each week (1792), and when fire consumed Glen Cove's Thorne Mill in 1806, over 10,000 bushels of grain were destroyed.

The early years of the nineteenth century saw new commercial enterprises evolve from the Island's agricultural base. About the time of the Revolution, Hendrick and Andrew Onderdonk constructed a paper mill in Roslyn to supply New York City's book and print sellers. Richard Conklin of Huntington opened another paper mill in 1782. By 1798 a strawboard and wrapping paper factory operated at Patchogue, followed by a twine mill in 1805. Cloth mills were soon started in Babylon, Smithtown, and Patchogue. In 1820 the Jones family erected a larger facility at Cold Spring Harbor which produced 120 pounds of broadcloth and flannel each day. Industrial production was not limited to cloth, paper, or grain. Captain Solomon Townsend, a New York sea captain, merchant, and iron master, built a forge on the Peconic River near Riverhead, and Jeffrey Smith manufactured bar iron in Patchogue. Water power drove most of these establishments, but where stream and tide proved insufficient, enterprising operators at Wheatley Hills and Huntington constructed windmills to saw lumber and spin thread. Although industry and commerce did not replace farming as Long Island's principal occupation, small-scale manufacturing had come to occupy an important niche in the local economy.

Increased business activity naturally generated demands for improved financial services. The Long Island Farmers Fire Insurance Company was chartered in 1833, followed by the Glen Cove Mutual Insurance Company four years later. Suffolk County's first bank opened in Sag Harbor in 1844.

Maritime industries also spurred Long Island's economic development. As available farmlands diminished, men increasingly turned to the sea to earn a living, while successful merchants sought new investment opportunities. Shipbuilding and coastal trading boomed, especially at Huntington, Northport, Port Jefferson, and Stony Brook. But the most profitable venture of all was whaling. From humble, coast-bound origins, it grew into a major industry, with large fleets operating out of Sag Harbor/Peconic Bay and Cold Spring Harbor.

Long Island's first whalemen were Indians who ventured offshore in dugout canoes, armed only with stone-tipped spears. The early English colonists followed their example and soon turned to shore whaling as well. Southampton's original whaling regulations date from 1644, and commercial companies were chartered by 1650. Villagers also manned beach stations at Rockaway, Tobay, and Jones Beach. In both Southampton and East Hampton Indian crews often enlisted for the winter season.

Jealous of their profitable whaling privileges, towns routinely forbid outsiders from invading their territorial limits, and disputes sometimes reached the Governor's Council. Citizens fiercely resisted taxation; smuggling was rampant. Governor Dongan confessed in 1686 that he had collected only ten gallons of whale oil.

Shore whaling was dangerous work. "About the fin," an early (1679) observer noted, "is the surest part for the harpineer (sic) to strike . . . As soon as the whale is wounded it makes all foam . . . so that if the men be not very quick in clearing the ways . . . it is a hundred to one that he oversets the boat."

As the quantity of coastal whales steadily diminished throughout the eighteenth century, sailors began travelling farther and farther in search of their quarry. By the 1780s the Sag Harbor ship *Lucy* had ventured off the coast of Brazil, and early in the next century, Long Island vessels reached Cape Horn and the Indian Ocean. Such extended voyages could last for years. The *Argonaut* departed Sag Harbor in September 1817 for a Pacific cruise and did not return until June 1819. But with whale oil selling at one dollar per gallon, the trips were lucrative indeed, attracting investors and captains from

*Opposite page: In 1842 Long Island historian Benjamin Thompson described Montrose as "equally well calculated for a country residence or for manufacturing and commercial purposes." True to its description, the area's water supply attracted mills and factories, and its nice weather lured summer residents. (SPLIA)*

*Right: Long Island was not completely bypassed by the Industrial Revolution; many local entrepreneurs attempted to apply new manufacturing methods to meet the growing demand for products of all kinds. (SPLIA)*

*Below: Windmills were often built where water power was scarce. This circa 1826 drawing depicts the mills of East Hampton. From Gillon,* Early Illustrations and Views of American Architecture, *Dover, 1971*

COLD SPRING

## Factory.

PERSONS sending WOOL to this Factory are requested to take notice, that in consequence of the difficulty and expense of collecting small accounts no credit can be given for a less sum than *Five Dollars*—and to prevent disappointment, those forwarding small parcels of Wool for carding, or Cloth for dressing, must prepare themselves accordingly.

### WANTED,

*MERINO WOOL—of the first quality,* For which the CASH will be paid on delivery.

*ALSO WANTED.*
*Several good*

## Weavers,

To whom constant employment will be given. Men of families will be preferred, and houses will be provided for them.
JOHN H. & W.R. JONES & Co.
Cold Spring, May 12, 1825.

# HENRY PACKER DERING

In contrast to neighboring villages, a cosmopolitan flavor developed early in Sag Harbor, the community Henry Packer Dering so ably served during its formative years. "Sagg's" deep, well-protected harbor was centrally located on both overland and water routes to New England and New York. Between 1760 and 1770 an active West Indies trade was established and at the end of the century Sag Harbor ranked not far behind New York as a maritime center. In 1789, at the first congressional session under the newly ratified Constitution, Sag Harbor was designated an official United States Port of Entry. Shortly thereafter, Henry Packer Dering was appointed to the prestigious position of collector of the port.

Dering's father, Thomas, had been a prosperous Boston merchant and his mother was heiress to the 1,200-acre Sylvester family manor on Shelter Island. When Thomas Dering took over Sylvester Manor's management, he was appointed inspector of trades and navigation for the Crown, thus becoming an important public figure on Long Island's East End. At the time of the Revolution he espoused the patriot cause and was twice delegate to the Provincial Congress for Suffolk County. Later, he was a member of the state constitutional convention of New York. After the Battle of Long Island in 1776 the Dering family fled to Connecticut

*Henry Packer Dering, depicted in a circa 1794 watercolor by William Verstille, held more than ten positions in the Sag Harbor community. (SPLIA)*

where Henry Packer Dering spent his adolescence.

After completing his preparatory studies, Henry entered Yale College, graduating in 1784. Following in his father's footsteps, he engaged in a number of mercantile pursuits. By 1790 he had settled in Sag Harbor and in 1793 married Anna Fosdick. Here the couple raised their nine children and Dering took on his role as community leader and public servant. In addition to his position as collector of the port, Dering was appointed United States postmaster, assumed the duties of assistant county clerk, acted as a notary public hearing oaths and arbitrating disputes, and served as a commissioner of highways and of schools. He was the federal agent for the area and as such was responsible for the lighthouses at Little Gull, Cedar Island, and Montauk. Dering issued papers attesting to sworn statements of registry and citizenship which were to serve as precautions against harrassment of sailors in the troubled days preceding the War of 1812. When war appeared imminent, Dering was put in charge of building and managing the Sag Harbor arsenal.

The late eighteenth and early nineteenth centuries witnessed a steady growth in Sag Harbor's importance as a center of trade and commerce. Having been exposed to a more cosmopolitan world outside the agrarian countryside of rural Long Island, Dering's concerns for the development of his home and his devotion to public service influenced the direction this growth would take. He was instrumental in founding schools, a lending library, a literary society, and other cultural organizations, and also attended to the more practical matter of furthering the development of the wharf area and public roads. It was Dering who invited David Frothingham to come to Sag Harbor, where in 1791 Frothingham established Long Island's first newspaper, *The Long Island Herald*. The paper ran articles on both local and international topics of interest and was filled with notices attesting to the variety of Sag Harbor's commercial life. Trading and passenger vessels making frequent trips to Boston and New York were advertised, local craftsmen offered their services, and businessmen of all sorts promoted their wares.

Despite his many roles, Dering's primary occupation continued to be that of a businessman who managed the family estate and engaged in numerous financial ventures. In an attempt to improve the quality of cloth in America, he imported Merino sheep from Spain, bred the animals, and sold the wool. The expanding whaling industry also took his interest and he made several investments in shipping and whaling expeditions, although they proved unprofitable. When Henry Packer Dering did meet with financial difficulties at the end of his life, forty-one prominent men of the area signed a decree releasing him from all debts because of his record of unwavering service to his community.

Dering died in 1822, having promoted the prosperity and sophistication of Sag Harbor, which had become Suffolk County's largest village in the nineteenth century.

Carolyn Marx

*Above: Sag Harbor was a flourishing sea-oriented community and a major whaling port. From Hazelton,* The Boroughs of Brooklyn and Queens, Counties of Nassau and Suffolk, N.Y., 1609-1924, *Lewis, 1925*

*Blacks had long been active in the whaling industry, supplying a much-needed, skilled labor force. This circa 1912 photograph shows a crew serving on the Long Island-built whaleship* Daisy. *Courtesy, Cold Spring Harbor Whaling Museum*

Suffolk's most prominent families.

An economic boom engulfed the East End. Between 1804 and 1837 Sag Harbor's ships harvested 380,000 barrels of oil and 1,600,000 pounds of whale bone as the village emerged the emporium of Suffolk County. Profits financed the construction of elegant mansions. Shipbuilding flourished; over 1,000 men labored in the fleet, and coopers manufactured 30,000 casks annually. The 1840s were the peak years, with Sag Harbor alone accounting for sixty-three sailings in 1846. Cold Spring Harbor supported a fleet of nine vessels and raucous seamen imparted the name Bedlam Street to its principal thoroughfare. Also active were the Peconic ports of Cutchogue, Greenport, Jamesport, and New Suffolk.

Whaling was not without its risks—storms, accidents, and disease were ever present. The *Governor Clinton* departed Long Island in 1833, but sank in a typhoon off the coast of Japan with the loss of twenty-nine crewmen. Anchored in Tahiti in 1836, the whaler *Telegraph* was struck by a sudden squall and wrecked on the reef. While the crew was saved, the ship and its entire cargo were destroyed.

Development of petroleum products and the American Civil War seriously curtailed the whaling industry, but in its heyday it had brought wealth to many Island families, prosperity to a half dozen communities, and adventure and employment for thousands.

Increasing population and prosperity also created numerous opportunities for Long Island's indigenous craftsmen. In the early years of settlement, wealthy families imported furniture and silver from European or American urban centers, while less affluent farmers made do with simpler country pieces executed by village cabinetmakers and smiths. By the time of the Revolution, however, local artisans had begun to supply the more elegant work associated with shops in New York or Boston. Distant from the city marketplace and patronized by a growing merchant elite, Suffolk artisans were among the most active. The Dominy clan of East Hampton became skilled craftsmen and clockmakers, while Ephraim Byron (1809-1881) of Sag Harbor developed a national reputation for his steeple time pieces and scientific instruments. Southold's John Paine (1737-1815) gained an impressive reputation as a furniture maker, but augmented his income by producing hatblocks, brick molds, coffins, and ropes. Talented silversmiths also flourished. Elias (1726-1810) and John (1755-1822) Pelletreau and John and David Hedges (active 1770-1859) of East Hampton sold their handiwork to leading East End families.

Some businesses grew quite large, benefitting from the prosperity generated by the whaling boom and increased trade. Cabinetmaker Nathan Tinker of Sag Harbor supplied the surrounding communities of Southold, Riverhead, Southampton, and East Hampton. His aggressive competitor, neighbor Henry Byram, even used public verse to attract customers:

*From Sideboards of the finest cut*
*  to workstands for the ladies*
*And stands whereon your candles put*
*  and cradles for your babies.*

Men like Byram and Tinker made extensive use of the growing number of country newspapers to advertise their wares. A more diverse local economy and society generated increased demands for news,

*Above: Nathan Tinker catered to the large and fairly sophisticated clientele of Sag Harbor and supplied a wide variety of furniture items. Unlike their rural counterparts, these well-to-do town dwellers were more aware of changing trends in the decorative arts. Courtesy, Mr. and Mrs. Louis R. Vetault*

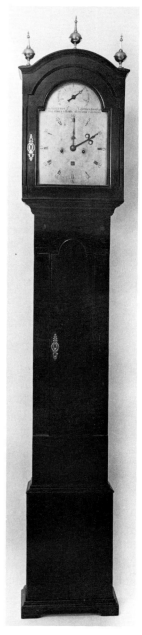

*Right: The Dominy family of East Hampton, successive generations of woodworking craftsmen active from 1714 to 1868, produced many fine pieces of furniture. This case clock was made by Nathaniel Dominy IV in 1790. (SPLIA)*

literature, and practical advice. These needs were filled through creation of numerous journals, beginning in 1791 with David Frothingham's *Long Island Herald.* Brooklyn replied with the *Long Island Advertiser* (1799) and the *Weekly Intelligencer* (1806). Other communities also responded, and by the 1850s dozens of papers were doing a booming business, providing clearinghouses for village news, instruction in agricultural techniques, farm market quotations, and word of national and international politics. Newspapers helped to break down the walls of parochialism and drew isolated villages together.

*Genre painter William Sidney Mount continually rejected offers of trips to Europe, staying instead on Long Island to paint its country life. From Cirker,* Dictionary of American Portraits, *Dover, 1967.*

Long Island's increasingly complex society could also claim one of nineteenth-century America's greatest artists: painter William Sidney Mount. Mount (1807-1868) spent nearly all his life in Suffolk County. Born of a farm family, he worked briefly for his older brother, a New York City sign painter, and later studied at the National Academy of Design. The young artist exhibited his first genre picture in 1830 and thereafter focused his talents on the country dances and barnyard scenes which enlivened his Stony Brook home.

Mount expressed a mystical concept of nature, observing, "We have nature, it speaks to everyone . . . My best pictures are those which I painted out of doors . . . The longer an artist leaves nature, the more feeble he gets." He also believed an artist should travel to observe ordinary men and women at work and play. So important was this conviction

that he constructed a horsedrawn studio with plate-glass windows and a woodburning stove.

A widely-read man, Mount's interests were not limited to art. He achieved proficiency on the fiddle, invented a "hollowbacked" violin, experimented with steamboat propulsion, and studied spiritualism in hopes of contacting deceased relatives. But it was his renderings of country people that made Mount the archetypical American genre painter. An early critic could truly say, "Mr. Mount's pictures are characteristic portraits of American rustic life . . ."

Despite improved transportation, the growth of local industry, and the influx of city residents, Long Island remained at heart a farming society. More, than 80 percent of the population earned its living from the soil, as rural hamlets stood at the center of local life. But even agriculture was beginning to shift its focus. Where once family-oriented homesteads held sway, commercial husbandry now dominated, especially as one neared New York. By 1820 Yale's President Dwight observed that the lands between Brooklyn and Jamaica were owned by farmers grown rich "with the aid of New York, their land under high cultivation . . . resembling a rich garden." From Jamaica to Hempstead cultivation was skillful, produce vigorous, and the influence of New York quite evident. As Brooklyn and Queens farmers held great marketing advantages, Dwight did not wonder "that therefore they are wealthy."

Suffolk County agriculture, distant from the city market and not yet served by the railroad, remained generally backward. Lack of adequate fertilizer was an additional impediment, while hogs often fed at a farmer's doorstep and watering ponds became "corrupted and unhealthy in summer seasons." A bemused traveller wondered in 1840 "in

what manner these people can live comfortably under this embarrassment?"

The arrival of the railroad alleviated many of these deficiencies, greatly expanding the zone of commercial agriculture. Trains provided cheap transportation to urban markets and a more convenient means of importing bone, ash, and manure fertilizers. One writer flatly predicted that "many portions of soil adjacent to the Long Island Rail Road will become highly valuable for agricultural purposes. Villages like Hauppauge, lying astride the line, could anticipate "an increase in population and great improvement in agriculture."

Progressive farmers promoted additional improvements and an exchange of information by creating the Queens County Agricultural Society in 1841. Its Suffolk companion, the Suffolk Society, came along seven years later. Farmers travelled many miles to attend fairs and display their prized livestock and produce. Thus, by disseminating ideas and urging growers to greater efforts, exhibits and societies hastened the shift to commercial agriculture. For another century or more, Long Island would remain true to its farming heritage.

Developments in the first half of the nineteenth century left Long Island a very changed place. Isolated villages and farmsteads were now linked to one another and to the city beyond through a network of rail, coach, and steamboat lines. Newspapers circulated information and advice. Commercial agriculture replaced traditional husbandry even as industry established a place in the local economy. The influx of vacationers and suburbanites was changing the face of village society. By 1860 Long Island was not quite part of the city, but it was no longer apart from it, either.

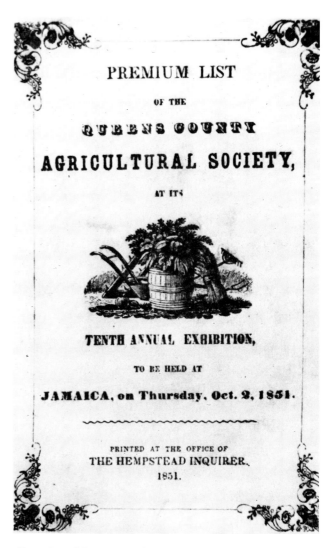

*Above: Long Island supplied much of the agricultural produce for the New York metropolitan area during the nineteenth century. According to the New York State census of 1840, the region's greatest crop was corn, followed by potatoes. (SPLIA)*

*Left: Improved markets and communication fostered development of agricultural societies in the nineteenth century. The Exhibition Hall of the Queens County Agricultural Society stood on its original site until it was demolished in the 1950s. (SPLIA)*

# SAMUEL BALLTON

One of the village of Greenlawn's most prominent citizens at the turn of the century was a black man named Samuel Ballton. Born in 1838 as a slave in Virginia, Ballton settled in Greenlawn after the Civil War, and though poor and uneducated, helped promote the growth of his adopted community by acquiring and developing property in downtown Greenlawn. Until the opening of the railroad in 1868, Greenlawn had been a quiet farming community known for growing cucumbers and cabbage. But the coming of the railroad fostered the establishment of several pickle and sauerkraut processing plants near the station, and by the late nineteenth century Greenlawn had begun to thrive. Displaying hard work, determination, and good business sense, Ballton tied his own fortunes to those of the town and managed to secure a measure of financial success while at the same time fostering the development of his new home.

Ballton's achievements showed him to be a shrewd man with a strong will to succeed. Ballton had already demonstrated his resourcefulness and determination when as a young man he escaped from a Confederate forced labor detail and managed to reach Northern lines. He even crossed enemy lines twice to see his wife, the second time bringing her with him to the safety of Union-occupied Virginia. He demonstrated a bold and cou-

rageous spirit when in 1864 he enlisted in the Fifth Massachusetts Colored Volunteers to preserve his country and ensure his freedom.

With the war over, Ballton, his wife Rebecca, and their family moved to Greenlawn to start a new life. Ballton's first job in the Greenlawn area was as a farmer for one of the town's wealthiest landowners, Charles D. Smith. There he began to establish a

reputation as a diligent and industrious worker. Later, he was employed as a sharecropper for Alexander Gardiner, who had the largest farm in Greenlawn, and Ballton gained much notoriety by growing record numbers of cucumbers and cabbages. Indeed, he was nicknamed Greenlawn's "Pickle King" as a result of growing 1.5 million cucumbers for pickling in one season.

*The Greenlawn Pickle Works was one of several processing plants in Greenlawn. Illustration by June Bassemir. Courtesy, Greenlawn-Centerport Historical Association*

Ballton's success in farming was just the beginning of a series of successful ventures. Moving beyond tenant farming, he was able to acquire some capital as a buying agent for a large Boston pickle house. Earning ten cents for every thousand pickles he bought, Ballton started into the business of land speculation. He also acquired some of his capital in the form of personal loans from wealthy local farmers, where his reputation for hard work probably stood him in good stead. With his money Ballton began to buy up valuable property, much of it along the railroad line in the then-growing village of Greenlawn.

Ballton's ventures in real estate demonstrated a creative and systematic method. He borrowed money from local farmers, bought land near the railroad, had houses built on the land, and then sold the houses to other farmers at a small profit. The confidence in his abilities which Ballton inspired is attested to by the long-standing business relationship he maintained with his first employer in the area, Charles D. Smith. Another of Ballton's ideas for Greenlawn's development was to bring laborers up from the South to work on the farms in the summer and build houses in the winter. Ballton did have setbacks, but managed to recover from the misfortune of having two of his houses accidently burn to the ground.

Not only Ballton, but his entire family, displayed the patience, resilience, foresight, and capacity for hard work which make a successful entrepreneur. Both Rebecca and their daughter Jessie worked as laundresses to make extra money for the family. Furthermore, while Ballton and his family were waiting for one of their houses to be built, they had to make do with living behind the unfinished house in a shed so tiny that it was later used as a washhouse.

By the turn of the century, sixteen years after moving to Greenlawn with no money or friends, Ballton had proved himself to be a success by the standards of his community. In spite of never having gone to school, he knew how to read and write. He lived in a home estimated to be worth $5,500. A member of the William Lloyd Garrison chapter of the veterans of the Grand Army of the Republic, and a member of the Greenlawn Presbyterian Church until his death in 1917, Ballton is still remembered as an outstanding founding member of the Greenlawn community.

Linda Day

# CHAPTER FIVE

# Brooklyn from First Suburb to Third City

While rural Long Island developed and matured in the first half of the nineteenth century, a great urban metropolis was rising at its westernmost extremity. From a small farming village, boisterous Brooklyn soon grew into America's third largest city. In the process, most vestiges of its earlier Dutch past were erased and, by mid-century, Brooklyn differed as much from its quaint predecessor as it did from its eastern Long Island neighbors. Accordingly, the youthful city faced a new and confusing assortment of distinctly urban problems: explosive population growth; inadequate sanitation, police, and roads; confusing charter reform; and the task of forging a separate identity in the face of Manhattan's persistent challenge. Half a century saw Brooklyn transformed from a bucolic village to an urban giant.

Every American city is a disunited collection of individuals going their own ways; yet each is a community with group loyalties and symbols, also. Many of Brooklyn's popular symbols derive from its nineteenth-century experience. Originally a city of homes and churches, concerned citizens created panoramic open green spaces like Prospect Park and Greenwood Cemetery. The city, too, gained fame for its busy docks, navy yard, Coney Island, the *Brooklyn Eagle,* and the storied Brooklyn Bridge.

Other attributes of Long Island's metropolis, while not so famous, were more distinctive. After the introduction of Robert Fulton's steam ferry in 1814, Brooklyn became the first modern suburb, but it quickly outgrew this role. No other American city ever developed from a suburb into a metropolis, much less in four short decades, and only Brooklyn eventually outgrew the center city that

*By the time of this 1840 illus-*
*tration the small rural*
*community of Brooklyn had*
*been submerged in a mixture*
*of new ethnic groups and com-*
*mercial activities. Fulton*

*Street appears in the center*
*background and Brooklyn*
*Heights is on the right. From*
*Thompson,* History of Long Island, *E. French, (1849) 1918*

initially nurtured it.

Urban historians often speak of a "dual revolution." Originally, several big cities existed but proportionately few people lived in them. Within a comparatively short period of time, however, rural masses were collected in small center-city parcels of land and then redistributed to adjoining suburbs. London housed a million people by 1810 and Great Britain was half urbanized by 1850. Brooklyn experienced both facets of the "urban revolution." From a suburban hamlet of only 1,603 people in 1800, and a town of barely 7,700 in 1820, the Kings County village mushroomed into an "instant city" of 266,000 in 1860. This overwhelming demographic phenomenon dominated every aspect of the city's nineteenth-century development.

Brooklyn's competitive relationship with nearby New York and the struggle to avoid being absorbed by its expanding neighbor provided the second prominent theme of early city history. Throughout the nineteenth century American communities fought tooth and nail for preeminence. New York generally emerged the victor in this contest, besting Philadelphia, Boston, and Baltimore. Meanwhile, Brooklyn gobbled up its own neighbors of Williamsburg and Bushwick, and aggressively jousted with

Manhattan for local dominance. Brooklyn's competitive experience, however, differed in scale from that of most other cities. While all battled for trade, industries, railroad lines, and immigrants, Brooklyn also fought to preserve its very identity and even its continued independent existence. Though Boston and Baltimore might lose some of their commerce to New York, they could not be incorporated into it. Brooklyn could be absorbed and knew it. Therefore, the fight for independence conditioned many facets of local behavior.

Brooklyn's battle to maintain its identity often proved an uphill struggle. Citizens opposed Manhattan's incorporation schemes and fought, instead, to gain control over their own ferries, to achieve separate status as a national port of entry, and to create viable churches, newspapers, and schools. Brooklyn's dynamic neighbor, however, cast a long shadow. Long Islanders often travelled to Manhattan for culture of all shades, work, business, fashion, capital, ministers to man the pulpits, and much else. By the time of the Civil War, at least 19,000 local residents daily commuted to work across the East River, where steamboat service had been established as early as 1814. Brooklyn Heights, home to the city's business and social leaders, looked out

*Opposite page: The first ferry between Brooklyn and New York departed from the foot of Fulton Street as early as 1642 and was operated by Cornelius Dircksen. This*

*1746 view features an old ferry house, with its stepped Dutch roof, built around 1700. From Ostrander,* A History of the City of Brooklyn and Kings County, *1894*

*Above: Built in 1850 and designed by Joseph C. Wells, Plymouth Church had a capacity of 5,000. Brooklyn would eventually earn the title "City*

*of Churches," and it was during mid-century that the majority of them were established. Courtesy, Library of Congress*

# HEZEKIAH BEERS PIERREPONT

*Above: Hezekiah B. Pierrepont was a leading figure in promoting Brooklyn's potential. From Stiles,* History of Kings County Including the City of Brooklyn, *Munsell, 1884*

*Opposite page: Brooklyn Heights, seen here from the bluffs of the East River, became New York City's first suburban community. From Hazelton,* The Boroughs of Brooklyn and Queens, Counties of Nassau and Suffolk, N.Y., 1609-1924, *Lewis, 1925*

Rare is the man who leaves any lasting memorial behind, much less a living one fully as exciting and impressive 150 years after his death as it was during his lifetime. Hezekiah Beers Pierrepont (1768-1838) was the exception. As the force behind the creation of Brooklyn Heights, one of the most beautiful urban residential areas anywhere, his good works continue to be enjoyed and appreciated by tens of thousands of people each year.

Pierrepont, grandson of the original minister in the New Haven colony, was a natural entrepreneur. By the time he was twenty-five, he had made a small fortune buying up national debt notes and had founded a firm to export goods to provision-scarce post-revolutionary France. He resided in Paris during the Reign of Terror, and saw Robespierre beheaded. In 1795 he bought a ship and sailed to India and China collecting valuable cargo; two years later, with Pierrepont on board, the returning ship was captured by a French privateer and both cargo and vessel were confiscated. Returning to New York in 1800, within two years Pierrepont had purchased a former brewery on the East River in Brooklyn Heights that had been burned during the Revolution, and turned it into New York State's only gin distillery. All these enterprises, however, were only a prelude to Pierrepont's great endeavor in Brooklyn Heights.

While in France, Pierrepont had met Robert Fulton, and he became an active participant with Fulton in establishing the first steamboat ferry between Manhattan and Brooklyn in 1814. Pierrepont realized that, with the inauguration of dependable ferry service across the East River, Brooklyn Heights could become New York City's first suburb, and a very fashionable one at that. He bought up as much of the Heights' land as he could, laid out wide streets, insisted that all new housing be of brick or stone, and in various other ways insured that development would result in a "select neighborhood and circle of society." Perhaps the following 1823 advertisement he placed for "Lots on Brooklyn Heights" best captures what Pierrepont both tried to, and actually did, achieve:

*Situated directly opposite the s-w part of the city, and being the nearest country retreat ... the distance not exceeding an average fif-* *teen to twenty-five minutes walk, including the passage of the river; the ground elevated and perfectly healthy at all seasons; views of water and landscape both extensive and beautiful; as a place of residence all the advantages of the country with most of the conveniences of the city ...*

*... Gentlemen whose business or profession require their daily attendance in the city, cannot better, or with less expense, secure the health and comfort of their families.*

Malcolm MacKay

uneasily across the water towards its powerful, prosperous, populous, and ambitious partner.

Nowhere was New York's exercise of power more irksome than in its control of the ferry franchises. Thanks to earlier colonial charters, New York City governed the vital East River right up to the Long Island shore. Under this detested arrangement, Long Islanders actually paid rent to Manhattan for local wharf space, such as the bustling Atlantic Basin docks. Outside control rankled; it sometimes meant poor ferry service to Manhattan, and that, in turn, damaged real estate development and construction activity on the Island in favor of growth in Manhattan. Kings County investors naturally sought to protect their interests, and beginning in 1836 they bought control of the ferries. After 1846 they championed state (outside) regulation. A three-way compromise resulted. By 1860 Brooklynites owned the ferries, New York City granted the franchises, and the state regulated some of their activities. By the era of Lincoln and Walt Whitman, East River vessels, especially Henry Pierrepont's Union Ferry Company, annually carried 32,850,000 passengers, suggesting that Long Island had certainly protected its realty and commuting interests.

It is impossible to say how much this vital transportation link aided Brooklyn's rise, but it is possible to gauge how the steam ferry facilitated the use of Long Island as a specialized part of what historian Edward Spann calls the "New Metropolis." Mid-nineteenth century observers believed that thousands of Brooklynites were no more than

"semidenizens" who spent most of their lives in Manhattan and merely returned across the river to sleep. Indeed, by 1855 Long Island's premier city had already earned the label "New York's bedroom."

The rest of the transit revolution came more slowly, but its impact was equally profound. Stage coaches and urban omnibuses, some capable of hauling thirty or more passengers, serviced the ferry sites by the 1830s, and in 1834 the Brooklyn and Jamaica (later Long Island) Railroad Company inaugurated the steam era. While the railroad exerted only a small impact on intracity commuting, the opening of the Brooklyn City (horsedrawn) Railroad line in 1854 was much more significant. The brainchild of Montgomery Queen, a prominent real es-

*Above: The number of private schools in Brooklyn greatly increased during the mid-nineteenth century. The Packer Collegiate Institute was built in 1854 as one of the state's highest institutions for the advanced education of young women. From Stiles,* History of Kings County Including the City of Brooklyn, *Munsell, 1884*

*Left: Brooklyn possessed an unrivaled waterfront with great capacity for expansion. The Atlantic Docks were laid out in 1844 on what had been a swamp marsh, and they eventually covered more than twenty acres. From Stiles.*

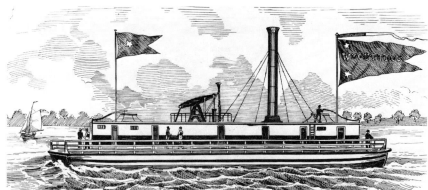

*Above: Although still a haven from inner-city congestion in this 1852 view, Williamsburg eventually became industrialized. Courtesy, The Long Island Historical Society*

*Right: By the 1840s many new ferry lines were opened with new and larger steamboats such as the* William Cutting, *named for Robert Fulton's partner. Courtesy, The Long Island Historical Society*

tate developer, the horse cars would dominate local transit until electrification arrived in the late 1880s. Taken together, ferries, horsecars, stages, and steam trains internally and externally integrated Brooklyn into the greater metropolitan areas.

Explosive and unrelenting population growth, aided by the rapid expansion of the transportation network, dominated nineteenth-century Brooklyn life. Local politics accurately reflected this phenomenon. Some leaders tried to stimulate growth through governmental reorganization; others attempted to accommodate the boom by providing streets, health, education, police, and fire prevention; still others sought to avoid the consequences of expansion by opposing taxes. But hardly anyone escaped the issue.

The imperfectly understood "science" of municipal government was barely able to harness such robust development. Like many nineteenth-century cities, the city sought metropolitan greatness. Its large natural hinterland, excellent port, and attractive Brooklyn Heights neighborhood lured many residents. Merchants, lawyers, bankers, and brokers by the score settled near the ferries that carried them to Wall Street every ten minutes. But for its natural advantages to be truly exploited, Brooklyn

would have to provide its new residents with fire protection, clean water, adequate police services, and competent government.

In an effort to bridge the gap between a growing city and a lagging government system, Brooklyn underwent four major and several minor political reorganizations between 1800 and 1865. In 1816 a village charter replaced the old town form of government. Although Manhattan real estate interests fought it, Brooklyn became a city eighteen years later. In both 1850 and 1855, the municipality's law was heavily amended. A considerable minority of citizens consistently favored reorganization by incorporation into New York City, but the Brooklyn-first party always triumphed.

Each charter change increased the range of government power. New municipal departments were spawned and outlying neighborhoods were annexed to the central city. In 1855, Williamsburg and Bushwick entered the boundaries. Brooklyn interests had long taken a jaundiced view of the rapid growth of potentially competitive Williamsburg; and fortunately for Brooklyn, the smaller city refused to raise taxes to fund its own growth. Thus, while evading the clutches of its imperial neighbor, the large Long Island city grasped a few districts of its

own. Its persistent efforts to move its boundary from the beach to the middle of the East River failed, however.

Enhancing the power of government did not necessarily solve urban problems. Most contemporary cities were poorly managed, though it is doubtful that Brooklyn fared worse than others. Moreover, urban developers suffered from unimaginable handicaps, of which unbridled and unregulated growth was the worst. Brooklyn's population doubled every decade from 1810 to 1840, and then tripled each decade thereafter until 1870. Thus, in every decade residents constructed at least one entirely new urban area equal to the one with which they started.

Such rapid development quickly altered the composition of the indigenous population. At the opening of the ferry era, most residents were of either British or Dutch extraction. They were soon joined, however, by tens of thousands of Irish and German immigrants who added a large Catholic population. These migrations created diversity and a cosmopoli-

*Above: The first volunteer fire company in Brooklyn was organized in 1785, with firemen chosen annually at a town meeting. By 1869 the first professional department had been established. Courtesy, The Long Island Historical Society*

*Opposite page, top: The development of pumping engines adequately supplied the city with water for fire, sanitation, and domestic needs. From* The Brooklyn Water Works and Sewers, A Descriptive Memoir, *1867*

tan air, and in 1860 about one-third of Brooklyn's population was foreign-born. Thanks in large measure to European and New York immigrants, Brooklyn's population was actually growing faster than Manhattan's.

A polyglot city, bursting at every seam, found the exercise in urban growth difficult indeed. Inexperience in everything from police administration to sanitation, a lack of civic loyalty, and an ingrained resistance to higher taxes complicated the process. It is therefore not surprising that the community often found itself only one jump ahead of disaster. On occasion the distance was even shorter. Fortunately, the catastrophes besetting so many other cities seemed rarer in Brooklyn.

Fire was an especially feared menace, and increasingly dense concentrations of tinder-dry wooden buildings frequently erupted in flames. Efforts to combat the danger were halting and usually inadequate. A fire district existed in 1800, but neither imaginary lines nor the fire wardens and citizen bucket brigades mandated by the 1816 charter brought much protection. Regulatory revisions in 1834 replaced primitive firefighting methods with new ones which were both more efficient and more exasperating. Under these arrangements, the city supplied equipment and firehouses, while volunteers provided the labor. Unfortunately, the engine, hose, and ladder companies (of which there were twelve in 1838) were also heavily involved in politics and not subject to strict city control. In 1843 one company refused to help another quench a blaze, resulting in the loss of twelve buildings. On other occasions the "fire laddies" rioted amongst themselves; and on still others they battled the police. With such a department and the absence of adequate equipment, small blazes could easily race out of control. An 1848 fire destroyed eight square downtown blocks. That disaster brought new regulations which were promptly ignored; the threat of large fires persisted until after the Civil War.

Brooklyn obviously required brick buildings and an efficient water supply to effectively fight fires and meet growing domestic demand. As the city expanded, its wells and cisterns were increasingly fouled by sewage and industrial pollution, highlighting the need for a distant source of water. From the time of its incorporation, Brooklyn tried to obtain such a supply, but competing engineering schemes,

rival water interests, and taxpayer opposition postponed the solution. In the meantime, city fathers procrastinated, digging but a few wells. Not until 1859, when the ailing and private Nassau Water Company forced the city to buy it out, did an adequate source appear. Nevertheless, Brooklyn's record was not all that bad, at least in comparison with other American cities. Manhattan did not receive its first Croton water until 1842, and many other urban centers were denied public supplies for a decade or two more.

Inadequate resources inevitably impacted public health, and the sanitary state of nineteenth-century cities is best described as horrendous. Crowded housing, pigs in the streets, sewage seeping into the water table, uncollected garbage and trash, infre-

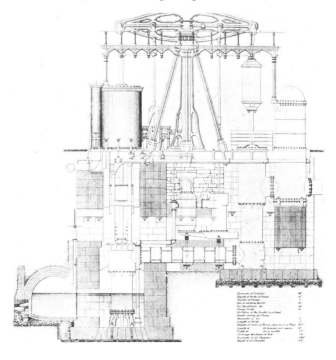

*Right: The Kings County Poorhouse was established in 1830 and by the 1850s consisted of a hospital, almshouse, and insane asylum. From Stiles,* History of Kings County Including the City of Brooklyn, *Munsell, 1884*

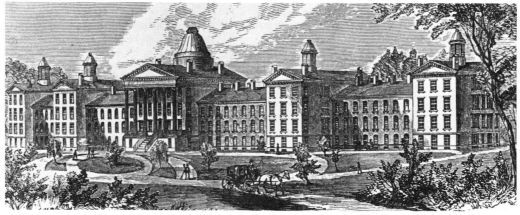

# WALT WHITMAN

*Above: Walt Whitman's extraordinary poetry spoke for an entire generation growing up with a young, prosperous nation. From Cirker, Dictionary of American Portraits, Dover, 1967. Courtesy, Library of Congress, Brady-Mandy Collection*

*Opposite page: Poet Walt Whitman was born in 1819 in this Huntington farmhouse built by his father. From the Clarence Purchase Photograph Collection, SPLIA*

In 1855, the poet Walt Whitman published the first edition of *Leaves of Grass.* That effort at self-realization, which would take him a lifetime to perfect, forever changed the course of American letters. Without Whitman as forerunner, most modern poetry could not have been conceived and written.

Born in 1819 on a small Huntington farm, Whitman was still a child when his family moved to

Brooklyn. Abandoning school in 1830, he worked first as an office boy, and two years later was apprenticed to a journeyman printer. By the late 1830s Whitman had returned to Long Island where he taught at several country schools. From 1836 to 1841 he taught single or double terms in Babylon, Long Swamp, Smithtown, Woodbury, Little Bayside, Whitestone, and Dix Hills. He also took time in 1838 to found the *Long Islander,* a weekly Huntington newspaper.

About 1840 Whitman again moved to Brooklyn and labored for a succession of newspapers, including the *Brooklyn Eagle,* and later in his life contributed historical and reminiscent articles on Brooklyn to the *Brooklyn Standard.* But in the early 1850s he abandoned publishing entirely to devote more time to his personal writings.

"Fish-shape Paumanok," Whitman called Long Island, using the old Indian name. As a small boy, he had roamed the hills and shores in and around Huntington, captivated by the colors, smells, plants, and animals that abounded in rural Long Island. As a young man, he roamed the "populous pavements" of Brooklyn in the same way, revelling in the sharp contrasts, the noise and commercial bustle and the smells of steam and sweat that belonged to the city. All these impressions, as Whitman tells us, became part of him; and out of these he made poetry. Not the carefully controlled and measured verse that was then being written and had always been written in English—but a new creation, entirely bold and free, without regular rhyme, without regular meter, without conventional form.

Whitman was the poet of democracy. He sings of simple people, working people, not just winners, but also "conquer'd and slain persons." Like many of his literary generation, he wanted to produce a truly American literature, one that expressed the values and virtues and wishes and fears of the young American nation. And more than any other poet of his generation, Whitman did speak for us—for all that was brawny and rambunctious, headstrong and open-armed about America in the nineteenth century.

Whitman's mark remains upon Long Island in the *Long Islander,* still published today; and in the old, weathered farmhouse at West Hills, Whitman's birthplace, where visitors cross a threshold and find themselves back in the nineteenth century. And through Whitman, Long Island makes its mark upon the world, as generations of readers absorb the thoughts and images that began there in the mind of one small boy.

Marilyn Oser

Mob violence often greeted such epidemics. In fact, yellow fever had come to Long Island in 1856 when an angry crowd drove an infected ship away from the quarantine station at Staten Island. Similar trouble threatened as cases appeared in Brooklyn, but cooler heads prevailed. Several local doctors gave their lives, and Mayor George Hall risked his health by nursing the sick, and confining the disease to New Utrecht.

These periodic scourges, together with more normal urban risks like tuberculosis (the great white plague), eventually generated a growing public health movement. A city-subsidized private hospital appeared in 1839, and Brooklyn's morgue opened in 1842. A public health care facility, city dispensary, and burial regulations followed in 1846, while the collection of vital statistics and control over swill (distillery waste) milk came in due course. After private contractors' neglect had turned the streets into a subject of local scorn and verse, a sanitation department appeared in 1855. Soon storm sewers began radiating outward from the center city. By 1867 demands for better drainage (as well as improved shipping) led to construction of the Gowanus Canal. As yet another cholera epidemic loomed in 1867, the Metropolitan Board of Health assumed sanitary responsibility for both Brooklyn and New York.

Similar fitful progress characterized the local police forces before 1857. Regulations in early nineteenth-century America dated from medieval times and were entirely unsuited to growing cities. In 1829 a modern model of police administration appeared in England, when Sir Robert Peel created London's famous Metropolitan Police Force (the bobbies). Brooklyn and other American cities then looked to Britain for inspiration, but generally evidenced little actual zeal for police reform. A large force was feared as both costly and threatening to American liberties.

Under Brooklyn's old village regime, local officials seemed to devote greater energy to clearing the streets of omnipresent pigs than to running off the criminals. Perhaps that emphasis reflected the large number of pigs and the small number of criminals, but by the 1840s many citizens were alarmed at increasing lawbreaking and violence. These twin threats caused Brooklyn leaders to effect modest reform.

quent bathing, faulty drainage, and commerce-borne microbes added up to perennial health emergencies. So did a lack of basic medical knowledge. Doctors bled, cupped, and leeched their patients, were blissfully unaware of the origins of disease, and usually ignored antisepsis.

Brooklyn's residents frequently suffered from these shortcomings, as health precautions were practically nonexistent. Intensified urbanization only heightened the problem of disease communicability; crises multiplied. A cholera epidemic terrorized Manhattan in 1832, causing 100,000 of its 250,000 inhabitants to flee. Its Long Island neighbor also felt the impact of the plague, but apparently not the panic. Historian Ralph Weld called this outbreak "the most terrible experience" in the history of the village. Several additional scourges soon followed. Smallpox struck in 1836 and 1845; cholera returned in 1849 and 1854. Yellow fever, which killed 11,000 in New Orleans in 1853, barely missed Brooklyn three years later, but suburban New Utrecht was hard hit and most of its residents fled.

A tiny police force of a dozen men in the 1840s grew to 159 officers in the 1850s, as the city's population mushroomed from 97,000 to 226,000. Officers also began wearing badges, but still resisted uniforms as too military. These limited efforts failed to satisfy the cries for reform; politicians exercised too much control over the force and the police chief, too little. The low level of professionalism was vividly illustrated in 1857, when the disgruntled Albany legislature merged the locals into a state-controlled metropolitan force. In Manhattan that move led to civil war between old and new officers, but Brooklyn apparently escaped the violence. Americans of the Civil War era evidenced a remarkably high tolerance of crime and disorder, and not until the latter part of the nineteenth century would a modernized police force patrol the city streets.

These same streets also acted as the arteries of a dynamic urban organism. Since Brooklyn was, in part, a product of the transportation revolution, it seems fitting that the city fathers spent so much time on street matters. The original town charter offered little guidance for an age of rapid expansion. Later village regulations mandated private maintenance of sidewalks and curbs. Street surveys were begun, as were public contributions towards grading, graveling, and filling municipal thoroughfares. City-sponsored reforms soon included paving, oil lighting, and numbering. Between 1851 and 1854 alone, 192,000 linear feet of streets were upgraded.

Structural improvement was directly tied to real estate development, and there was plenty of that. Tens of thousands of new residents needed homes and shops; the demand for vacant land was enormous. A Gowanus farm worth $18,000 in 1831 sold for $102,000 just four years later. Ex-New York Mayor Phillip Hone called Brooklyn real estate speculation "one of the bubbles of the day." Yet, streets often were laid out haphazardly, and many areas remain unsurveyed. A monotonous square plot governed the plans. Still, given the limited competence of municipal experts and legislators, it is probably well that they did not attempt anything fancier.

By 1861 Brooklyn had laid the foundations of a modern metropolis. Population was booming. Eight miles of commercial waterfront faced Manhattan. Local docks serviced more ships than New York and Hoboken combined. Townhouses and brownstones crowned Brooklyn Heights, radiating in all directions. Local shipyards built elegant clippers and warships for the Czar's navy. Poet Walt Whit-

*Opposite page: Born in New York and educated at Erasmus Hall, George Hall was the first mayor of the original city of Brooklyn (1834-35), as well as the first mayor of the consolidated city (1855-57). From Stiles, History of Kings County Including the City of Brooklyn, Munsell, 1884*

*Left: Reflecting its new status as a city, Brooklyn's Borough Hall was originally envisioned as an elaborate marble structure. Public outcry over the extravagance of such a costly design prompted the building in 1846 of this smaller and more subdued version. From Hazelton, The Boroughs of Brooklyn and Queens, Counties of Nassau and Suffolk, N.Y., 1609-1924, Lewis, 1925*

*Above: This mid-century view of East New York, with its newly laid thoroughfares and expanding urban center, would have certainly surprised the area's early Dutch settlers. East New York would eventually grow into a large metropolitan section, spurred by a large influx of German immigrants in the 1860s and 1870s. Courtesy, The Long Island Historical Society*

*Opposite page: Opened in the winter of 1862, the Union Pond Skating Rink in Williamsburg catered to Brooklyn's growing middle class and their increasing interest in leisure pursuits. Courtesy, The Long Island Historical Society*

man sang the city's praises.

In other, less physical spheres, Brooklyn's achievements were, as yet, modest. Modern observers often condemn this record, especially a persistent inability to solve the complex issues of growth. But Brooklyn's urban pioneers labored under burdens inconceivable to today's city managers or critics. The wonder is that Brooklyn kept up as well as it did. No one, rich or poor, wanted higher taxes; and in a political culture which featured annual elections, vigorous party competition, an unbridled press, a weak executive system, and a strong tradition of violent protest, cities had little choice beyond modest, evolutionary change. Republican sentiments were so ingrained that even issues as trivial as the introduction of police uniforms sparked heated controversy. Sheer ignorance also impeded progress. Nineteenth-century physicians knew little about disease and even less about how to eradicate it. Quarantine restrictions often provoked mob violence. Given these facts, one must conclude that Brooklyn did far better than is generally thought.

The Long Island city's animated rivalry with Manhattan abated temporarily with the outbreak of the Civil War. Although Brooklyn voted against Lincoln in 1860, it stood ready to fight for him and the Union in 1861. After the fall of Fort Sumter, a rainbow of flags cloaked the city; 50,000 citizens gathered at Fort Greene to pledge their support; men flocked to the colors; and the sanitary and Christian commissions soon appeared to succor the wounded. A total of 30,000 men served in the Union armies, often in ethnic or vocational regiments like the Schwartze Jaegers, the Irish Legion, or the 173rd Infantry (Brooklyn and Manhattan police). At Bull Run these citizen soldiers fared badly, but at Gettysburg and the Wilderness they fought like heroes.

Also important, though in a less sanguine way, were the efforts of the Greenpoint shipyard, which built the ironclad *Monitor,* and the nearly 6,000 employees of the nearby Navy Yard. Moreover, despite the harsh judgment of some historians that Brooklyn was under-policed, residents proved generally unwilling to join the draft riots that greeted conscription in Staten Island and Manhattan. Its citizens must have enjoyed a good chuckle as their militia set off to squelch New York's upheavals.

The Brooklyn throngs who welcomed the return of peace did so from the streets, neighborhoods, and factories of a now-great American city. The fifty-year odyssey from Anglo-Dutch village to the nation's third metropolis had been astonishing, but the most spectacular era still lay ahead.

# Of Grand Hotels, Great Estates, Polo, and Princes

enjamin Thompson was so impressed with the then six-year-old Marine Pavilion at Far Rockaway, "a large and splendid edifice, standing upon the margin of the Atlantic," that he made special mention of it in his *History of Long Island.* The novel two-story seaside lodging with "sleeping apartments" for 160 and a 200-foot piazza had been erected in 1833. It was the brainchild of a group of New York investors, headed by Governor Dewitt Clinton's brother-in-law, aiming to accommodate the increasing number of vacationers who wished to experience "fresh inspiration and increased vigor by repeated plunges in the ocean." Longfellow, Washington Irving, and John Trumbull were among the notables who frequented the new watering spot and helped to make Far Rockaway one of the nation's most famous pre-Civil War resorts. The Pavilion burned in 1864, but it was to be the precursor of dozens of seaside hotels, starting at Coney Island and stretching east to the Hamptons and Peconic Bay. On the North Shore from College Point to Wading River, each new resort claimed to be bigger than the last. The Rockaway Beach Hotel, which opened in 1881 near the site of the Marine Pavilion, announced that it was the world's largest hostelry with 1,188 feet of facade, 100,000 square feet of piazza, and a 1,300-foot ocean pier. By the turn of the century, five of these giant havens, the Manhattan Beach, Oriental, Edgemere, Arverne, and Long Beach hotels, could house between 400 and 1,000 guests. Many of the large resorts had their own railroad depots, since convenient transportation links were often the key to success. Not surprisingly, the Long Island Rail Road had a large stake in this burgeoning business. When Austin Corbin, builder of the Manhattan Beach and Oriental, became the

*The Marine Pavilion, con-
structed in Rockaway in 1834,
was one of the earliest resort
hotels in the country. Only a
coach ride from New York
City, its country setting and*
*magnificent beaches attracted
summer inhabitants from
that increasingly urbanized
area until a fire destroyed the
resort in 1864. Courtesy, The
Long Island Historical Society*

firm's president in 1881, he revitalized the line and formed the Long Island Improvement Company. The new organization constructed the remarkable Argyle at Babylon, a hotel, cottage, and casino complex in a seventy-acre landscaped park. Under Corbin, the Long Island Rail Road became the principal publicist of the area's resort potential. The annual visitor's guides, produced by the passenger department, were impressive, lavishly illustrated directories which touted this "expanse of ocean-bounded country where beauty of landscape and health go hand-in-hand." Corbin's projects and promotional instincts also helped to keep Long Island in the press. When shore erosion threatened the Brighton Beach Hotel in 1888, the entrepreneur sent his railroad to a much publicized rescue. Laying sections of parallel track, a team of locomotives moved the 500-foot structure to safety.

Despite Corbin's efforts, the new hotels could not begin to fill the need for accommodations during the height of the season. Many of Long Island's eighteenth-century country seats, such as Rock Hall at Lawrence and the Joseph Lloyd Manor House at Lloyd's Neck, were pressed into service as boarding houses. Village residents began taking in boarders. Mrs. J.C. Hawksworth of East Islip, for instance, had room for eight guests in her home during the 1903 season. She charged eight dollars per person

per week. By the turn of the century, the resort business had grown to such proportions that the railroad guides reported accommodations for 24,000 vacationers in Nassau and Suffolk County alone. This represented one room for every five residents in the two-county region, or, by another yardstick, twice the number of lodgings believed available for tourists in 1984.

Proceeding apace with the development of resort hotels was the construction of mansions or country houses for the rich. In this respect Long Island, with its mild climate, had always been a favored locale for country escapes. As previously mentioned, such early notables as Governor Dongan and Mathias Nicoll had established estates as early as the seventeenth century in what is now Nassau County. By the start of the Revolution, Long Island was peppered with the manors and country homes of such city-oriented families as the Martins, Gardiners, Lloyds, Joneses, Coldens, and Smiths. What began to manifest itself in the mid-nineteenth century, however, was an entirely different phenomenon: the establishment of summer retreats on relatively small parcels of land which had no agricultural (i.e., income producing) function. The recurrent warm weather epidemics, increased congestion, and rapid industrialization of New York City had made the prospect of vacationing in Gotham less appealing to many well-healed New Yorkers. Hence, such early summer residents as William Cullen Bryant, who acquired a place in Roslyn on Hempstead Harbor in 1843, and John Banvard, the panorama artist who built a wooden castle in Cold Spring Harbor in the 1850s, pioneered a wave of summer house development which was to begin in earnest during the Civil War—against a backdrop of draft riots, urban tension, and national uncertainty. While Gettysburg was still raging, carpenters in Oyster Bay were putting the finishing touches on Long Island's first sophisticated country house, an architect-designed villa in the Rural Gothic style, for one of New York's most prominent citizens, James W. Beekman. After renting a house in the hamlet of Oyster Bay where his fellow members of the Union League Club also summered, Beekman decided to build.

The factors that transformed this sleepy village into the North Shore's first resort foretold estate development in later decades. As with hotels, the growth of the Long Island Rail Road was the pri-

*Above: The Long Island Rail Road helped to popularize the Island's growing resorts and communities. The line published numerous colorful brochures containing photographs and glowing accounts of the Island's attractions. (SPLIA)*

*Left: Columbia Grove on Lloyd's Neck, depicted in this 1881 painting by Edward Lange, was one of Long Island's resort attractions during the 1880s and 1890s. Courtesy, Andrus T. Valentine*

# AUSTIN CORBIN

Had Austin Corbin not been killed in a carriage accident in 1896, Montauk might have become a transatlantic terminus for ocean liners, and construction might have commenced on a subway system for New York a generation earlier. Corbin was a remarkable man. An energetic financier with great vision and what his contemporaries termed a capacity for details, Corbin ushered in the age of the resort on Long Island, attracting foreign capital to build huge seaside hotels and reorganizing the transportation system that made it all possible, the Long Island Rail Road.

Born and educated in New Hampshire, Corbin graduated from Harvard Law School in 1849 and first went west, establishing a suc-

cessful banking business in Davenport, Iowa. Moving to New York City at the close of the Civil War, he established the firm that became known as The Corbin Banking Company and at the same time reorganized the Indianapolis, Bloomington and Western Railroad, earning a reputation as a wizard in railroad affairs. By 1886, Corbin was president of four railroads and had reorganized the Philadelphia and Reading line for J.P. Morgan.

The financier's involvement with Long Island is said to have begun while he was visiting an infirmed son who was recuperating at a small hotel on Coney Island. Walking east on the sparsely settled beach, Corbin sensed the resort potential of Long Island's ocean

*The Argyle Hotel in Babylon was one of several large and fashionable summer hotels built by Austin Corbin, a pioneer in resort building. It was completed in 1882 and could accommodate over 700 guests. Courtesy, Vanderbilt Historical Society*

frontage. In 1876, Corbin began developing Manhattan Beach, building a rail line to the remote area from Bay Ridge. Corbin's Manhattan Beach Improvement Company then built two immense shore hotels, The Manhattan Beach and The Oriental, as well as a theater, stadium, bandstand, and other amenities. Next came the exclusive Argyle Hotel at Babylon, built by another Corbin enterprise, the Long Island Improvement

Company, in the midst of a seventy-acre casino and cottage complex. In 1885, Corbin added The Long Beach Hotel to his resort empire, acquiring the rail line to Point Lookout and untold property in the process.

Corbin became acquainted with "the slow and uncertain movement" of the Long Island Rail Road while commuting to his summer residence in Babylon near the Argyle. Realizing that a well-run railroad could be immediately profitable and would open up new areas of Long Island for the summer trade, Corbin organized a syndicate of Boston and London capitalists that bought a controlling interest in the LIRR in 1880. As president of the LIRR, Corbin embarked on revitalizing a railroad that was over a million dollars in debt and in such bad shape that one railroad man had called it "two streaks of rust and a right of way." The banker-turned-railroadman replaced the old iron rails with new steel track, built new lines while abandoning unprofitable links, upgraded narrow gauge roads to standard gauge, introduced air brakes and automatic couplers, bought new equipment, built new stations, and within two years had restored the line to profitability. *The New York World* was to hail the LIRR in 1886 "for speed, safety, promptness" which was "unsurpassed on any road."

Corbin was to continue as president of the LIRR until his death, but this man of vision focused his energy on other projects in the late 1880s. He hired an English engineer to design a subway system for New York and proposed the construction of tunnels under the East and Hudson rivers more than a generation before these plans were eventually realized. In 1885, he proposed a scheme which would have shortened transatlantic travel. Corbin wanted ocean terminals constructed at Fort Pond Bay, Montauk and Wilford Haven, Wales. Rail links to New York and London would then have cut hours off travel time to Europe and the LIRR's passenger business would have received a major boost. Corbin made frequent trips to Washington, D.C. to convince Congress of the merits of his plan since federal approval was required to create new ports of entry. Unfortunately, the plan did not survive the visionary's untimely death and the opposition of New York City interests, but Corbin's legacy to Long Island was already in place—a fully developed and completed railway system, the new resort industry, and a large number of investors interested in Long Island's growth potential. Indeed, Austin Corbin did more than almost anyone else in bringing Long Island out of its nineteenth-century agrarian isolation.

Robert B. MacKay

mary determinant; its decision to extend a spur to Syosset in 1854 made Oyster Bay accessible to a rail head for the first time. Surviving papers of the Edward Swan family, among the first summer residents of Oyster Bay, indicate that the train was preferred over the steamship. The vessels were seasonal at best and had trouble running on schedule. So rapid was the railroad, on the other hand, that the average trip made by Caleb Swan in 1854 from the Syosset depot to his lower Manhattan residence was only twenty minutes longer than it is today. When one considers that Swan had to cross the East River by boat and travel to his downtown house by horse-drawn omnibus, the feat seems all the more remarkable. In general, the railroad was making Long Island accessible for resort development in a way that couldn't have been imagined even a generation before. The decision to build a spur to Glen Cove (1867), the projection of the South Side Railroad to Patchogue (1869), the electrification of the Port Washington line (1898), and the completion of the East River tunnels (1910) are among the more notable milestones in the great litany of progressive rail improvements. With the completion of the East River bridges, Long Island's transportation advantages continued to build in the early years of the automotive age. The Queensboro or 59th Street Bridge (1909) was particularly important, since it dramatically shortened the trip from midtown Manhattan to the North Shore via Route 25 or 25A. Extending to the south and east, it also connected to William K. Vanderbilt's new Long Island Motor Parkway, commissioned in 1906. The area's transportation edge over other resort locales

*Above: By the 1900s Long Island's two main centers of fox hunting were the fashionable Meadow Brook Club and the Rockaway Hunting Club. This painting depicts a hunt about to begin on the Meadow Brook. Courtesy, Mrs. Betty Babcock*

*Right: Completed in 1909, the Queensboro Bridge linked Queens and Manhattan, facilitating the spread of population and commerce across the East River. Its influence was immediately felt as many large industrial plants began to seek sites in Queens and Long Island. (SPLIA)*

in the tri-state, not to mention more distant watering spots such as Newport, was then considerable. Long Island was a place where the man of affairs could vacation while not losing contact with developments in the city and office.

The development of recreational interests was another factor contributing to the resort phenomenon. Young New Yorkers began renting farm houses in the Oyster Bay area in the 1860s for the sole purpose of participating in the informal sailboat races that took place there every summer. The nation's first open amateur regatta was sponsored by the Seawanhaka Corinthian Yacht Club, organized in Oyster Bay in 1872. Many of the youthful yachtsmen had been among the first undergraduates to participate in intercollegiate athletic contests, deeply believing in the concept of Corinthian (or amateur) sports. They were soon joined by the equestrians, who reestablished on Long Island the late eighteenth-century pastime of fox hunting. The Queen's County Hounds, which gathered at the Garden City Hotel in 1877, were the first pack of drag hounds in the United States, while the Rockaway Hunt, founded in 1878, is believed to be America's oldest such organization in continuous operation, edging out Jericho's Meadow Brook Club by three years. The latter was one of the earliest precursors of this nation's modern country clubs.

Long Island sporting groups did not limit their interests to fox hunting, however. Polo, first played in the United States in 1876, made its local debut at the Mineola Fair Grounds in 1879, and was being played at the Rockaway and Meadow Brook clubs by the early 1880s. Every American to swing a mallet in the twelve international matches against Great Britain from 1886 to 1939 was to be a Long Islander. Golf, a later development, nevertheless, was another pastime in which Long Island made history. Southampton's Shinnecock Hills Golf Club was the first American golf club which owned its grounds, had links laid out by a professional, and a clubhouse specifically designed for the sport. While lawn tennis was also introduced elsewhere in America, the Brooklyn Heights Casino can lay claim to being the country's first indoor club to accommodate that game. The West Side Tennis Club at Forest Hills later became the largest and most prominent tennis club in the United States, holding the U.S. Open matches between 1915 and 1920. After its opening in 1923, the Forest Hills Stadium,

with a seating capacity of 13,000, became the preeminent national tennis arena, hosting both the Davis Cup challenges and the U.S. Open. Even aviation was thought to be something of a gentleman's sport by the New York Aeronautic Society, which had facilities in Mineola as early as 1909. The Long Island Aviation Country Club at Hicksville, which flourished between the two world wars, had no precursors whatsoever. By the end of the first decade of the twentieth century, Long Island had become the cradle of many of America's nascent recreational pursuits, a great national playground where grand prix sporting events were often taking place concurrently. During the 1910 or 1911 summer season, for instance, one could have seen the "Big Four" take on the British for the America Cup, polo's greatest contest, at the new, specially-built, 40,000-seat stadium on the Hempstead Plains; witnessed aerial acrobatics at the first International Air Show at Belmont Race Track where a new

*Above: Smartly dressed members of the Meadow Brook Club prepare for a fox-hunting meet at Sagamore Hill circa 1895. Courtesy, Meadow Brook Club Album*

*Left: Forest Hills Stadium, completed in 1923, and the West Side Tennis Club form a complex that has attracted thousands to its Davis Cup and U.S. Open matches since the 1920s. From Hazelton,* The Boroughs of Brooklyn and Queens, Counties of Nassau and Suffolk, N.Y., 1609-1924, *Lewis, 1925*

*The Vanderbilt Cup races, held on Long Island from 1904 to 1910, attracted huge crowds. The mounting number of accidents and deaths involving both racers and spectators eventually led its promoters to discontinue the event. Courtesy, Vanderbilt Museum*

world altitude record of 9,714 feet was set; thrilled to the maneuverability of the competing speedboats at the International Races in Huntington Bay which could be viewed from such elegant surroundings as the terrace of the new Beaux Arts Casino; observed the spectacle of a great squadron of yachts and America's Cup candidates depart for the annual cruise of the New York Yacht Club from the Club's new "station" at Hempstead Harbor; watched some of the world's greatest drivers tune up their engines at Robert Graves' novel garage-hotel in Mineola before putting their "motors" to the test in the Vanderbilt Cup Races; bet on "Sweep," the winner of the 1910 running of the Belmont Stakes, the greatest prize of the season at one of the most important thoroughbred tracks in America; or one could have attended one of the myriad horse shows, hunt meets, steeplechases, or other sporting events that were focusing national attention on Long Island.

The decision of many of these clubs to establish permanent grounds and facilities for the pursuit of recreational interests became the primary contributor to the later stages of the estate boom. The founding of the Southside Sportsmen's Club in 1865 by frequenters of Snedicor's Hotel at Oakdale, a South Shore hunting lodge, encouraged members to build mansions nearby. The Frederick Bourne Estate (now LaSalle Military Academy), the William K. Vanderbilt Estate (today's Dowling College), and the Bayard Cutting Estate (presently the Bayard Cutting Arboretum), are but three Islip-Oakdale survivors of the phenomenon. So momentous for the North Shore was the decision of the Manhattan-based Seawanhaka Corinthian Yacht Club to build a waterfront facility on Oyster Bay's Centre Island in 1892, that within the next thirty-five years, over forty of its members had built mansions in the vicinity. These individuals, including

*Left: Reminiscent of a European cafe with its alfresco dining area and apron-clad waiters, the Beaux-Arts Casino and Cafe in Huntington was an elegant turn-of-the-century gathering spot. (SPLIA)*

*Below: Many Long Island estate grounds were laid out by well-known architects, and mature trees were imported and transplanted by such nurseries as the Hicks Brothers of Westbury, shown here at the Herbert Pratt estate circa 1912. Courtesy, Hicks Photograph Collection*

J.P. Morgan, whose residence was demolished in 1980, and Marshall Field, whose homestead is currently part of Caumsett State Park, had no previous connection to Long Island. A further comparison of construction dates and polo team rosters indicates that almost all the great country estates erected between Old Westbury and North Hills during this period were for aspiring players wearing the sky blue shirts of the Meadow Brook Club. By the turn of the century, sporting interests determined the building sites of mansions. Competition between the organizations was quite real. After continuous boundary disputes, the Meadow Brook Club and the Rockaway Hunt "divided" Nassau County's foxing grounds along an east-west line at Mineola.

So rapid was the pace of mansion construction that in the eighteen years between 1900 and America's entry into World War I, 325 country houses of over twenty-five rooms were constructed east of the Queens line. New York City firms were forced to open Long Island branches in order to handle the volume of business. Many leading contractors spe-

cializing in country houses picked centrally located Hicksville for their headquarters. Lewis and Valentine, the landscapers with offices at 47 West 37th Street in New York, boasted no less than four Long Island nurseries by the 1920s. Architects generally viewed Long Island as synonymous with country house design; 146 firms are recorded to have built mansions in Nassau and Suffolk counties in the eighty years leading up to the Second World War. One company of landscape contractors, the fa-

*Left: Built in 1899 by the prominent architect Richard Howland Hunt, William K. Vanderbilt, Sr.'s Idle Hour was an elaborate country estate that included a 110-room mansion, a boat house, coach house, tea house, bowling alley, indoor tennis court, glass conservatory, and a farm complex. (SPLIA)*

# WILLIAM CULLEN BRYANT

Best remembered as a poet and the editor of the *New York Evening Post,* William Cullen Bryant (1794-1878) first received national attention with the publication of the poem "Thanatopsis" at the tender age of seventeen. Perhaps the most famous of his works, this poem's weighty subject, the contemplation of death, caught the attention of nineteenth-century literary notables, including Richard Henry Dana. Surprised at its excellence in expression and style, Dana, then editor of the *North American Review,* published the work, which received wide critical acclaim. It is considered today to be the first significant and true example of American poetry. In addition to his great literary prowess which produced hundreds of published poems, Bryant authored numerous essays and travel books, and even translated such classics as Homer's *Illiad* (1870) and *Odyssey* (1871).

As the editor of the *Post,* Bryant was the first to utilize the editorship of a major newspaper to promote numerous social and political causes. The main issues that placed Bryant in the national forefront were the antislavery movement and the labor movement. In addition, Bryant was the leading proponent of the creation of Central Park, strongly supporting the selection of Frederick Law Olmsted as its landscape architect.

Having been born and raised in

the countryside of Cummington, Massachusetts, Bryant frequently tried to find a country home close to his work in New York City. Drawn initially to the North Hempstead area by a land development promotion in 1837, Bryant subsequently purchased "Springbrook," a simple farmhouse built in 1787, from historian Joseph W. Moulton in 1842. The house, situated in what is now Roslyn Harbor, had been extensively altered by this time to reflect the fashionable Greek Revival style favored by its former owner. Bryant pro-

ceeded in what would be a lifelong undertaking to enlarge and embellish the estate's natural beauty. It was about this time that Bryant changed the name of his estate to "Cedarmere," as it is known today, and altered the structure to mirror his tastes and needs. He enlarged the main house to accommodate the large number of friends and associates who were invited to Cedarmere during his fifty years of residence along the harbor.

Bryant's guest list included many of the nineteenth century's most prominent figures from the world of art, literature, and politics. Among them were actors Edwin Forrest and Edwin Booth, tastemaker Andrew Jackson Downing, and artists Thomas Cole, Asher B. Durand, Daniel Huntington, and Robert Weir. Orville Dewey, probably the most prominent American theologian of the first half of the nineteenth century, was a frequent visitor and his younger sister, Jerusha, later became Bryant's tenant. Bryant continued to write poetry at Cedarmere and this interest attracted Dana and poet Fitz-Greene Halleck, novelists James Fenimore Cooper, Carolyn Kirkland, and William Gilmore Simms, and America's most famous sculptor, Horatio Greenough.

Possessing an almost congenial aptitude for architecture and landscape design, Bryant contributed greatly to the beauty and growth of his newfound community, which he helped rename Roslyn in 1844. As Bryant continued to work on his own house, he also completed or altered a number of other buildings on the estate. Quite early in his ownership, probably in 1844, he built "Golden-Rod Cottage," which served as his house while Cedarmere was being altered. Later it became the home of his daughter Fanny and her husband, Parke Godwin.

In one way or another Bryant participated in the construction or alteration of at least twenty buildings in and around Cedarmere. In 1869 Orville Dewey wrote, "Don't look down from your lordiness, of owning a dozen houses, and three of them you own to live in." Singleton Mitchell's survey of the Bryant property in 1875 recorded fifteen buildings, including two mills. One of these, a board-and-batten structure with superb vergeboards, seems to have been built circa 1860 in large part as a garden ornament, as it is spectacularly sited on a hillside between the pond and the harbor. The architect of this "Gothic Mill" is not known; possibly it was designed by Bryant himself. It is generally accepted today that the estate's dramatic, romantic landscape was designed as well as developed by Bryant. All this activity in the development of the natural and built landscape at the highest possible level contributed immeasurably to the architectural quality of Roslyn and its surroundings, which survives to this day. Happily, most of Bryant's houses still stand. Some, like "Golden-Rod," have been vastly altered, while others like George Cline's "Stone Cottage" have experienced few changes and the superb "Gothic Mill" remains untouched. Cedarmere, now called "Cedar Mere," is owned by the Nassau County Department of Parks and Recreation and plans are being developed for its restoration.

Dr. Roger Gerry
Anthony Cucchiara

*Opposite page: William Cullen Bryant (right) confers with Long Island manufacturer and inventor Peter Cooper at Cedarmere in 1875. They discussed Cooper's plans to run for President on the Greenback ticket. Courtesy, Nassau County Museum*

*Left: Writing to a friend, William Cullen Bryant exclaimed, "At last, I have a house and land on Long Island, a little plain house in a most beautiful neighborhood ..." He continually enlarged and embellished Cedarmere during his lifetime. From the Clarence Purchase Photograph Collection, SPLIA*

Left: Pembroke, the home of wealthy businessman J.R. DeLamar (1843-1918), is a striking example of one of the many elaborate mansions and country estates built on Long Island at the turn of the century. From Town & Country Magazine, December 1921

Opposite page: Technically innovative and later emulated, the Long Island Motor Parkway was the first limited access concrete toll road ever built on such a grand scale. Its twelve gate houses and inn were designed by architect John Russell Pope. (SPLIA)

Right: Long Island's country estates were the sites of banquets, balls, and weddings, such as this wedding reception for Helen and Ernest Dane at the Pratt estate in Glen Cove. Courtesy, Lawrence and Anne Van Ingen

mous Olmsted Brothers of Brookline, Massachusetts, were commissioned to design the grounds of no less than fifty Long Island estates. Cromwell Childs, in a 1902 *Brooklyn Daily Eagle* article, marvelled at the pace at which these special homes were being built:

*No side of the life of New York is more interesting than the splendid way men of wealth and fashion have thrown themselves into making country places. One year a bare hillside, a field, a rugged short front; then rumors of its purchase from the farmers who have owned it for generations go about; suddenly a sale is recorded at the county seat, and the next year a transformation has been wrought where but a few months before there was undeveloped country, now a summer home stands, all but complete.*

To agriculturalists, baymen, and merchants the resort boom appeared to be an invasion akin to the coming of the seventeenth-century Europeans. Hundreds of farms were displaced by the phenomenon. When assembling his Manhasset estate, Payne Whitney purchased five such tracts, uprooting families who had owned the land since the eighteenth century. Willie Vanderbilt bought six or seven farms to build his Lake Success place, Deepdale. Perhaps the greatest construction feat occurred when utility magnate John E. Aldred and New York attorney W.D. Guthrie bought up the entire village of Lattingtown, comprising over sixty structures, to build their adjoining estates. The hamlet was then demolished, as Guthrie later told the *World Telegram*, "to get the view we wanted." Westbury nurseryman Issac Hicks wrote in 1900 that the "wealthy ones" were paying more for the land than its agricultural worth. Farming production fell rapidly in the estate areas, and by 1904 *The Long Islander* of Huntington reported that only one packet carrying agricultural produce now made runs to New York in season, where formerly there had been three making trips year-round.

Displacement was not the only effect of the resort boom. Whole industries, such as the Duryea starch works at Glen Cove and the brickyards in Cold Spring Harbor, disappeared due to labor and raw material problems linked to the boom. Bitter shore rights disputes erupted between opulent landowners and town governments. Baymen working the Centre Island beaches cut holes through estate docks which blocked their horse carts. Not even Main Street was pleased with the new realities. In a 1904 editorial, *The Long Islander* expressed the views of many of its merchant subscribers, stating: "When farms have been cut up and sold in plots" for "summer villas" the change had been "beneficial," but "where large tracts of hundreds of acres are monopolized for the enjoyment of a single owner, the change is to be regretted."

In time the estates did win a large measure of acceptance from Long Islanders whose world had been altered by their arrival. Willie Vanderbilt had predicted as much in 1902, when the citizens of North Hempstead had expressed concern that his proposed acquisition of Lake Success would prevent the men who cut ice there from making a living. Didn't they realize, Vanderbilt told the press, how many people would be employed in the castle he planned to build? A staff numbering in the teens was required to run even a modest country house, and fifty was not an uncommon number. Four hundred were allegedly put to work during the heyday of the Pratt Oval, the service complex for the adjoining Pratt family estates in Glen Cove. For many, the estates offered year-round employment at better wages. The brick works in Cold Spring Harbor, for example, is said to have closed after its workers left for better paying jobs on the area's new estates. To agrarian Long Island, which had been in decline since the opening of the Erie Canal and the era when railroads brought cheap western staples to the New York markets, the estates promised increased opportunities. Indeed, Long Island's entire service and transportation infrastructure originated with the resort period. We have already explored

the connection between the expansion of the Long Island Rail Road and the resort hotel. The Vanderbilt Motor Parkway, in which dozens of estate owners held stock, was conceived partially as a commuter road, a precursor of the Robert Moses-era parkways which were heavily influenced by it. Just think of it, noted A.R. Pardington, the chief engineer, in a 1907 article in *Harper's Weekly*:

*Think of the time it will save the busy man of affairs, who likes to crowd into each day a bit of relaxation. He will leave downtown at three o'clock in the afternoon, take the subway to a garage within striking distance of the new Blackwells Island-East River Bridge. In twenty minutes a 60 horse-power car will have him at the western terminus of the motor parkway. Here a card of admission passes him through the gates, speed limits are left behind, the great white way is before him, and with throttle open he can go, go, go and keep going fifty, sixty or ninety miles an hour until Riverhead or Southampton is reached.*

The Nassau Light and Power Company, the nucleus of what became the Long Island Lighting Company in 1922, began with E.D. Morgan's desire to obtain electricity for his Wheatley Hills Estate in the 1890s. The hand of the seasonal resident is also seen in the spread of telephone service commencing as early as 1884 in the summer community of Glen Cove.

The Nassau Hospital (now Winthrop University Hospital) in Mineola, Long Island's first voluntary,

In cultural life, Long Island's first art museums, the Heckscher at Huntington and the Parrish at Southampton, were the gifts of prominent summer residents. The hand of the estate owners is even seen in the development of Long Island's primary industry of the twentieth century—aviation. When flying was still thought to be something of a daredevil's sport with few practical applications, these individuals invested in aeronautics. Nelson Doubleday's popular magazine, *Country Life in America,* chronicled the leisure activities of the rich and gave monthly coverage to the exciting new pastime of flying. August Belmont, a director of Orville and Wilbur Wright's airplane company, was behind the first international air show at Belmont Park in 1910. Its top prize of $10,000 had been put up by another Long Island millionaire, Thomas Fortune Ryan of Manhasset. The summer community even brought attention to the area through politics. On becoming the Democratic nominee in 1924, John W. Davis of Locust Valley rounded out a quarter of a century of Long Island presidential aspirations begun by Theodore Roosevelt.

In developing new employment opportunities and improved public services, the resort period also put Long Island on the map. A barrier island, this agrarian outpost which had been passed over by the industrial revolution for lack of falling water to power mill turbines, suddenly found itself featured in every periodical in America. By the time "the Gold Coast," as the press began to call the North Shore, was at its height, the editors or publishers of the Brooklyn *Daily Eagle,* and the New York *Sun, Post, World,* and *Tribune* all summered there. Conde Nast, who was to own *Vogue, House and Garden, Glamour* and many more magazines, resided at Sands Point. Ralph Pulitzer and William Randolph Hearst spent the warm months on Long Island for a while, as did various members of the Lamont, Whitney, and Guggenheim families, newspaper owners at one time or another. The heads of publishing houses were also very much in evidence. Ormand G. Smith, of the huge dime novel house of Smith and Street, lived on Centre Island. Not far away was the Mill Neck Estate of Nelson Doubleday, whose Country Life Press was head-quartered in Garden City. Great Neck also became the favored world of writers and Broadway luminaries. Ring Lardner and F. Scott Fitzgerald summered

*Alva Vanderbilt Belmont became a leading figure in the women's suffrage movement, implementing an experimental agricultural school for women on her Hempstead estate in 1911. From Brown Brothers Endpapers*

non-profit hospital east of the city line, moved in 1900 from temporary quarters to its first permanent buildings. Located near the railroad tracks, it allowed patients to be brought in from the more distant reaches of Suffolk County. The edifice was designed by no less a figure than Richard Morris Hunt, architect of the Vanderbilt "cottages" at Newport and Oakdale, and Nassau's first wards were named for its major patrons, the Vanderbilts, Harpers, and Belmonts. Estate owners were also involved in the development of community hospitals. Yet, no one did more to establish advanced health care on Long Island than the Whitneys, who largely funded later expansion of the Nassau Hospital and the growth of the North Shore University Hospital at Manhasset.

there, the latter writing much of *The Great Gatsby* in a room over the garage of the Spanish Colonial house at Six Gateway Drive which he and Zelda had rented in 1922. Sinclair Lewis also toured Long Island, as did P.G. Wodehouse and Frances Burnett, who had a substantial estate in Plandome. Many parties were held at both Eddie Cantor's and George M. Cohan's places. Basil Rathbone, Lew Field, Ed Wynn, and Jane Cowl frequented the North Shore, to mention just a few celebrities. Will Rogers hit his head on a rock while diving in the Great South Bay during one of the many summers he resided at the Massapequa estate of vaudeville actor Fred Stone. Some of Stone's other friends who summered in the Freeport and Massapequa areas were Annie Oakley, Eddie Foy, Victor Moore, and George "Spider" Murphy. The Astoria Studios made Long Island an early filming center, and many of the producers, including the president of the American Vitagraph Corporation, Albert E. Smith, lived in Nassau County. Near Smith's Centre Island estate there survives a unique boathouse in the form of a ship's stern, said to have been built as part of a 1914 movie set.

Long Island's varied topography and scenic qualities also attracted the attention of artists. East Hampton on the "East End" of the Island had been an early mecca for a loosely based art colony drawn to sandy beaches, a rural atmosphere, and the ever-changing play of light on sea and dunes. One of the first to arrive and build a studio was the painter and etcher, Thomas Moran. He and his artist wife, Mary Nimmo Moran, were to be followed in the 1870s by other artists including Lockwood de Forest, Winslow Homer, Charles Henry Miller, and Childe Hassam. Wealthy summer residents also encouraged the prominent painter and teacher, William Merritt Chase, to form a studio and art school in Southampton in the 1890s. This group of artists, often collectively called the "American Barbizon," painted the Long Island landscape in a wide range of styles, and the East End to this day has continued to attract contemporary artists and painters such as William de Kooning and Lee Krasner.

Cold Spring Harbor was the site of another type of artist colony, more a retreat than a school, formed briefly in 1920 by Louis Comfort Tiffany at his summer estate, Laurelton. As an artist who worked in many fields, including painting, jewelry, stained

*Irene and Vernon Castle were a well-known dance team who popularized the tango and other dances. They had a country home in Manhasset near F. Scott Fitzgerald, and epitomized the glamour and excitement of the 1920s. (SPLIA)*

glass, textiles, interior decoration, and landscape architecture, Tiffany conceived and designed this lavish mansion. Both inside and out, it represented his love of the exotic and was greatly influenced by Oriental and Moorish art. Under the aegis of the L.C. Tiffany Foundation, the artist had his carriage

# THEODORE ROOSEVELT: LONG ISLAND'S PRESIDENT

*Theodore Roosevelt speaks to women suffragists at Sagamore Hill in 1917. Courtesy, Sagamore Hill National Historic Site, Oyster Bay*

Theodore Roosevelt, descended from a long line of sturdy Dutch Knickerbockers, was the seventh generation of his family born on the island of Manhattan. He is often called "Long Island's President," however, and rightfully so, because Roosevelt's life since boyhood was linked to Oyster Bay, on Long Island's North Shore.

Cornelius Van Schaack Roosevelt (1794-1871), Theodore's grandfather, is considered the founder of the "Oyster Bay Roosevelts." The old patriarch, who lived on Union Square in New York City, spent summers in Oyster Bay, and he was followed to the North Shore by his sons and their families. Theodore loved Long Island, and after he married he decided to build a home in Oyster Bay. In 1883 Roosevelt, then an assemblyman from Manhattan, bought land on Cove Neck, a small peninsula to the east of the village of Oyster Bay. The following year he began construction of a spacious house, completed in 1885 and called "Sagamore Hill," after the Sagamore (or chief) Mohannis who had lived with his Indian tribe on the land centuries before. Other Roosevelts, too, built on Cove Neck, and eventually (long before the Kennedy compound in Hyannis Port) there were four Roosevelt households and sixteen Roosevelt children in Oyster Bay.

Roosevelt took up residence at Sagamore Hill in 1887, after marrying his childhood friend Edith Kermit Carow, who had shared summers with the Roosevelts on the North Shore. At Sagamore Hill, Theodore and Edith raised a lively brood of six children: Alice (born to Roosevelt's first wife in 1884), Theodore, Jr. (born in 1887), Kermit (1889), Ethel (1891), Archibald (1894), and Quentin (1897). When Roosevelt became President in 1901—at forty-two he was the youngest President in history, before or since—Americans for the first time had a "first family," as the nation affectionately embraced the youthful Chief Executive and his winsome family. The Roosevelt family of Sagamore Hill was considered by Americans at the turn of the century to be the perfect model of all that was culturally revered in home life.

Much history was made at Sagamore Hill. There the nation watched the return of the colonel of the Rough Riders, after his Spanish-American War regiment was mustered out at Montauk Point, Long Island. There committees of Republicans came to officially notify Roosevelt of his nomination for governor of New York in 1898, for Vice President in 1900, and, after he entered the White House following the assassination of William McKinley, for

President in 1904. During the Roosevelt administration, 1901-1909, Sagamore Hill served as the "summer White House," the first of the noted presidential establishments outside the nation's capital. Many important meetings and conferences were held there, including the preliminary negotiations for the Portsmouth Treaty, which ended the Russo-Japanese War and earned Roosevelt the Nobel Peace Prize. There, after Roosevelt left the Presidency, supporters and reporters continued to come, day after day, to hear what "the Colonel" had to say about the affairs of the nation and the world. And there, on January 6, 1919, at the age of sixty, Roosevelt died.

The day before his death, Roosevelt had remarked to his wife, "I wonder if you will ever know how much I love Sagamore Hill." Sagamore Hill had a special place in the hearts of many Americans, too, and after Mrs. Roosevelt's death there at the age of eighty-seven in 1948, the house was purchased by the Theodore Roosevelt Association. It opened to the public in 1953. The Association gave Sagamore Hill to the National Park Service in 1963, and the house, one of the most famous in American history, is today probably the most popular public site on Long Island.

The early part of Theodore Roosevelt's life, when he was a summer sojourner on the North Shore, coincided with the rise of Long Island as a popular summer resort area. Roosevelt's adult years, when he made his home in Oyster Bay, witnessed the transformation of Long Island into a land of estates and suburbs. The Roosevelts were among the first to migrate eastward from New York City to enjoy the pleasant Long Island summers, and to take up yachting on the Long Island Sound. And later Roosevelt, who did not have the money to maintain a separate residence in New York City, was part of the first generation of commuters—people who lived on Long Island but worked in New York City or elsewhere. Roosevelt's prominence put Long Island in the public eye as perhaps never before, and his life spanned much of the making of modern Long Island, in which he played an important role.

Theodore Roosevelt's accomplishments, interests, and activities were many and varied; he was a naturalist, historian, hunter, intellectual rancher, explorer, soldier, writer, politician, conservationist, and public official. Roosevelt had a lifetime interest in natural history, and while still a student at Harvard he published a paper, "Notes on Some of the Birds of Oyster Bay, Long Island" (1879), one of the early works on Long Island ornithology. Near the end of his life, in 1915, he was the founder and first president of the Long Island Bird Club. Roosevelt studied, collected, and wrote about wildlife in North America, Africa, and South America. His interest in natural history led to his involvement with conservation; as President, Roosevelt established five national parks and set aside eighteen national monuments, including the Grand Canyon. He increased the federal forest preserves by over 300 percent and created the first federal wildlife refuges, including fifty-one for birds. A man of letters as well as an outdoorsman, Roosevelt wrote histories, biographies and numerous volumes on public affairs and his many adventures.

TR was a major figure in American politics for nearly forty years, and served as New York State assemblyman in the early 1880s; United States Civil Service commissioner, 1889-1895; president of the Board of Police Commissioners of New York City, 1895-1897; assistant secretary of the Navy, 1897-1898; governor of New York, 1898-1900; Vice President of the United States in 1901; and President of the United States, 1901-1909. As President, Roosevelt busted the trusts, built the Panama Canal, and promoted consumer protection and the regulation of big business. Long Island's President was, said the writer Julian Street, "the most interesting American."

John A. Gable

L.C. Tiffany (1848-1933), son of the founder of Tiffany & Company, was an artist who worked in many mediums, most notably stained glass. His eighty-room mansion at Cold Spring Harbor was the scene of many social events; here Tiffany is dressed as an Eastern potentate for one of his elaborate masquerade balls. Courtesy, Mrs. Collier Pratt

house converted into a studio and used his estate to encourage young artists. Although it did not last long for financial reasons, Tiffany's art community was based on a new concept in which artists working in different mediums were brought together to "study decoration from nature." Bellport on the ocean side of the Island also drew its share of artists. From 1907 to 1930 four large summer hotels attracted such visitors as painters Everett Shinn, William Glackens, Ernest Lawford, and John Sloan, as well as such journalists and editors as Walter Lippman, Frank Crowninshield, and Edna Woolman Chase.

By the time *Forbes Magazine*'s founder, B.C. Forbes, wrote his 1919 bestseller, *Fifty Men Who Are Making America,* twenty-five titans of American industry and finance either summered on Long Island or had children who owned country houses east of the Queens line. The names of these "movers and shakers" read like a *Who's Who* of the monied communities, and include George F. Baker, Jr., son of George F. Baker, known as the "Sphinx of Wall Street" and President of First National Bank of New York; J.P. Morgan, Jr., heir to the immense banking house; Nicholas Brady, financier and utility magnate who contributed to the formation of Consolidated Edison; Mortimer Schiff, son of Jacob

Schiff, head of Kuhn, Loeb and Company; John C. Ryan, financier Thomas Fortune Ryan's scion; and Howard Gould, son and heir to the brokerage and financial assets of Jay Gould. Among the industrialists were Walter P. Chrysler, founder of the Chrysler Corporation; Henry Ford II; the sons of Andrew Carnegie's partners, Henry Phipps and Henry Clay Frick; and the Graces of shipping line fame. Charles Pratt, of Pratt Institute and Standard Oil, created a unique family compound in Glen Cove that comprised twenty-one estates. As already mentioned, the Vanderbilts, who inherited a transportation empire that included railroads and shipping lines started by Commodore Cornelius Vanderbilt, and four of the seven sons of Meyer Guggenheim, the mining magnate, sometimes called Long Island home. Over 900 mansions dotted the landscape from the city line to Montauk. The area had become the great national playground, "a slender and riotous island," as F. Scott Fitzgerald put it, basking in a visibility it had never before known. Even a future king of England, Edward, Prince of Wales, was impressed when he came to the Island for 1924 polo matches. "My American hosts spared no expense in demonstrating the splendor of a modern industrial republic," he said. Edward was later to note that "compared to the creature comforts Americans took for granted, the luxury I was accustomed to in Europe seemed almost primitive." The Prince saw Long Island as the showcase for "a country in which nothing was impossible." As late as 1946, *Life* was to call it "the most socially desirable residential area in the United States," and *Holiday* reported that "while time is making some changes," it was clear that the "estates of Long Island's North Shore are close to an American ultimate in elegance, exclusiveness and display."

*The highlight of the 1924 social season on Long Island was undoubtedly the visit from Edward, Prince of Wales. The prince was feted and entertained on a grand scale by a number of prominent Long Islanders, including the Burdens and Pratts. From* Spur *magazine, September 1924*

The factors which were to bring the resort period to a close, however, had begun long before the post-World War II period. In his 1968 treatise, *Dynamics of Community Change,* author Daniel Sobin has chronicled the litany of transformations which ended Long Island's great estate period. Contributing factors included the 1916 appearance of the federal income tax, the establishment of the gift tax in 1932, the 1924 restrictive immigration law effecting servant procurement, the rise in local property assessments, the development of air travel, the construction of the Robert Moses parkway system, and passage of the G.I. Bill. *American Magazine* was informing its readers in 1948 of the great "Bargains in Dream Houses" on Long Island. Henceforth, the most frequent buyers of mansions were to be developers planning subdivisions. The epoch of the great estates was over, but their legacy would continue to shape life on Long Island in the future. Even the majority of the mansions would survive, finding a wide range of adaptive reuses. Largely as country clubs, educational facilities, and cultural institutions, the splendid palaces leave Long Island with a unique architectural heritage and a rich patina of history.

*Many of the titans of business and industry summered on Long Island. Pictured from left to right are Matthew S. Sloan, James Cox Brady, Nicholas F. Brady, Thomas E. Murray, Thomas A. Edison, and Walter P. Chrysler. Edison summered in Quoque from 1913-19, and the Sloan estate at Sands Point was the scene of many parties during the 1920s. Nicholas Brady's estate in Manhasset has become a Catholic retreat, while Chrysler's Kings Point estate is now the home of the U.S. Merchant Marine Academy. From Chrysler,* Life of an American Workman, *1937*

# CHAPTER SEVEN

# Brooklyn from the Civil War to the Great Renunciation

Nineteenth-century Brooklyn was a city in motion, continually changing from a place that was relatively small, simple, and stable into one that was large, complex, and volatile. With every year that passed, the emerging metropolis grew more like its rival across the East River and less like the surrounding villages and farms of eastern Long Island. Nowhere were the changes more pronounced than in the size and composition of Brooklyn's famous neighborhoods. Way back when Robert Fulton was proposing his first ferry scheme, most Brooklyn residents were of either Dutch or Anglo-American extraction. Beginning in the 1840s, however, large numbers of German and Irish immigrants arrived, and by 1860 just under 40 percent of the population was foreign-born. Over 55,000 Irishmen constituted the largest foreign-born group, while 23,000 Germans added a large non-English speaking contingent. Catholics, once a tiny minority, accounted for about half of all churchgoers. By 1860 Brooklyn was only slightly less "ethnic" than the nearby melting pot of Manhattan and its population was growing even faster than that of New York City.

The astonishing growth of Long Island's major city accelerated after the Civil War as a population of 266,000 quadrupled to over 1,150,000 at the turn of the century. And Brooklyn's population continued changing as it mushroomed. By 1890 the Germans constituted the largest ethnic group, while immigration from southern and eastern Europe brought numerous Jews, Italians, and Slavs. In fact, the number of Brooklyn's foreign-born citizens at the close of the nineteenth century equalled its total population forty years earlier. Valuing mutual support, familiar customs, and the same language, ethnic groups colonized particular neighborhoods:

The Brooklyn Bridge, standing amidst the fireworks on its opening night in May 1883, is still considered to be one of the most beautiful bridges in the world. Its construction sparked the imagination of an entire generation and reflected Brooklyn's potential. Courtesy, The Metropolitan Museum of Art, gift of Edward C. Arnold

*Left: Dr. Susan Smith McKenney-Steward (1847-1918) was the first black female physician in Brooklyn and in New York State. Born in Weeksville, she was an important figure in black Brooklyn's intellectual and social circles during the late nineteenth century. Courtesy, The Long Island Historical Society*

*Below: At one time covering 145 acres, the Brooklyn Navy Yard was kept busy during every major conflict since the Civil War. The* Indiana, *part of the U.S. fleet in the Spanish-American War, is depicted here in 1898. Courtesy, The Long Island Historical Society*

the Germans in Williamsburg, the Jews in Brownsville, and the Italians in Red Hook and South Brooklyn. Nearly 19,000 blacks lived in Brooklyn, too.

Underlying such rapid growth, and giving great vitality to the entire Brooklyn experience, was the surging nineteenth-century economic boom that transformed Manhattan's first suburb into a major city in its own right. Like its population, Brooklyn's economy became ever more dynamic. This development owed much to regional and national factors which spurred dramatic urbanization: the transportation revolution, European immigration, the growth of transatlantic commerce, the opening of western lands and resources, the spread of southern cotton culture, the rapid development of technology, and the rise of factory production.

But the Long Island metropolis also benefitted from its closeness to neighboring New York. A direct consequence of this proximity was the explosive growth of Brooklyn's real estate industry, thriving on the population boom and the region's popularity as a residence for middle-class New Yorkers. Brooklyn also controlled Long Island's gateways to Manhattan and flourished with the

trade, transportation, and transshipment functions which occurred at the entrepot. By the same token, Manhattan's commerce soon outgrew its own wharves and spilled across the East River. The Atlantic Docks in South Brooklyn, designed to warehouse grain, symbolized this development. Commerce likewise attracted the resources for manufacturing, and local industry benefitted greatly from these trends. Sugar refining prospered, especially the famous firm of Havemeyer and Elder, which later became Amstar. Brooklyn's shipyards built yachts, cargo vessels, and a host of warships, including the famous Civil War *Monitor.* Though Brooklyn in 1860 trailed far behind New York and Philadelphia in manufactures, it equalled Boston, and led Chicago, Baltimore, and St. Louis.

The same expansive economic trends continued unabated during the second half of the century and by 1900 had transformed Brooklyn into the fourth largest manufacturing center in the United States, a sugar refining giant, and a brewing, warehousing, and meat packing center. Furthermore, local docks handled the bulk of New York's cargo. From an agricultural village in 1800, Brooklyn developed into a commercial and industrial goliath.

Transit construction helped energize and facilitate Brooklyn's economic and population growth. By 1890, 2,500 cars drawn by 8,000 horses served the city, but their days were numbered and that same year the first all-electric trolley line opened to Coney Island. Most other lines were electrified in the next five years. The same era witnessed the introduction of elevated steam railroads (1885), and in 1896 the Brooklyn Rapid Transit Company organized a near monoply of the city's lines to become one of the largest transit companies in the world.

In the pre-automobile age, trollies and elevated trains were indispensable. They not only carried millions of passengers monthly, but hauled freight, removed trash, carted the mail (Brooklyn was the first city to do so), and even hosted parties in special parlour cars which rented for fifteen dollars an evening. These conveyances unfortunately proved rather dangerous for pedestrians, enough to make the "Trolley Dodgers" nickname more than a little grim. Nevertheless, they provided the framework for growth in an interdependent metropolis. Riders increasingly travelled somewhere to play or relax.

Nineteenth-century urban America produced no more profound change than the "Leisure Revolution." By concentrating masses of people and separating them from their former rural pastimes, urbanism both encouraged and necessitated the development of alternate forms of recreation. Brooklyn assumed a leading role in this recreation movement with Prospect Park, the sporting mania, and Coney Island playing the most important roles.

New and better recreational facilities were paramount. Local park reformers expected a lot from their natural settings—an antidote to urban living, encouragement of upright values, and a prestige symbol in the struggle with Manhattan. Early efforts centered on saving Brooklyn Heights as a promenade. This campaign failed; but in the 1830s and 1840s the first city park was built on reclaimed land near Wallabout Bay, and Washington Park

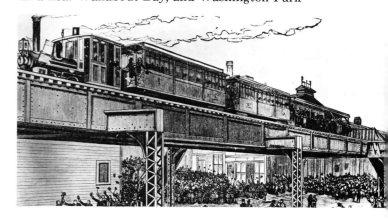

*Above: The elevated railroad or "el" greatly improved Brooklyn's rapid transit. It also boosted real estate development, for in the year that it opened 2,000 new houses were built along its routes. Courtesy, The Long Island Historical Society*

*Left: The E.W. Bliss Machine Shop and Foundry, built in 1879, exemplified Brooklyn's industrial growth during the 1880s. In just a few years Bliss had built up a prosperous business manufacturing iron, brass, and tin for household and commercial use. From Stiles,* History of Kings County Including the City of Brooklyn, *Munsell, 1884*

Above: Frederick Law Olmsted (1822-1903) developed the use of natural landscape resources in the construction of urban parks and recreational grounds. He designed more than eighty public parks in the United States. From Cirker, Dictionary of American Portraits, Dover, 1967

Below: Prospect Park's Brooklyn Plaza, later to become Grand Army Plaza, was designed and built in many stages. The park itself had just been completed when this photo was taken circa 1875. Courtesy, George B. Brainerd Photograph Collection, Brooklyn Public Library

opened in 1847. Nineteenth-century urbanites considered rural cemeteries to be parks as well as burial grounds. Creation of Greenwood Cemetery in 1838 put Brooklyn in the forefront of this movement. These initial successes, plus the example of Manhattan's Central Park in the 1850s, led to a decision in 1860 to build a great park system. Designed by Calvert Vaux and Frederick Law Olmsted, the architects of Central Park, Brooklyn's Prospect Park was completed in 1874 and soon became one of the nation's finest pleasure grounds, a fitting tribute to both its landscape architects, park commission president James S.T. Stranahan, and the Brooklyn elite which had espoused parks reform since the 1830s.

The completion of Prospect Park came just in time to encourage another part of Brooklyn's leisure revolution, the rise of participatory sports. Such pastimes existed earlier in the century, but from the 1880s onward a sporting mania developed. As in other cities, local aristocrats fostered the introduction of sports to Brooklyn both individually and through organizations like the prestigious Crescent Athletic Club. While tennis, golf, yachting, and equestrian activities remained upperclass monopolies, baseball, basketball, bicycling, and football soon became popular with middle- and working-class groups. Ethnic fraternities retained their own special activities like the gymnastics of the Germans, the handball of the Irish, and the Highland Games of the Scots. Since Brooklyn enjoyed easy access to nearby open spaces, older rural sports like boating, hunting, and fishing also persisted longer there than in other urban areas.

*The original Dutch farmsteads so numerous in Brooklyn were slowly succumbing to urban sprawl by the time of this nostalgic 1864 watercolor by James Ryder Van Brunt. Courtesy, The Long Island Historical Society*

*In this 1880 watercolor of Smithtown Bay and the mouth of the Nissequogue River, Long Island artist Edward Lange captures nineteenth-century Long Island with picnickers on the beach, horse drawn carriages, and sloops and schooners plying the river. Courtesy, private collection*

*Right: Rapid strides in public transportation spurred Brooklyn's growth during the late nineteenth century. The Brooklyn Bridge, the elevated railway, and streetcars are depicted in this turn-of-the century postcard. (SPLIA)*

*Below: Newspapers, magazines, and postcards such as this one quickly made the Brooklyn Bridge well known throughout the world. (SPLIA)*

*Circus Parade on Main Street,
Huntington, circa 1903. Photo
by Ben Conklin, Huntington
Historical Society*

With over ten shipyards operating at one time, Northport
was a busy harbor community
through the greater part of the
nineteenth century. This 1880
watercolor by Edward Lange
depicts Northport's Lower
Main Street running eastward
from the dock. Courtesy, Mrs.
D.C. Bushnell

The interior of Louis C. Tiffany's Cold Spring Harbor estate uniquely expressed his
interest in Oriental and
Moorish art. The central court
featured a crystal water foun-
tain crowned with a dome of
Tiffany glass. (SPLIA)

*Prominent among the many artists who summered on Long Island, William Merritt Chase (1849-1916) was considered one of the foremost landscape and portrait painters of his day. He painted many views of the Island's East End, such as "Bayberry Bush," which depicts the Shinnecock Hills. Courtesy, Parrish Art Museum, Southampton*

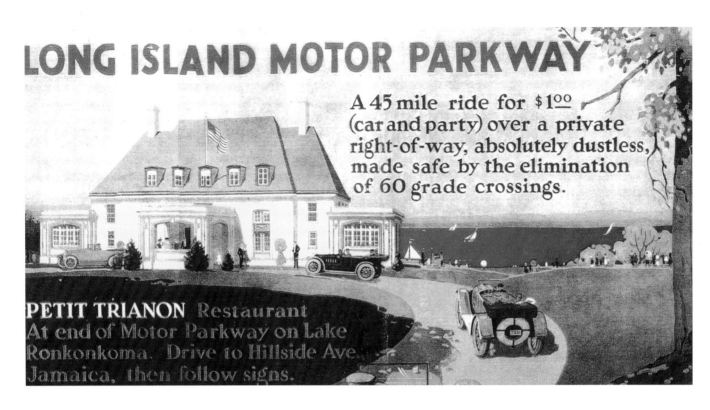

# LONG ISLAND MOTOR PARKWAY

A 45 mile ride for $1.00 (car and party) over a private right-of-way, absolutely dustless, made safe by the elimination of 60 grade crossings.

PETIT TRIANON Restaurant At end of Motor Parkway on Lake Ronkonkoma. Drive to Hillside Ave., Jamaica, then follow signs.

*Opposite page top: Long Island
Motor Parkway poster. Cour-
tesy, The Suffolk County
Vanderbilt Museum*

*Opposite page bottom: Jones
Beach Bathers. Courtesy,
SPLIA*

*Above: Poster for the Vanderbilt
Cup Race early in the 20th
century. Courtesy, The Suffolk
County Vanderbilt Museum*

*Left: Flags on the central mall at
Jones Beach. Courtesy, SPLIA*

*Steamboat* Seawahaka *is pictured in this 1868 oil on canvas by James Bard (1815-1897). Courtesy, SPLIA*

*The home of the Brooklyn Dodgers for over forty-four years, Ebbets Field opened in 1913 with a seating capacity of 35,000. Named after Dodgers owner Charles H. Ebbets, the stadium was razed in 1960 to make way for an apartment complex. Courtesy, The Long Island Historical Society*

# CHARLES PRATT

Horatio Alger had nothing on Charles Pratt (1830-1891). One of eleven children of a Watertown, Massachusetts cabinetmaker, he left home at the age of thirteen to become a clerk in a Boston grocery store. Twenty-four years later, he founded the Astral Oil Works on Bushwick Creek and the East River in Williamsburg (now Brooklyn). Business boomed. Pratt's Astral Oil, a high-quality kerosene used in lamps that was notably less prone to explode than most competing fuels, became a great international success. In 1874, the Pratt combine was acquired by John D. Rockefeller, and Pratt became a major force in the Standard Oil Company. When he died, he was almost certainly the richest man in Brooklyn, and one of the wealthiest in the United States.

There are several explanations for Pratt's success. Astral Oil was, quite simply, a superior product, and the demand for a high-quality yet safe illuminating oil was virtually insatiable. Also, more than most refiners, Pratt found markets for the many petroleum by-products that were separated out during the refining process: varnish, turpentine, naphtha, paraffin, asphalt, and so forth. Perhaps even more important in his success was his creative use of machinery and his emphasis on efficient production. The Astral Oil Works was considered the model refinery in the industry.

*Charles Pratt, industrialist and philanthropist, was one of Brooklyn's leading citizens in the late nineteenth century. Courtesy, Pratt Institute*

Pratt took his philanthropic concerns seriously. His greatest interest was in what we would today call vocational education. In 1887 he founded Pratt Institute in Brooklyn for the training of skilled artisans, designers, and draftsmen; there were twelve students the first year, over 600 the second year, and several thousand a few years later. Pratt was insistent that the institute serve "all classes of workers, artists, artisans, apprentices and homemakers." Courses would "give every student practical skill along some definite line of work, and at the same time reveal ... possibilities for further development and study." Admission was open to those of every educational background, and "persons of both sexes." The first black student enrolled in 1888. Tuition, $2.50 per course in the early years, was kept well below cost.

Ever practical, Pratt built the Institute so that it could be converted into a shoe factory if the original purpose was unsustainable; fortunately for hundreds of thousands of students over the last century, this conversion alternative proved unnecessary. Early course offerings included drawing, mechanical arts, and training programs for milliners, tailors, librarians, and kindergarten teachers. Today, Pratt Institute has an international reputation in design, the arts and sciences, architecture, and engineering. Other Pratt philanthropic endeavors included the Astral Apartments, a model worker housing project in Greenpoint near the oil refinery (and still standing at 184 Franklin Avenue), the first free public library in either Brooklyn or New York City, and a savings bank for working class families.

Pratt, like Rockefeller, was a devout Baptist and very much a self-made man, living relatively modestly on Clinton Avenue in Brooklyn. His house, and those of three of his children across the street, still stand. Just before his death, he bought "Dosoris" in Glen Cove, which served until recently as a summer retreat for the Pratt family. From the time of their arrival in Glen Cove, the Pratt family played an active civic and philanthropic role. In addition to employing as many as 400 local residents in the management of the family estates between 1900 and 1935, the Pratts donated land and money for a high school, were instrumental in the founding of the North Shore Community Hospital, and donated the land and architects' fees for the Glen Cove City Hall and Glen Cove Post Office, as well as land for a twenty-five-acre public park.

Malcolm MacKay

Women participated in the sporting boom, too, but were confined to less strenuous activities, such as croquet, bowling, and bicycling. They also participated as spectators in other sports, even the emerging national game of baseball. Invented in New York City, what was to be called "America's favorite pastime" quickly spread to Brooklyn. In 1858 the two cities fielded all-star teams, playing for a mythical world championship. Manhattan won this contest, but Brooklyn dominated the series for the next decade. Professionalism appeared later, and the famous Trolley Dodgers won a pennant and tied for the world's championship in 1889 and 1890. Though baseball went into temporary eclipse in the 1890s, other forms of leisure boomed. Whether it was watching the America's Cup Races which started off from Fort Hamilton, the Battery-to-Coney Island swims, the Trolley Dodgers, or the Highland Games, Brooklynites enjoyed increasingly diverse sports.

Just as the nineteenth century drew to a close, Brooklyn's most famous leisure institution entered its heyday. Coney Island had been used for recreation purposes as early as 1829, when its first hotel was built. Thirty years later, Brighton Beach and Manhattan Beach had developed into pleasure resorts for the more genteel classes, while West Brighton increasingly catered to the masses. At the turn of the century, three new amusement parks—Luna Park, Steeplecase Park, and Dreamland—brought Coney Island its era of greatest fame. An outrageous collection of outsized humans and animals, fantastic rides, never-ending shows, and the excitement of the crowds allowed urban dwellers to experience a world of make-believe. As historian John Kasson described it, the world was turned upside down—class order was disregarded, roles were shunned, mores were loosened, spontaneity replaced regularity and order, and exuberance supplanted cold calculation. Whether to escape the rigors of urban-industrial existence or to enjoy the excitement of modern life to the fullest, millions of middle- and working-class Americans streamed to Coney Island, helping to create what many have termed a new mass culture.

In a similar vein to the leisure revolution, Brooklyn's population growth and economic development were accompanied by an increasingly complex and varied cultural life—churches, schools, and other institutions multiplied to serve the needs of residents and contributed to an emerging sense of community identity. This Long Island metropolis had always claimed its share of small public halls and meeting places, yet nineteenth-century New York City had outshadowed it in terms of more diverse cultural events. However, from mid-century the creation of concert halls, museums, colleges, private clubs, and art associations signified the arrival of the Brooklyn community to full urban status. Many factors contributed to Brooklyn's burgeoning cultural fluorescence: rapid population growth and urban development generated a need for improved educa-

*Left: The proximity of Coney Island's wide beaches to New York City and Brooklyn attracted thousands, although in this 1877 view from the pier the usual mob is conspicuously absent. Courtesy, George B. Brainerd Photograph Collection, Brooklyn Public Library*

*Below: Organized in the 1850s, the Academy of Music became Brooklyn's cultural center. This photo depicts the second Academy building, erected in 1907 and still standing today. From* Hazelton, The Boroughs of Brooklyn and Queens, Counties of Nassau and Suffolk, N.Y., 1609-1924, *Lewis, 1925*

well-known cultural establishment during this period was the Brooklyn Academy of Music (1859). The Academy became Brooklyn's cultural center and most of the great musical artists, actors, and performers in the country (including Edwin Booth and Jenny Lind) were heard under its roof. Performances continue today, attracting not only Brooklynites, but thousands from New York City and surrounding regions.

The mid-1800s also saw the expansion of schools of higher learning and specialized instruction to meet the increasing demand for improved training. Many of Brooklyn's earliest cultural and education-

tional facilities, immigration fostered its own ethnic and cultural diversity; and most importantly, improved transportation enabled people to get around to a degree unimagined in earlier decades.

For most of the eighteenth and nineteenth centuries a secondary education was generally a luxury of the middle and upper classes. As late as 1850, Brooklyn had few secondary schools and no colleges. The apprenticeship system had been one of the most important institutions for educating the young during the previous century, but this type of training had declined with the rise of industrialization. One of the early responses to this change was the founding of the Brooklyn Lyceum in 1833 as part of a national movement to stimulate discussion of science, art, and humanitarian subjects. It offered lectures by Brooklynites on many diverse topics. Speakers included Horace Greeley, Ralph Waldo Emerson, and Henry Ward Beecher, among others. These early cultural institutions continued to grow and expand throughout the century: the Mercantile Library, formed in 1857, was intended for working people and sponsored a library, study classes, and lectures and eventually became the Brooklyn Public Library; The Long Island Historical Society, organized in 1863 by several prominent men to document their city's history; and the Brooklyn Institute of Arts and Sciences (Brooklyn Museum), founded in 1881 and housed in an impressive building designed by the nationally known architectural firm of McKim, Mead & White. Perhaps Brooklyn's most

al institutions were founded by a new breed of residents, self-made business leaders who had come to the city in the wake of its rapid growth and possessed a strong sense of social and community responsibility. Such men as Henry E. Pierrepont, A.A. Low, Charles Pratt, and Isaac Frothingham gave impetus to the movement. Some of the institutions they helped to foster were the Polytechnic Institute (1853), with a curriculum geared to the expanding industrial city; the Long Island College Hospital (1858); St. Francis College (1859), established to serve sons of Irish Catholics; St. Johns College (1871); and Pratt Institute (1887), focusing on manual and industrial training, as well as high school education.

In the area of art, literature, and crafts, Brooklyn during the latter part of the nineteenth century was emerging as a cultural center to be reckoned with—in addition to poet Walt Whitman, its artistic community included Brooklyn native Harry Roseland (1866-1950), who enjoyed a successful career as a portraitist and genre painter. The well-known architect, George B. Post (1837-1913), contributed importantly to the city's architecture, designing the Williamsburg Savings Bank (1875), the Long Island Historical Society Building (1878), and the Hamilton Club (1888). The Brooklyn Art Association was formed during this period as a way for artists to show their work, and private clubs devoted to art and literature flourished, one of which, the Rembrandt Club (1880), is still in operation. In addition, a growing crafts industry catered to the emerging middle class and affluent residents of Brooklyn, producing objects of high quality and artistic value. The Union Porcelain Works at Greenport manufactured ceramic objects that won the admiration of connoisseurs. In fact, as late as 1880, it was the only firm in the country producing such high-grade porcelain. The Flint Glass Works and Christian Dorflinger Greenpoint Glass Works produced everything from fine stemware to street lamps.

Whether for amusement, cultural, economic, or residential pursuits, urban crowds required ever-increasing public works to accommodate them; Brooklyn built several by 1900. Between 1867 and 1873 new docks and anchorages were constructed out of the marshes of Wallabout Bay, and Washington Avenue was built across the wetlands to link Brooklyn and Williamsburg. Prospect Park opened

in 1874, while rapid transit began in 1885. However, the most massive public work of the age was the construction of the "Great Bridge" bewteen 1869 and 1883. Residents had talked of building a structure across the East River since 1800, but costs, engineering problems, and lack of perceived need postponed the work for some sixty years. The technical problems had then been mastered, a substantial population base could bear the cost, and a large commuter group clamored for better service. Steam ferries were crowded, slow, dingy, and sometimes closed due to ice or wind storms. A bridge would eliminate these annoyances and tie the metropolis together, opening new markets for businessmen, making Brooklyn real estate more accessible, and, as usual, allowing the city to upstage New York. These promises, plus a calculated underestimate of the cost, were enough to overcome the opposition of many skeptics: engineers, warehouses, shippers, Navy men, taxpayers, and economizers worried over structural, navigational, and financial problems.

To a later age the conquest of a mere tidal strait may seem inconsequential, but in its day, the

*Above: By 1890 Brooklyn had a population of over 700,000, one-third of which was foreign born and hard-pressed to find adequate housing. These tenements were built in the 1870s by philanthropist Alfred T. White in an early effort to provide low-cost, non-profit housing. Courtesy, The Long Island Historical Society*

*Below: In this early view, ferries can still be seen vying with the Brooklyn Bridge as a means of public transport. In 1920, when pedestrian tolls were discontinued and subways were developed, the ferry industry rapidly declined. Courtesy, The Long Island Historical Society*

Brooklyn Bridge was an astounding construction feat. In 1867, when it was chartered, suspension bridges were by no means universally accepted, and for good reasons. One such model over the Ohio River at Wheeling lasted only five years before crashing in 1854; and in 1879 the monumental Tay Firth Bridge (non-suspension) collapsed into the sea during a storm. Though engineer John Roebling had built durable structures at Cincinnati and Niagara Gorge, the public remained anxious all the same.

The East River Bridge did not fall, but it did have numerous crises. Twenty men perished on the span, including John Roebling, the first fatality,

*After completing two suspension bridges, German immigrant John Augustus Roebling began work on the Brooklyn Bridge. He died from tetanus in 1869. From Cirker,* Dictionary of American Portraits, *Dover, 1967*

who succumbed horribly to tetanus contracted in a work accident. Several others fell to caisson sickness (bends). Washington Roebling, who succeeded his father and supervised most of the work, almost died from this disease. Bends and accompanying nervous disorders confined him to his house for much of the later stages of construction. Accidents also plagued the project, and on one occasion the heavily timbered roof of a caisson caught fire, requiring massive flooding to extinguish it. Completing the list of disasters and near misses, a sailing ship mast struck the bridge floor while passing beneath. Amidst cheers of the workmen, the suspension structure stood, while the mast went down.

When construction problems abated, political difficulties took their place. Tammany Boss William Marcy Tweed tried to gain control of the bridge and its construction jobs; Boss John Kelly held up New York's share of the funds; the bridge trustees squabbled endlessly; and Brooklyn Mayor Seth Low even tried to fire the chief engineer. Roebling sur-

vived, but he always considered the political headaches greater than construction difficulties. Cable wire problems illustrate the point. The trustees insisted on giving the contract to a Brooklyn manufacturer, who began supplying defective wire. Roebling later discovered this outrage, but refused to revoke the contract with J.L. Haigh. Fortunately, the chief engineer had built the bridge with a sixfold margin of safety.

The press fully aired these episodes, perhaps too fully. Nevertheless, the bridge soon captured the imaginations of Brooklynites and, indeed, all Americans. The spectacle of hundreds of men working in a pressurized caisson, sinking ever deeper into the earth as the weight of the masonry towers accumulated above them; of the laborers toiling away, with hand picks, shovels, and powder against mud, sand, and boulders; of a specialized machine reeling out fifty miles of wire a day; of two huge, Gothic-arched masonry towers dominating the skyline, all seemed endlessly fascinating to the public. Moreover, the accident victims being carted off to the tenements where they lived and the equally heroic chief engi-

*Above: Difficulties with contracts and expenditures slowed work on the Brooklyn Bridge, and politicians and promoters on both sides of the river constantly bickered. The distant possibility of a completed bridge was a theme of popular songs and newspaper jests, as seen in this 1883 caricature from* Puck *magazine. Courtesy, The Long Island Historical Society*

*Opposite page: For Brooklyn's poorer residents, the bridge was not only a means of transportation but also a part of their social life. Promenading across the bridge on summer evenings and weekends provided some relief from the heat and offered a chance to watch the city life around them. (SPLIA)*

neer fighting the bends, nervous exhaustion, and a horde of politicians as he desperately tried to supervise the work from his house on the Heights via his charts and telescope, gave the bridge a drama shared by few other events of the time.

The bridge also claimed many firsts, not the least of which was the role played by Roebling's wife, Emily, who took over so much of the supervision from her stricken husband that the public often mistook her for the real engineer. Fittingly enough, she and her coachman were the first citizens to ride across the finished structure in the spring of 1883. Brooklyn's celebration of the bridge's opening was outlandish even in a century much more given to urban fanfare. Enormous crowds pressed for admittance on each side, and some enterprising souls rode the ferries back and forth for hours to see the ceremonies.

The completed bridge symbolized many things to many different people. To Henry Cruse Murphy and William Kingsley, who initiated the project in 1866, it was a personal triumph; for realtors it meant increased property values; to immigrants the twin Gothic stone towers represented the gateway to North America; commuters perceived the same landmarks as the entrance to suburbia; to modern historians, the bridge symbolizes the dawning of the age of steel and electricity; and to ordinary citizens of the two great cities, the span offered a release from the confined quarters of the city, a place to stretch the legs, lungs, and soul, and to see the larger community of which they were a part. So popular did the bridge become, and so boisterous were the throngs of eager sightseers, that a tragedy soon resulted. On Memorial Day, 1883, one week after the official opening, twelve people were trampled to death when a crowd of 20,000 pedestrians raged out of control at the steps leading to the bridge promenade. Despite the tragedy, the Roeblings' masterpiece proved itself a hundred times over. Nine million people rode the trains the first year. And the bridge did connect the neighboring urban giants, open the suburban frontier, and bring fame to the city of Brooklyn.

Local politics also brought notoriety to Brooklyn, but of a different kind. During the village and early

# SETH LOW

Seth Low (1850-1916), political reformer, college president, businessman, and philanthropist, was perhaps Brooklyn's most outstanding citizen at the start of the twentieth century. A native of Brooklyn and the son and grandson of highly successful China trade importers, Low was valedictorian of Columbia College in 1870, two-term mayor of Brooklyn (1882-1886), president of Columbia College (1890-1901), and mayor of the recently consolidated City of New York (1901-1903). In these difficult jobs, as well as in running his family's importing firm, his performance was exemplary.

As a very young mayor of Brooklyn, he championed various civil service reforms, including the institution of competitive hiring and promotion examinations. At Columbia, he initiated the move from its Forty-ninth Street site to Morningside Heights, personally contributed one million dollars for the construction of the Low Library, forced greater coordination among the various academic departments, created the Columbia Union Press, and brought within the university corporation the College of Physicians and Surgeons. As an anti-Tammany mayor of New York City, he trimmed the city's budget and lowered taxes while strengthening the old departments of health, charities, and tenement housing. Unlike some reformers, however, Low was generally op-

posed to municipal ownership, emphasizing the awarding of city franchises to private companies on a competitive basis. As mayor, Low pushed the planning of the first subway to Brooklyn and the Pennsylvania tunnel to Long Island, as well as the completion of the electrification of the New York Central within city limits.

After being defeated for reelection in 1903 by Democrat George B. McClellan, Jr., the Civil War general's son, Low spent the rest of his life deeply involved with problems involving blacks, labor, and New York City: he served as chairman of the Tuskegee Institute; president of the National Civic Federation; a member of the Colorado Coal Commission, appointed by President Wilson to investigate labor unrest in that state; and president of the New York Chamber of Commerce. The house in which he was born, grew up, and lived most of his life still stands at 3 Pierrepont Place in Brooklyn Heights, appropriately looking out over the harbor and lower Manhattan.

Malcolm MacKay

*Brooklyn mayor Seth Low appointed men on the basis of merit rather than patronage and instituted long-needed reforms in the city's administration. From Stiles,* History of Kings County Including the City of Brooklyn, *Munsell, 1884*

city eras, the governing powers initiated paltry efforts to offer basic services, curtail expenses, and regulate liquor licensing. By mid-century, however, Brooklyn's explosive growth came to the fore. Rapid expansion sharpened the conflicts over provision of expensive new services, governmental reorganization, bossism versus reform, and Brooklyn's proper relationship with Manhattan.

Before the Civil War an ineffective city council dominated the local government. Curtailing expenditures remained the prevalent issue, but expenses continued to rise in line with the demands of urban growth. Brooklyn then responded to fiscal woes with a further and counterproductive diffusion of government power. Under the Charter of 1873, local aldermen were given added responsibilities, a move designed to establish checks and balances in a system which already possessed too many. The resulting government lacked cohesion and accountability and was prey to every imaginable kind of corruption. Inefficiencies loomed ever larger because a lack of political responsibility strengthened the hand of Democratic boss Hugh McLaughlin. With easy access to patronage jobs and public works contracts, he was little different from other city bosses who emerged across mid-century America, except that his tenure lasted far longer, from the late 1860s until 1903. Like most of his peers, McLaughlin was not obsessed with tyrannical power, but he certainly wielded more clout than any other Brooklyn politician of his era, and not always in the best interests of the city. In classic machine fashion, he traded favors for votes, jobs for influence, and franchises for cash.

Recent nostalgic writers have invested political bosses with Robin Hood-like qualities—they uplifted the poor, they got things done, they provided illicit but popular services. Perhaps some of these traits are valid. Yet, machine politicians frequently stole vast sums. In Brooklyn's case both the school fund and monies allocated to poor relief mysteriously disappeared. Local citizens finally refused to stomach any further misdeeds, and began protesting these outrages in a series of reform movements. Former Brooklyn mayor Frederick Schroeder initiated the process in 1879 when he secured from Albany a new, "single-head" charter that centralized authority within the city government and enhanced the power of the mayor. This innovation quickly

*Brooklyn did not have an organized police department until 1857, when the Metropolitan Police law placed New York City and Kings County under a single system of police enforcement. In 1870 Brooklyn acquired a separate police department and the city was divided into precincts. At the time of this circa 1890 photograph the force consisted of over 700 men. Courtesy, The Long Island Historical Society*

*T. McCants Stewart (1854-1923) was a prominent black lawyer and intellectual in Brooklyn. He was appointed to the Brooklyn Board of Education in 1891. Courtesy, The Long Island Historical Society*

*The Brooklyn Orphan Asylum was established in 1833, and this building was erected in 1872, accommodating 400 children. Courtesy, George B. Brainerd Photograph Collection, Brooklyn Public Library*

forced reformers to seriously contest the 1881 mayoralty race, lest the newfound power fall into the waiting hands of boss McLaughlin. Reformers found a winning candidate in the popular and aristocratic Seth Low. As mayor, Low exercised tight control over his department heads and successfully insisted on home rule. He proved an energetic reformer as well. Previously, McLaughlin had kept taxes at a minimum by selling franchises to private contractors who provided terrible service while corrupting local government. Not only did Low refuse to cut taxes, breaking with the more narrow, privileged view of reform, but he insisted on collecting scandalously large sums of tax arrearages. The mayor then used the money to provide better health, police, fire, and especially, educational services. He quickly opened the schools to Brooklyn's Negro population, ended the practice of looting the education department, and supplied free textbooks to all children. Low also insisted on competency testing for office holders, established a civil service system, and outlawed the custom of squeezing officials for political contributions at election time. Finally, the mayor was first and foremost a Brooklyn booster, favoring development over tightfisted fiscal practices. He was one of the first of a new breed of urban executives who combined sensitivity for the poor with solicitude for the city's economic welfare.

Low's policies transformed Brooklyn into a model imitated by reformers across the country, yet he failed to please all the taxpayers, or even members of his own Republican party. He retired in 1885, the Democrats captured the office again, and the duel between boss and reformers resumed. A new rapid transit company concluded that it need not pay taxes and fraudulently escaped with a payment of only $282,000 out of a $1,500,000 assessment. Such flagrant abuses soon brought the reformers back into power in the 1890s, just as the issue of metropolitan consolidation replaced honesty and efficiency as the leading political question.

The concept of a Greater New York had been discussed for decades, but never caught on, especially in Brooklyn. Rather, Long Islanders had been busy creating a Greater Brooklyn through the 1894 absorption of Flatbush, Gravesend, and New Utrecht; the New Lots and Flatlands takeover in 1896; and consolidation with Kings County the same year. These and other acquisitions raised Brooklyn's pop-

Manhattan, but by a perilously thin margin. This election also revealed a curious ethnocultural, class, and partisan split. The pro-unification coalition, embracing wealthier Germans, Irish, Anglo-Americans, and many residents of distant neighborhoods who needed city improvements, won by 277 votes. Opposition forces were led by Brooklyn's Protestant, Republican reform elite, but supported by the normally Democratic German and Irish working-class wards. Out of the referendum of 1894 grew the League of Loyal Citizens who feared that the creation of a Greater New York would destroy Brooklyn's special character. They also predicted a rise, rather than fall, in taxes and fretted over the impact of Manhattan's corrupt Tammany Hall on Brooklyn's good government efforts. St. Clair McKelway and the Brooklyn *Eagle* spearheaded the

*Below: Henry Ward Beecher (1813-1887) was the leader of Plymouth Church for forty years. Like his sister, Harriet Beecher Stowe, he endeavored to arouse public awareness of the evils of slavery. From Hazelton,* The Boroughs of Brooklyn and Queens, Counties of Nassau and Suffolk, N.Y., 1609-1924, *Lewis, 1925*

ulation to more than one million. Manhattan's final push for a Greater New York was simultaneously gaining strength, fanned by the conviction that their city was about to be eclipsed by Chicago and possibly even Brooklyn, itself. In 1888 New York Mayor Abram Hewitt opened the debate. Andrew H. Green, the real father of consolidation, carried it forward. Manhattan elements expected several gains from a massive annexation-control over the entire metropolitan harbor, central public works planning, the prestige of being the world's greatest city, and a chance to implement their good government ideas.

While Brooklyn retained a sturdy sense of its own identity, Manhattan's blandishments nonetheless attracted many local residents. Some citizens hoped that Manhattan's greater wealth might lower Brooklyn's taxes and widen its bonding power, bring a second East River Bridge, hasten growth in the outer neighborhoods, and ease a local water crunch through access to upstate Croton water. Pro-consolidationists included many of Brooklyn's leading citizens: realtors, bankers, insurers, manufacturers, merchants, street railway operators, and builders. In 1892 they formed the Brooklyn Consolidation League to promote their cause. An 1894 advisory referendum favored unification with

*Opposite page, top: Convicts work inside the Kings County Penitentiary, also known as "Crow Hill." Courtesy, The Long Island Historical Society*

*Right: The Brooklyn* Daily Eagle, *whose original offices are seen here on the left, was the city's largest newspaper in the nineteenth century. From Stiles,* History of Kings County Including the City of Brooklyn, *Munsell, 1884*

anti-consolidation forces. Despite their cause, attitudes and events tended towards merger.

Local forces thereafter lost control of the issue, as New York State boss Tom Platt was not about to let such an important matter pass the legislature without some conformance to his own political needs. In 1896 Platt ramrodded the necessary laws through the senate and assembly. A commission soon drafted a metropolitan charter which took effect on January 1, 1898. Although Brooklyn Firsters lost the larger battle, they obtained several important compromises which guaranteed local autonomy through the borough system. They gained citywide equalization of taxes and maintained control over the school system. Brooklyn now formed the largest part of America's greatest city, brought into being by the most awesome urban consolidation in American history.

The Long Island city's surprising renunciation of independent status was almost unique among nineteenth-century American municipalities. In an age of urban expansion and conflict, these jurisdictions competed in nearly all facets of life: in sports, population growth, industry, culture. Brooklyn was well prepared for the race to urban greatness. Its growth rate placed it among the very largest American cities; Coney Island made it famous; the Brooklyn Bridge loomed as a symbol to all America and even the world; its industry ranked fourth in the United States. Seth Low and his reform colleagues pushed the city to the forefront of American urban reform, and communities all across the nation looked to it for guidance.

Long known as a mecca of churches and homes, Brooklyn's residential neighborhoods were possibly the best in the country, certainly surpassing those of nearby Manhattan. The fame of Brooklyn Heights minister Henry Ward Beecher alone would have been enough to distinguish the city's religious establishment. Beecher helped his congregation accept and understand the urban revolution swirling around them. His popularity was so great that he earned an annual salary of $20,000, preached to audiences of 2,000, and caused the ferries that carried his flock to be dubbed "Beecher Boats."

These varied factors represented just a partial list of Brooklyn's major assets, enough to have given a lesser city delusions of grandeur. Hence, the "great renunciation of 1898" becomes even more mystifying. Just as Greater Brooklyn was within reach, Long Island's own metropolis dropped out of the race.

# CHAPTER EIGHT

# Broader Networks of Modernization

Despite the heavy influx of excursioners and estate owners, turn-of-the-century Long Island retained much of its rural character. Agriculture and fishing flourished, small-town life predominated, and local inhabitants viewed themselves very differently from their urban neighbors. Indeed, their rural state of mind helped foster the creation of a new county, Nassau, formed out of Queens' three eastern towns on January 1, 1899.

Yet, amid the placid landscape change was evident as well. Daily commuters already travelled to New York by railroad and steamboat, and a proposed tunnel under the East River promised to increase the flow. Although farming remained the single most important economic activity, its position on western Long Island had begun to decline. Instead, real estate development accelerated. Within a generation automobiles, trolleys, and commuter trains would combine to create the archetypical American suburb.

Suffolk County experienced the same forces, but the pace was slower and the intrusion of modern urban life less persistent. As late as the 1930s, many local farms lacked electricity and running water, and Suffolk's population growth lagged in comparison to that of its exuberant neighbor. Not until after World War II would Long Island's East End fully enter the twentieth century.

Small towns and rural villages, sustained by the agricultural and fishing economy, set the tone for life throughout turn-of-the-century Long Island. Nassau County contained over 1,650 farms spread across 70,000 productive acres. A town like New Hyde Park was termed "rich farming country" by a contemporary guide book, while Syosset was known for "its really good farms and better fruit." Milk,

An old form of horse power confronts a new one on a Port Washington street in 1910. The myriad technological developments of the early twentieth century altered patterns of life on Long Island that had seen little change in over two centuries. Courtesy, Nassau County Museum

*Left: The growth of Port Jefferson can be attributed almost entirely to its excellent harbor and to shipbuilding. The Bayles Shipyard (pictured here in 1875) turned out approximately 140 vessels between 1836 and 1917, when it was sold. Courtesy, George B. Brainerd Photograph Collection, Brooklyn Public Library*

*Below: Like so many other coastal communities, Greenport (depicted in 1879) was adversely affected by the decline of the whaling and shipbuilding industries. Once one of the busiest whaling ports on Long Island, the boats moored at its dock today are pleasure boats, not schooners. Courtesy, George B. Brainerd Photograph Collection, Brooklyn Public Library*

potatoes, and vegetables for city tables proved profitable, and in 1898 the H.J. Heinz Company opened a plant in Hicksville to process pickles, sauerkraut, ketchup, and vinegar.

Suffolk County, more distant from New York, was even more agricultural and shipped tremendous quantities of cabbage, pickles, and potatoes to urban markets. Tiny Calverton made a specialty of growing "that indispensable delicacy, the cranberry." Duck farms flourished, too. The first seven "Peking" ducks were imported from China in 1873, and within a generation Long Island and the water fowl were synonymous. Riverhead boasted the world's largest duck farm by 1898.

Fishing and the maritime trades, widely practiced since colonial times, contributed greatly to local economic life and character. Oyster Bay boatmen planted tons of seed oysters every year and South Shore baymen harvested millions of bushels of shellfish annually. Coastal Freeport shipped over one million pounds of fresh seafood to the New York City market. Greenport was Suffolk's fishing leader, supporting scores of processing plants and a large sailing fleet. And Greenport was not alone in its maritime ways. Bridgehampton across Peconic Bay was described by one chronicler as a "rare old town, full of sturdy mariners who wrest a living from the sea." Shipbuilding remained an important industry in Rockaway, Northport, Port Jefferson, Greenport, and additional bay towns.

Other reminders of earlier times were also evident. In many villages gristmills and sawmills, some survivors of the seventeenth and eighteenth centuries, continued to turn. Annual agricultural fairs, dating from before the Civil War, saluted the Island's farming heritage. In numerous one-room schoolhouses, teachers were not only expected to educate, but also to fill kerosene lamps, clean chimneys, carry coal for the stove, and fill the water buckets. Village general stores stocked groceries, dry goods, paints and oils, and hardware, while gaily painted delivery wagons or horsedrawn sleighs carried their wares out into the countryside. Shops for blacksmiths and harnessmakers crowded many streets.

The march towards industrialization, which affected nearby Brooklyn and Queens so heavily, barely touched Long Island. The 1900 census counted only 1,650 employees of 321 small Nassau manufacturing establishments; Suffolk supported even fewer. Though an occasional large firm thrived, such as the Plymouth Lace Mills in Patchogue or the Ladew Leather Works in Glen Cove, they were most conspicuous by their rarity.

As befit their semi-rural ways, Long Islanders generally lived in small villages and towns. Hempstead, Nassau's retail and transportation hub, counted barely 3,600 inhabitants in 1900, and its main street remained unpaved. The size of Suffolk's largest population centers were equally unimpressive: Huntington contained 3,500 residents; Patchogue 2,900; Greenport 2,400. Riverhead, the county seat, numbered but a few thousand, and horses and wagons crowded the central business district. Most Islanders, in fact, resided in even smaller places. Villages like Glenwood Landing, Bellmore, Massapequa, Medford, and Yaphank counted a few hundred inhabitants each. In the words of one observer, Suffolk's Miller Place, Rocky Point, Shoreham, and Wading River all appeared to "have been bodily transported from the Massachusetts shore, so rural and simple are their ways."

*Above: In spite of their rural, unassuming character, village centers such as Main Street in Sag Harbor provided a base for the Island's economy. Supplying services and goods to a growing population, each village's cluster of businesses usually included grocery, hardware, and clothes stores, feed dealers, blacksmiths, and ice and coal suppliers. (SPLIA)*

*Left: While country clubs and sports clubs catered to the wealthy, the circus was for everyone. These boys approach circus tents set up in Jamaica circa 1915. Courtesy, Clarence Purchase Photograph Collection, SPLIA*

This rural atmosphere and its accompanying social and political attitudes helped create a new and independent Nassau County. Occurring just before the start of the century, this action ended fifty years of contention among Queens County residents. The differences between the inhabitants of eastern and western Queens ostensibly centered around the location of the county courthouse, but actually reflected the contrasting development experienced by the two regions. Directly adjacent to New York City, the western towns of Newtown, Flushing, and Jamaica had grown increasingly industrial, urban, and Democratic, while the eastern towns of Hempstead, North Hempstead, and Oyster Bay remained largely agricultural and Republican. As a result, the more populous area wished to move the county seat away from rural North Hempstead and closer to its own growth centers.

After more than a decade of political sparring, the state legislature in 1871 selected a new site in Long Island City, close to Manhattan. Resentment in the eastern towns was widespread. A generation later, in 1896, the legislature passed another important bill, this time consolidating several cities, towns, and counties into a unified New York City. The act included Queens' urbanized western towns, but excluded the rural eastern ones. Eastern residents then faced the unpleasant prospect of being part of Queens County, but not part of New York City. How could their interests possibly be protected? With the encouragement of local leaders, and despite the strong opposition of City and Democratic politicians, the legislature agreed in 1898 to separate the eastern towns and create an independent Nassau County. Henceforth Long Island would be divided into two distinct entities, a New York City portion to the west comprised of Brooklyn and Queens, and a rural component to the east consisting of Nassau and Suffolk counties.

Even as many Long Islanders attempted to preserve their independence from New York City, signs of change rapidly developed, especially in Nassau

*Above: Fahy's Watch-Case Factory, built in 1881, was one of the largest manufacturing plants of solid silver and plated ware in the nation. After the whaling industry languished in the 1870s it became Sag Harbor's principal industry, employing over 800 in its heyday. (SPLIA)*

*Left: Founded in 1855 by Hendrick Vanderbilt Duryea, Duryea's Starch Works in Glen Cove played a leading role in the development of nineteenth-century Long Island industry. It employed hundreds during its peak years, and this 1880 lithograph depicts its bustling activity. Courtesy, New-York Historical Society*

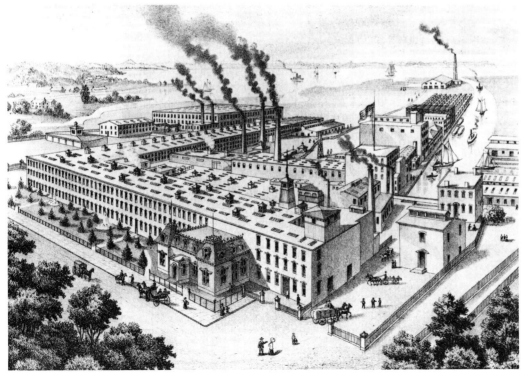

*Governor Theodore Roosevelt speaks at the cornerstone laying ceremonies for the first Nassau County Courthouse in Mineola on July 13, 1900. Photo by J. Burt.*

At the turn of the century, village social life for most Long Islanders included agricultural fairs, church socials, Sunday outings, and holiday parades, such as this 1916 Decoration Day parade in Jamaica. Concerts and plays were performed at the Huntington Town Opera House and the Music Hall in Riverhead, while vaudeville drew large crowds at the Freeport Theatre. Courtesy, Clarence Purchase Photograph Collection, SPLIA

Opposite page: William K. Vanderbilt, Jr., seen here on the left in 1908, was instrumental in promoting the automobile and auto racing in America. To encourage U.S. auto manufacturers to improve their product and compete with European markets, he instituted the Vanderbilt Cup Races on Long Island. (SPLIA)

County with its close proximity to the metropolis. This phenomenon was especially evident in the realm of modern technology. Telephones appeared in Glen Cove in 1884, and in Hempstead by the 1890s. In 1900 nine Nassau exchanges counted 446 subscribers.

Electric power was another important innovation. Established in 1890 to supply electricity to nearby North Shore estates, the Roslyn Light and Power Company soon combined with similar firms in Floral Park, Oyster Bay, Port Washington, and Glen Cove to form the Nassau Power and Light Company. A growing cosmopolitan element in the local population demanded urban services, and the trend quickly affected Suffolk County, also. Babylon received limited electric power in the late 1880s, and Northport followed less than a decade later. By 1911 several Suffolk firms had united to form the Long Island Lighting Company (LILCO). Under the leadership of financier Ellis Phillips, LILCO then purchased the Nassau-based utilities, creating an island-wide power grid.

Transportation improvements also altered local habits. By 1898 a cross-island trolley sped from Huntington to Amityville in just one hour for a fare of thirty cents. Other lines ran as far east as Patchogue. A similar network appeared in Nassau. After a dramatic political battle, the Mineola, Hempstead, and Freeport Traction Company bested its rivals and commenced service in 1901, running through fourteen towns and villages, with branch lines to Queens. Nassau's second line, serving Roslyn, Port Washington, and Mineola, opened in 1907.

Automobiles began to appear, as well. While only a few thousand vehicles were registered on the Island before 1915, visitors from New York City often travelled eastward. As a result, many county roads were graded or improved. Several resort villages experienced what seemed a never-ending stream of weekend traffic.

Change was also evident on the old Long Island Rail Road. First conceived as a through route to Boston, the line was now almost exclusively an excursion and commuter train. At the end of the 1800s, residents of Garden City, Freeport, and Rockville Centre already rode the morning train to their jobs in the city. Even Huntington Station in Suffolk County serviced about thirty daily commuters.

All these turn-of-the-century changes paled, however, beside the social revolution wrought in the next three decades by the interaction of transportation improvements and intensive real estate development. Between 1900 and 1930, Nassau's population leaped from 55,000 to over 300,000, while the number of Suffolk residents more than doubled from 77,000 to 161,000. The railroad stood at the heart of this boom. Throughout the last quarter of the nineteenth century, the Long Island Rail Road tirelessly promoted the concept of commutation—working in the city and living in the country. But the time-consuming East River ferry crossings discouraged extensive local development. A 1900 edition of *Nassau County Review* noted that "the cool fields, ample beaches, and picturesque hills offer room for tens of thousands of cottages if only people could be assured of rapid transit."

The call was heard, and that same year new railroad management committed itself to "supply swift express trains to commuters, enabling them to live out on Long Island all year round." Plans were also announced to dig an East River tunnel and build a huge terminal on Seventh Avenue in Manhattan. The railroad kept its promises and New York's Pennsylvania Station opened in 1910. Another new terminal arose in Brooklyn and electrification of the tracks to Hempstead and Babylon began. *Putnam's Magazine* observed, "If Long Island does not blossom like a rose, it will not be the fault of the . . . Railroad." By 1914 the number of daily trains serving growing towns like Freeport, Lynbrook, Valley Stream, and Great Neck had doubled. Even realtors in Babylon, thirty-seven miles distant from the city, touted their lots as "within commuting distance, convenient to the express depot."

Equally important in transforming Long Island from a semi-rural neighbor to a bedroom suburb was the rise of the automobile and construction of a modern road network. First came improved access to Manhattan via three new East River bridges: the Williamsburg, completed in 1903, and the Manhattan and Queensboro, both opened six years later. Farther east, millionaire racing enthusiast William K. Vanderbilt II sponsored a series of highly promoted auto races. Competing for the prized Vanderbilt Cup, drivers from all over America roared through Long Island's country towns, setting records and attracting immense publicity. Between

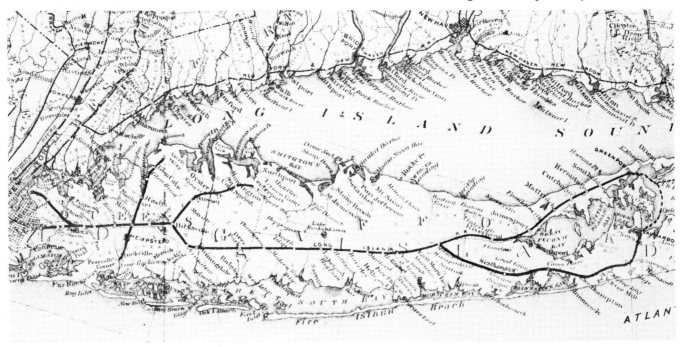

1908 and 1914, Vanderbilt and his associates also constructed a modern two-lane motor highway running forty-eight miles from Flushing to Lake Ronkonkama in central Suffolk.

The automobile really caught on after the First World War, and the 1920s witnessed a wide-ranging construction program and an enormous leap in traffic. Older country routes like the Jericho Turnpike and Merrick Road were paved. Along the south shore, a new thoroughfare was laid out atop New York City's old water line right-of-way. Designed to service the rapidly growing commuter villages, the first leg of this "Sunrise Highway" opened in 1928. Under the direction of master builder Robert Moses and his Long Island State Park Commission, modern high-speed parkways were constructed, designed to transport urban residents to new state parks like Jones Beach (1929) and local commuters to their jobs in Brooklyn, Queens, and Manhattan. By 1930

# ROBERT MOSES

Although never elected to public office, Robert Moses was one of the most powerful men in America, using that power to physically reshape New York's metropolitan and surburban environment to an inner vision conceived of and controlled by him alone. During his forty-four years in public service he personally conceived and carried out over twenty-six billion dollars in public works projects, including the building of bridges, parkways, expressways, state parks, and both private and public housing projects across New York State. Moses was to become famous as America's greatest road builder and the father of the New York State Park system. His influence on Long Island's development was immense.

A look at any current map of Long Island will indicate the impact of Moses' vision, energy, and determination on this relatively small, 120-mile-long strip of land. To cross any bridge, to drive on any parkway or expressway, to swim or boat at any state park on Long Island involves utilizing a project that owes its existence, directly or indirectly, to Moses. Moses was fond of Long Island, summering for most of his life in Babylon. He considered the park and road projects on Long Island as one of his greatest achievements. By the end of his career Long Island had over fifteen state parks and a network of roads,

*Above: Robert Moses speaks from the porch of the Taylor Mansion in Islip at the dedication ceremonies of Heckscher State Park on June 2, 1929. Courtesy, Long Island State Park Commission*

*Opposite page: The Long Island State Parkway system consists of limited access roadways extending from Queens into Suffolk County. Courtesy, Long Island State Park Commission*

bridges, and parkways connecting it to the larger metropolitan area. Perhaps more than any other single individual, Moses was instrumental in transforming the physical landscape of the Island. Some of the more famous projects he planned and built on Long Island include the Northern State, Southern State, Wantagh, Sagtikos, Sunken Meadow, and Meadowbrook parkways; a myriad of parks including Jones Beach, Hither Hills, Sunken Meadow, Fire Is-

land, Captree, Bethpage, and Hempstead Lake; and bridges such as Throgs Neck and Triborough, among others.

Born in 1888 into a well-to-do Jewish family, Moses went to Yale and just a few years out of college was appointed to his first state job by Governor-elect Al Smith in 1918. In 1923 Smith did something that would eventually change the direction of park systems throughout America—he appointed Moses as park commissioner and a year later Moses became president of the newly formed Long Island State Park Commission. Moses was far ahead of his time in his ideas about city and urban planning and was one of the few who understood the complexity of the problem posed by the need for parks and the roads to get to them. In the early 1920s, twenty-nine states didn't even have a single state park and road conditions in general verged on the primitive. Moses was quick to notice the beauty of Long Island with its miles of unused beaches and open wooded areas, and he immediately envisioned a sophisticated recreational system encompassing the whole island that would be linked to the city by a network of roads and scenic parkways.

A facet of Moses' personality that to a large extent helped accomplish this grand vision was his willingness, even eagerness, to battle entrenched interests. Moses sensed the difficulty (and the great challenge) in getting groups with vested interests to relinquish any land for the purpose of building public park facilities and connecting roadways. When the report on Moses' plans for Long Island was made public in 1924, he found himself battling the state legislature, town boards, chambers of commerce, civic associations, and wealthy North Shore residents whose estate lands would be disturbed by the building of the

Northern State Parkway. With his vast amount of energy, Moses obtained easements and rights of way, solicited donations from philanthropists such as August Heckscher, negotiated deals and compromises with wealthy landowners such as Otto Kahn, and made sure that friends and allies were appointed as presidents of each of the regional commissions. He discovered estates and searched out abandoned government properties that would make ideal Long Island state parks—600 acres on Fire Island; land in Hampton Bays and at Montauk Point; land on the Sound at Sunken Meadow, Wildwood, Lloyd's Neck, and Orient Point. Moses also eyed, and eventually acquired, two large parcels of land in the center of the Island, the Belmont and Yoakum estates, that would eventually become state parks. In total over 40,000 acres were identified as potential state parks, and an ingenious system of eleven parkways was

designed to joint the parcels together. The "ways to the parks" were designed to portray a rustic look and each had handsome stone overpasses that were deliberately kept low to prevent use by trucks or buses.

When Moses was appointed president of the Long Island State Park Commission in 1924, there was only one 200-acre state park, on Fire Island. By the end of August 1928, Long Island had fourteen state parks. Although Moses' career was not without controversy and his fair share of critics, his legacy to Long Island is best exemplified in these public parks that provide oases of unspoilt woodland and beachfront and hours of recreational pleasures for millions of people every year. In 1964 the creation of Robert Moses State Park and the Robert Moses Causeway paid homage to the man called America's greatest road builder.

Tim O'Brien

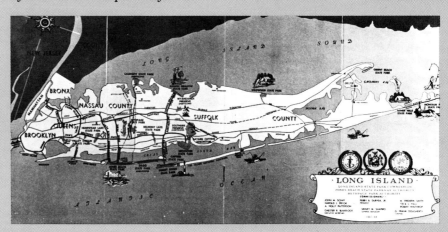

Rapid technical improvements and lower prices after World War I had transformed the automobile from a rich man's toy to a transportation necessity. This change required highways such as those in this 1931 view to be continually enlarged and improved. From Long Island: The Sunrise Homeland, 1931

*The Motor Parkway was begun in 1906 by William K. Vanderbilt, Jr., and other wealthy Long Island residents to facilitate their love of auto racing and touring. Running from Lake Ronkonkama westward to the metropolitan area, the toll road operated until the public parkway system developed in the 1930s. (SPLIA)*

Nassau's auto population surpassed 110,000, up from only 8,800 just fifteen years before. Such dramatic changes in transportation were intimately linked to the burgeoning real estate boom then altering the very face of the Island.

Real estate development on Long Island had extended antecedents. As early as the 1840s, immigrant entrepreneurs Frederick Heyne and John Heitz purchased 1,000 acres of Hicksville farmland and attempted to settle fellow Germans there. After the railroad reached Rockaway in 1869, Thomas and Samuel Marsh began laying out building lots. So did brothers Alfred, George, and Newbold Lawrence; one South Shore town still bears their name. Retailing magnate A.T. Stewart created a model community in central Nassau and called it Garden City. At Breslau (later Lindenhurst) Thomas Welwood and Charles Schleier formed the Breslau Cooperative Building Association and during the 1870s marketed thousands of small house lots. But until direct routes to Manhattan were completed, growth remained relatively slow. Nassau's population increased by a modest 8,500 in the 1880s and again by 9,500 in the 1890s. Suffolk County expanded only slightly more rapidly, adding 24,000 residents in the same period.

After the opening of the New York City bridges and tunnels, the picture changed entirely and the human floodgates opened. Railroad suburbs soon sprouted everywhere. Promoters called Floral Park an ideal spot for commuters "where short travel hours and good train service are the essence." Hempstead was only thirty-eight minutes from Manhattan via electric express. Even towns in Suffolk County boasted of their excellent rail connections.

The villages closest to New York, such as Great Neck, Port Washington, Valley Stream, and Freeport, naturally attracted much of the initial influx. One Port Washington resident soon noted, "Our population is largely made up of New York businessmen." Every developer was selling the suburban dream. Builder John Randall asked, "Why pay rent in a crowded city when you can secure a beautiful

# ALEXANDER TURNEY STEWART

The history of Garden City is closely tied to the unique vision and force of one individual. Alexander Turney Stewart (1801-1876), known as the "merchant prince" of New York, was an immigrant of Scotch-Irish heritage who arrived in New York City in 1818. After teaching for a year he started a small retail dry-goods business. Through unstinting labor and astute management practices (he was the first to advertise "fire and remnant" sales), Stewart became an undisputed leader in merchandising and one of the world's wealthiest men. His famous six-story "iron store" on Tenth Avenue, the largest retail store in the world at the time, and his mansion at Fifth Avenue and Thirty-fourth Street, called the "Marble Palace" by New Yorkers, were designed by John Kellum, a native of Hempstead. Stewart had a plan to build a model suburban community, a relatively new idea at the time, and it was probably Kellum who informed Stewart in 1869 that the residents of the town of Hempstead were willing to sell a large area of the unused Hempstead Plains. A special town meeting was called on July 17, 1869, to consider Charles T. Harvey's bid of forty-two dollars an acre, but Stewart's last minute cash offer of fifty-five dollars and his willingness "to expend several millions of dollars in improving the Plain land" received an overwhelming vote. Some 7,170

acres of town land and an additional 2,000 acres purchased from individuals that extended from Floral Park through Bethpage became Stewart's, and the history of Garden City began.

Stewart immediately had Kellum prepare plans for a model village of 500 acres to provide a beautiful suburb of "pleasant and reasonable" housing on a rental

*Above: This circa 1860 painting is the only known portrait of Alexander T. Stewart. Courtesy, Garden City Archives*

*Opposite page: These simple and austere wood-frame residences, Garden City's "Disciple" homes, were built for the working classes. Courtesy, George B. Brainerd Photograph Collection, Brooklyn Public Library*

basis for the executives and clerks who worked in his stores. The village proper was laid out on an orderly geometric pattern of wide streets with houses, stores, and other public buildings. Stewart's own home would double as a small hotel. To make it a real "garden" city, the entire village and park were planted with thousands of trees and shrubs, most obtained from Prince's Nursery in Flushing. As part of his grand plan, Stewart also built the Central Railroad Company to connect the village with existing railroad lines, and a brickwork at Bethpage to supply building material for the developing community.

By 1874 the four-story hotel and a dozen large, mansard-roofed houses known as "The Twelve Apostles" were built in the latest Victorian style. Smaller houses, called "The Disciples," stores, a huge brick stable, and the largest well on Long Island created a semblance of a community. Stewart, however, was not to live to see his

model village completed. His death in 1876 ushered in a period of faltering development. In 1885 Garden City had a total population of only 550 and was mocked as "Stewart's Folly."

Perhaps the most impressive building projects of Garden City were constructed not by Stewart, but by his wife, the former Cornelia Clinch. The Cathedral of the Incarnation was designed by architect Henry G. Harrison and completed in 1885 as a memorial to Stewart from his wife, who provided a permanent endowment for its maintenance. The cathedral, the seat of the Episcopal bishop of Long Island, is an impressive example of Gothic revival architecture and is considered Harrison's finest ecclesiastical work. Before her death in 1886, Cornelia Stewart was instrumental in developing plans for an entire ecclesiastical complex including the twin cathedral schools, St. Paul's and St. Mary's, and the bishop's residence.

In 1893, prospects for the growth

of Garden City began to improve. In that year, Stewart's lands were acquired by several companies, including the Garden City Company which had been formed by a number of Stewart's heirs, and vigorous development of the village began. Previously, houses and stores had been available for rent only; now Garden City would develop like other communities. With its new hotel, designed in 1894 by Stanford White, husband of one of the heirs, and its casino and golf and gun clubs, the village became a center for fashionable New Yorkers and Long Islanders to gather for sport and recreation. In 1907 a large tract of the original Stewart holdings was sold to a separate company that developed what is now known as Garden City Estates. While Stewart's vision of an ideal suburb was not realized in his lifetime, his imaginative plan laid the basis for one of America's finest suburban villages.

Edward Smits

cottage with all the improvements?" Each town and village seemed to have an eager promoter. As late as 1906, Nassau Boulevard was a mile-square expanse of open fields. Then the Garden City Development Company stepped in, building streets, parks, and homes, all converging on a central railroad station. In 1912 nearby Malverne was a rural hamlet. That same year Alfred Wagg organized the Amsterdam Development and Sales Company, bought up eight farms, and began building. By 1920, 100 homes had been erected and a newly incorporated village was born. This story was repeated a dozen times.

Some men even created entirely new cities. William Reynolds and others spent over four million dollars to develop the Atlantic Ocean resort of Long Beach. At times 1,500 workers and a herd of elephants dredged channels, stabilized beaches, and erected boardwalks, apartments, and houses. The cumulative effect of all this real estate activity was dramatic. By 1920 Nassau's population had more than doubled from its 1900 base to 125,000, surpassing geographically larger Suffolk County for the first time.

The outbreak of war in 1917 did not materially affect the social and economic trends already underway, but did impose a temporary moratorium on the rising level of activity. Instead, local energies were directed towards the great military bases situated on the Island. At Camp Mills in Garden City, the 42nd Rainbow Division trained for duty overseas. Nearby Mitchell and Roosevelt fields constituted the largest flying center in the East. Out at Camp Upton in Yaphank, the 77th Infantry Division practiced with broom handles instead of rifles, while clearing stumps and brush and struggling to erect shelter. Among Camp Upton's most illustrious

# THE MEADOWBROOK MODEL

THE Meadowbrook is a favorite Bossert design offering an amazing number of ingenious variations both in plan and design, all of which are most economical, because, the building being square, the greatest amount of floor space is enclosed with the least amount of wall area.

The front entrance can be on the side or on the gable end of the building.

Porch is of ample size and is made unusually attractive with pergola beams and flower trellises. From this porch handsome double French doors open directly into the spacious well-lighted living

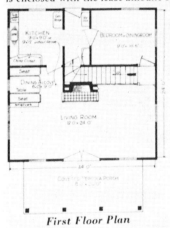

**First Floor Plan**

### READY-CUT OR SECTIONAL

#### FLOOR PLAN

1. Width, 24 ft.
2. Depth, 24 ft.
3. It has five rooms and bath, with a dining alcove.
4. The porch is 20 x 8 ft.
5. Living-room, 24 x 12 ft., with a dining alcove 6 x 9 ft. and space provided for fireplace.
6. A dining-room or bedroom on first floor is 9 x 10 ft.
7. The kitchen is 9 x 9 ft.
8. A china-closet is provided in the kitchen.
9. A butler's pantry and rear entrance, 5 x 9 ft., with ample space for ice-box and stores with door to kitchen and dining-room and entrance to cellar.
10. Second floor, two bedrooms, each 9 x 12 ft.
11. A bath 6 x 5 ft. 6 inches.
12. From each bedroom are two large closets for storage.
13. Each bedroom has four windows.

**Second Floor Plan**

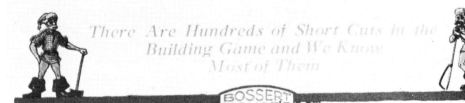

*There Are Hundreds of Short Cuts in the Building Game and We Know Most of Them*

BOSSERT HOUSES

*Opposite page: Camp Mills in Garden City, like Camp Upton in Yaphank, was a military training center during World War I. It became a principal embarkation center for troops going to Europe. Courtesy, Garden City Archives*

*Left: Firms like Louis Bossert & Sons, Inc. offered simple design and inexpensive prices while providing a variety of choices to new suburbanites. From Louis Bossert & Sons, Inc., Bossert Houses, 1926*

residents was a young soldier named Irving Berlin who was inspired during his stay to write "Oh, How I Hate to Get Up in the Morning."

With the return of peace, local energies turned away from military requirements and resumed, instead, the great peacetime activity of growth and development, setting the stage for the fantastic decade still known as the "Roaring Twenties."

The impressive development activity of the pre-war years only anticipated the fabulous 1920s when Nassau became America's fastest growing county. National prosperity, ever-improving roads, slick advertising, and continually expanding rail service all combined to create a land boom of feverish proportions. Almost 200 companies and 16,000 construction workers labored mightily to meet the demand for new housing. One outfit, the Zenith Land Corporation of Hicksville, auctioned 242 building lots in October 1923 on "the day of days for all those who believe in the future of Long Island." Apparently, there were many believers. The population of

Floral Park quintupled to 10,000. Lynbrook added 7,500 new residents and Garden City, 5,000 more. Total Nassau population surged to over 300,000 before the great stock crash.

The number of commuters rose also, as Nassau was truly transformed into a bedroom suburb. Perhaps 75 percent of the local labor force worked outside the county. By the end of the decade, nearly 110 daily trains stopped at Valley Stream, eighty at Mineola and Rockville Centre, seventy-six at Lynbrook, seventy-two at Babylon. George LeBoutillier, a senior vice president of the Long Island Rail Road, proudly noted in 1925: "Fast, clean and adequate railroad services for more than a generation is primarily responsible for the marvelous growth Long Island has enjoyed for many years."

Such voracious development naturally required extensive acreage, and many farms were quickly converted to building lots. Although the amount of agricultural land had been slowly shrinking since the 1870s, the decade of the 1920s was one of espe-

*Opposite page: Immigrants farmed, built roads, worked in early industries, and served as domestic servants and gardeners on the large estates. These men worked at the Hicks Brothers Nursery in Westbury circa 1900. Courtesy, Hicks Photograph Collection*

*Above: A growing suburban population imposed considerable land requirements during the twentieth century, causing farm acreage to drop. Views such as this lone farmer on his land circa 1920 would all but disappear. Courtesy, Clarence Purchase Photograph Collection, SPLIA*

cially swift conversion: total Nassau farmland diminished by almost two-thirds to about 25,000 acres. Operators of the county fair noticed the difference. Visitors seemed less intrigued by agricultural exhibits and showed far more interest in simple entertainment.

Though somewhat removed from the frantic Nassau scene, many Suffolk communities also felt the quickening pace of development, especially those North and South shore villages along the railroad right of way. Population, while not growing as swiftly as in Nassau, still jumped by 50,000 to 165,000 during the 1920s, the largest increase in Suffolk's history. Clusters of new homes appeared. Promoter T.B. Ackerman converted a "Bay Shore gentleman's estate into a high class suburban residential park where those of modest means may enjoy all the advantages." Realty Trust of New York City actively developed properties in Babylon, and in Brightwaters "choice 100' X 150' plots" sold for as little as $500. Villages like Amityville, Lindenhurst, Babylon, Patchogue, Islip, Bay Shore, and Huntington all experienced significant growth. Even some newspapers got into the act. The New York *Daily Mirror* offered eighty-nine-dollar lots in Rocky Point for less than five dollars down. They also threw in a free six-month subscription.

Further east at Montauk Point, brash promoter Carl Fisher promised something much grander. Fisher had previously built the Indianapolis Speedway, backed coast-to-coast motor highways, and earned a quick fortune developing Miami and Key West real estate. Turning his attention to eastern Long Island, he purchased 9,000 sandy acres for $2.5 million and dredged Lake Montauk to create a deep water harbor. Fisher then erected a seven-story office tower amidst the dunes and built the huge $1 million Montauk Manor hotel. On one summer day in 1927, over 25,000 visitors in 10,000 cars came to watch. Fisher's great scheme, however, ended in failure, for the Depression soon intervened. Land values plummeted, his companies went bankrupt, and when the super promoter died in the late 1930s, his real estate empire was only a tattered memory.

Long Island in the boom years attracted more than just commuters who shuttled daily to city offices and factories. A colorful and flamboyant show business colony of considerable proportions also developed, drawing strength from the Broadway stage and the motion picture studios in nearby Astoria, Queens. Performers, producers, writers, and directors like Fanny Brice, D.W. Griffith, W.C. Fields, Paulette Goddard, Ring Lardner, and Groucho

Marx clustered along the North Shore, especially in Great Neck. The Long Island Rail Road even ran a special late evening train to accommodate homeward-bound entertainers.

When the Vitagraph Company of Brooklyn opened a studio at Bay Shore in 1915, an artists' colony blossomed there too, including Marie Dressler, Norma Talmadge, and Fatty Arbuckle. Long Island's geographic diversity also provided varied backdrops for many on-location films. Much shooting was conducted at Roosevelt aviation field, while Rudolph Valentino's "Sheik" galloped across the dunes at Montauk Point.

Even more colorful than the movie stars who es-

*Opposite page: Great Neck played summer home to many celebrities of the New York entertainment and publishing industries. W.C. Fields, who lived on Long Island, is depicted here in 1925 touring with director D.W. Griffith. From the Film Stills Archives, Museum of Modern Art*

*Above: Long Island's landscape began to change drastically in the 1930s as an unprecedented influx of suburban dwellers beseiged the area. Some Island communities, such as Baldwin in Nassau County (depicted circa 1931) clustered the new homes around small industry. Courtesy, Baldwin Historical Society and Museum*

*Left: Glenn Curtiss' experimental flights at Mineola in his "pusher plane," a small biplane looking somewhat like an enlarged box kite, helped make Long Island the center of aviation development. It continues to be one of the Island's largest industries. Courtesy, Nassau County Museum*

# THE DOUBLEDAYS

As with the great painters, it is perhaps best to describe the Doubledays through the breadth of their work. This three-generation book empire, headquartered in Garden City, introduced to the annals of literature works by W. Somerset Maugham, Rudyard Kipling, Daphne du Maurier, Joseph Conrad, H.G. Wells, Theodore Dreiser, Norman Mailer, and Alex Haley.

Without the support and guiding hand of the Doubledays, the world might never have had *Rebecca, A Tree Grows in Brooklyn,* and *Roots.* Indeed, the contributions of what became the world's largest book publishing firm are hard to overestimate. There are fifteen book clubs, including The Literary Guild. There are 600 new titles a year. There were, at times, 30 million books printed annually.

Like many of today's Long Island residents, the Doubledays came from New York City and migrated out to the country east of the Queens County line. Frank Nelson Doubleday, the founder of the book dynasty, was the son of a poor Brooklyn hatter and began his book career as a three-dollar-a-week staffer at Scribner's in 1881 at twenty-three years of age.

Eight years later, Doubleday struck out to form his own company, publishing some of Kipling's first works and forming a lifelong friendship with the author. Kipling had nicknamed Doubleday "Ef-

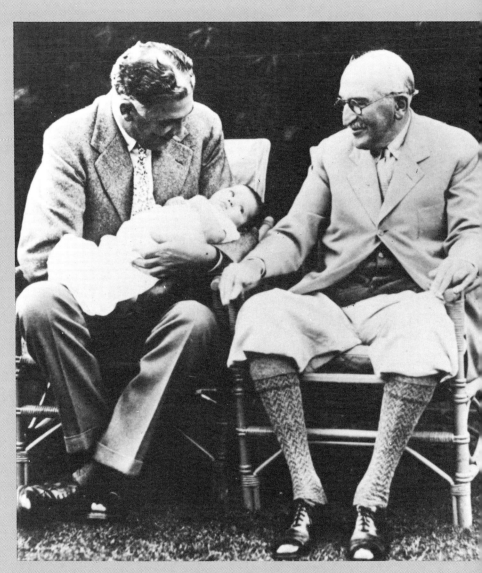

fendi," a Turkish title of respect and a play on the book magnate's initials, F.N.D. The city, however, could not provide the quiet and open spaces to which the publisher was suited, so in 1910 he moved the entire operation to a forty-acre site in Garden City.

Many of Doubleday's workers

*Three generations of Doubledays established and maintained a book empire: Nelson Doubleday, Sr., holds Nelson Doubleday, Jr., as patriarch Frank Nelson Doubleday looks on. Courtesy, Doubleday & Co., Inc.*

first came out on the Long Island Rail Road, and their special train stop, Country Life Press, exists today. By 1930 the plant was producing 40,000 books and 150,000 magazines a day.

Doubleday's sensibilities attracted a continual stream of talented writers and famous admirers. Formal garden parties at the exquisitely landscaped Garden City headquarters attracted the likes of industrialist John D. Rockefeller and President Theodore Roosevelt. Doubleday and his wife, Neltje De Graff, an author of nature books, and their two children, Nelson and Neltje, made their home in Mill Neck on Long Island's famed Gold Coast.

In the 1920s Nelson began assuming increasing amounts of responsibility in the firm and in 1928, at the age of thirty-nine, became president. He became chairman of the board in 1934 when his father died at the age of seventy-four. Nelson Doubleday was a shrewd and innovative businessman, developing the idea of selling month-old, high-quality magazines at half price. He started a mail-order book business and in 1929 bought the fledgling Literary Guild, then two years old. Nelson helped start a Canadian branch of Doubleday and revolutionized book publishing by striving to print large numbers of books at ever-lower unit costs. He often transacted business at his home on Long Island and at his plantation in Yemassee, South Carolina.

But Doubleday remained a prod-uct of Long Island and New York City, having been educated at Friends School, Holbrook Military Academy, and New York University. In 1932, after his first marriage ended in divorce, he married Ellen McCarter, daughter of Thomas N. McCarter, the president of the Public Service Company of New Jersey.

Nelson Doubleday died in 1949 at the age of fifty-nine, and his son, Nelson Jr., took over the business. Educated at Princeton, the younger Doubleday wrote his senior thesis on paperback books. While some of Doubleday's main offices have moved off Long Island, its Garden City building remains as the accounting division and Nelson Jr. remains active in Long Island affairs. Much of the Doubleday family still lives on Long Island, from East Hampton to Glen Cove.

Kimberly Greer
Stuart Diamond

*The Doubleday headquarters in Garden City, designed to resemble England's Hampton Court by the firm of Kirby and Petit, was dedicated by Theodore Roosevelt in 1910. Courtesy, Doubleday & Co., Inc.*

*Painted in 1937 for the Hempstead Post Office, Peppino Mangravite's mural was commissioned through the Works Progress Administration's effort to counteract severe unemployment during the Depression. In addition to working on art-related projects, Long Islanders built roads, drainage systems, and county facilities such as Bethpage State Park in Nassau. The mural illustrates the arrival of the first airmail by the British dirigible R34 in 1919. Courtesy, National Archives*

tablished homes on Long Island were the intrepid aviators who made the flat, open landscape their own. Aviation first reached the Island in 1908 when the infant New York Aeronautical Society purchased one of Buffalo inventor Glenn Curtiss' rickety pusher biplanes. In June 1909, after first rejecting a Bronx site, Curtiss surveyed the broad Hempstead Plains of Nassau and liked what he saw. He quickly commenced a series of exhibition flights, and soon Mineola and Garden City buzzed with the sounds of young adventurers trying to emulate his feat.

The following summer witnessed the great international air meet at Belmont Park. Twenty-five French, British, and American aviators competed before a huge audience, seeking fame and $75,000 in prize money. One of the most dramatic events was a race around the Statue of Liberty. That same year air mail service was initiated between Minoela and Garden City, a distance of about six miles. Shortly afterward the New York Aeronautical Society established a 1,000-acre flying field, complete with grandstand and twenty-five hangars. By 1916 Nassau was the undisputed leader of East Coast aviation. The First World War provided further impetus when the Army Air Service constructed huge complexes at Roosevelt and Mitchell fields, while naval aviators and flying boats were stationed at Far Rockaway and Bay Shore. A host of aircraft manufacturers also began production, spurred by wartime demand.

Though the postwar years were strewn with cor-porate bankruptcies caused by the collapse of military orders, they were also the most exciting in the history of Long Island flight. In 1919 a Garden City-built Curtiss flying boat travelled to England by way of the Azores and Portugal. That same year Roosevelt Field hosted Britain's huge R-34 dirigible after a 108-hour non-stop flight from Scotland to New York. During the early 1920s, the Curtiss Company developed several record-breaking racing planes which dominated international competition. Among the most successful Curtiss pilots was James "Jimmy" Doolittle, later to win further fame for his "Thirty Seconds Over Tokyo."

Roosevelt Field, by now converted to civilian use, thronged with weekend crowds who came to watch assorted daredevils, wing walkers, and parachute jumpers, or to experience a thrilling ten-minute "joy ride." Roosevelt Field also became a take off point for several transatlantic expeditions, the most famous being Charles Lindbergh's epic 1927 hop from New York to Paris. Out east lesser known pilots used their fragile planes for less newsworthy missions, like the bootlegging of illegal whiskey from Canada.

America's Great Depression sharply affected the suburban boom. Land speculation virtually ceased, while homebuilding slowed to a trickle. Perhaps one worker in six was laid off. Unemployment soon stalked the Island, and federal, state, and local governments eventually responded with a variety of programs. Emergency work bureaus hired tens of thousands to perform a wide range of assignments: traffic accident surveys, road sign installation, historic surveys, adult education courses. Major public construction projects (including courthouses, post offices, roads, and military buildings at Mitchell Field) were also initiated. For those unable to work, home relief often helped put food on the table.

Despite the suffering and drastic slowing of the local economy, some growth continued. By 1940 Nassau's population had swelled to 400,000. Depression or not, Nassau County was no longer a sleepy neighbor or even a country retreat for the urban masses. It had instead become a bedroom community for the New York metropolis. Everywhere new houses, roads, schools, and shops appeared, while farming and all the old ways that went with it contracted dramatically.

One measure of the changes wrought was a comprehensive governmental overhaul instituted at the county level to address modern problems of explo-

sive growth. After a struggle lasting two decades, antiquated county institutions were replaced in 1938. Local voters adopted a new charter which created the centralized office of County Executive, a unified budget, a county welfare department, a remodelled Board of Supervisors, and a countywide tax assessment board.

Suffolk County, still relatively isolated from New York City, also succumbed to the economic collapse. The impact was especially severe where agriculture and fishing predominated. Several older communities like Port Jefferson, Greenport, and Southampton actually lost population and the overall county growth rate plummeted 50 percent. Despite the heightened real estate activity of the 1920s, Suffolk remained essentially agrarian in outlook, decentralized in government. A new and even more dynamic brand of post-World War II suburbanization would be required to wrest the county from its nineteenth-century past.

*Charles Lindbergh and his Spirit of St. Louis captured the wonder and imagination of a generation of Americans when he flew from Long Island on May 20, 1927, and landed in Paris 33½ hours and 3,640 miles later. Courtesy, Nassau County Museum*

# CHAPTER NINE

# Long Island As Its Own Empire

The decades which followed World War II witnessed Long Island's greatest and most rapid transformation, as a tidal wave of suburban growth overwhelmed Walt Whitman's Paumonok, leaving no aspect of the local landscape untouched. Nassau County, greatly developed in the 1920s and 1930s, rapidly assumed a role as one of America's leading suburbs. Population spurted from approximately 400,000 in 1940 to over 1,300,000 by 1960. The often cantankerous Long Island Rail Road truly earned its nickname as "The Route of the Dashing Commuter." Suffolk, still largely rural at war's end, experienced a somewhat delayed, but equally energetic, surge that carried local population from 275,000 in 1945 to 1,125,000 in 1970.

Both counties confronted similar challenges: explosive expansion and all the pressures which accompanied it, followed almost immediately by the very different dilemmas which characterized consolidation, aging, and sharply curtailed growth. In only two decades vast housing developments, hundreds of new schools, dozens of retail shopping centers, and miles of highways opened. So did major universities, cultural institutions, and a host of recreational facilities. Surprisingly, within just a few years, some of those very same schools bolted their doors for lack of students, and foreclosure signs dotted certain subdivisions.

Farming, long an economic mainstay, virtually disappeared in Nassau and fell under increasing pressure in its eastern neighbor. In place of agricultural activities came a host of manufacturing and financial pursuits, led by giant aerospace corporations. Industry finally took root in the Long Island economy. Along the way, the area's relationship with New York City changed from nearly complete

*Cold Spring Harbor Labora-
tory, founded in 1890, stands
at the vanguard of cancer
research and molecular genetics, preserving its historic*
*buildings while accommodat-
ing the needs of modern science. Photo by Dave Mikloso.
Courtesy, Cold Spring Harbor
Laboratory*

dependence to far greater autonomy. As the *New York Times* rightly concluded: "From behaviour to politics, ecology to economics, there is virtually nothing this outward migration has not changed."

Triggering the postwar suburban phenomenon was a fantastic housing boom generated by the pent-up demands of millions of ex-G.I.s. Both the depression of the 1930s and stringent wartime priorities combined to limit home construction in the metropolitan area. But now the vets were coming home, clamoring for houses with which to shelter their new families. Sensing the opportunity, developer Abraham Levitt and his son, William, announced plans in May 1947 to build hundreds of small, inexpensive homes on a tract of farmland in central Nassau County. The response was overwhelming. They received 6,500 applications within a few weeks, and the first houses were completed by October. Plans to sell the small capes and ranches—originally designed as rental units—were facilitated by the growing availability of veteran's financing and long-term mortgages. Terms were easy: ninety dollars down and fifty-eight dollars per month purchased a $7,000- to $10,000-domicile. When construction ceased in November 1951, over 17,440 houses had been sold and a new community born. In 1940 Levittown counted only a few hundred residents, but by 1955 the population had reached 56,000, including 19,000 schoolchildren.

As other developers quickly emulated Levitt's methods, the remaining farmland of central and southern Nassau County rapidly gave way to homes, streets, and playgrounds. Potato and vegetable fields in Hicksville, Plainview, Syosset, Massapequa, and elsewhere soon sprouted capes, ranches, and colonial-style houses. East Meadow quadrupled its population to 57,000 in only six years. In the same period, Hicksville added 30,000 residents, Massapequa, 25,000. There seemed no end to the demand for housing, as the stream of new homeowners from Brooklyn and Queens became a flood. In just ten years Nassau welcomed 650,000 new citizens.

Such explosive expansion, however, could not possibly be sustained indefinitely. As the quantity of easily developed land diminished, so did the rate of construction and population growth. The peak occurred in 1958 when 7,200 new homes were built. Thereafter volume slipped to 4,160 dwellings in 1960, 3,000 in 1965, and barely 1,000 by 1970. Pop-

ulation trends mirrored the construction slowdown. After spurting by nearly 100 percent in the 1950s, Nassau grew by a much more modest 10 percent in the 1960s.

Yet even while Nassau's expansion slowed, nearby Suffolk's accelerated. In the first burst of postwar energy, the county's population jumped by 75,000 in the late 1940s and by almost 400,000 more within the next decade, as Nassau's frantic economic activity spilled across the border into the westernmost towns. By 1960 Suffolk's own boom was roaring along and the number of county residents leaped from 667,000 to more than 1,125,000 in the next de-

*Art lovers enjoy the Huntington Art League's annual summer show held on the historic village green. The exhibits display a wide range of media and attract over 5,000 visitors. Courtesy, Huntington Township Art League, Inc.*

*Coney Island continued to draw huge summer crowds after World War II, as seen in this view from the parachute jump at Steeplechase Park in 1950. Courtesy, National Archives*

# WILLIAM J. LEVITT

His name is identified with the quintessential suburb and with America's first great post-World War II community. Like Henry Ford with cars, he revolutionized the building of houses and, perhaps more than any other individual, he gave Long Island its modern identity. He is, of course, William J. Levitt, the builder of Levittown. "Any fool can build houses," Levitt said as his community neared completion in 1948. "What counts is how many you can sell for how little." In 1950, *Time* magazine called Levitt "the most potent single modernizing influence in a largely antiquated industry."

Born in 1907 in Brooklyn, William Jaird Levitt, one of two sons of attorney Abraham Levitt, dropped out of New York University after his junior year and started building homes. "I wanted to make a lot of money," he said. His father started Levitt and Sons builders in 1929, and in the 1930s Bill Levitt and his brother, Alfred, an architect, were building custom houses for the upper middle class on the North Shore of Nassau County. These early communities included the Strathmores in Manhasset, developed between 1933 and 1949 on former Frank Munsey and Virginia Graham Vanderbilt properties, a Strathmore community in Rockville Centre, and a development in Roslyn. But the move that would lead to fame occurred during World War II when

*In 1946, William J. Levitt became a household word when he converted a Hempstead potato field into a sprawling community of 17,447 Cape Cod houses. Courtesy, Newsday, Inc.*

Levitt learned Navy techniques of quickly building identical slab houses as an officer in the Seabees.

Departing from the age-old and costly technique of crafting each house individually, Levitt divided home building into twenty-six separate steps and trained teams of workmen in each step so the houses could be built in assembly-line fashion. For each working day over a three-year period, an extraordi-

nary average of thirty homes were finished. The four-room expandable homes sold for $6,990 each—$2,000 below those of competitors. None had basements, another feature that enabled the homes to be built more quickly and more cheaply, but all had a complement of appliances, including refrigerators, ranges, and washing machines. Levitt also planted more than 500,000 trees that would grow along with young families. And eventually there were swimming pools, ballfields, shopping centers, churches, schools—a complete suburban community.

The Levittown formula has been transferred to many places, both in the United States and abroad. Not only have replicas of Levitt's models been built throughout Long Island, but there are senior citizen Levittowns in Florida and Levitt communities in France, Puerto Rico, Nigeria, and Venezuela; in all, there are more than 140,000 of his homes. There was even to be a Levittown in Iran, called Levittshar, but the property was taken over by the revolutionary government when the Shah of Iran fell, prompting a still-pending thirty-four-million-dollar lawsuit by Levitt in international court.

Although the houses in Levittown have largely been modified and expanded by their owners so that they no longer look alike, the imprint of Levitt endures. So valuable has this imprint become that when the company, Levitt & Sons, was sold to International Telephone and Telegraph Corporation for ninety-two million dollars in 1968, Levitt was barred for a time from using his own name on his new projects.

Kimberly Greer
Stuart Diamond

*Levittown, depicted circa 1948 before lawns and trees were planted, began a unique episode in the development of American communities. Courtesy, Newsday, Inc.*

cade.

Real estate developers began looking eastward after the end of the war, and shortly thereafter new or enlarged communities appeared at Huntington, Islip, East Northport, and Lindenhurst. Speculators then snapped up nearby farmland, anticipating the same growth then transforming neighboring Nassau. Their predictions were correct. A farming hamlet like Centereach counted only 628 residents in 1950. Ten years later there were tracts of development homes, new schools, and modern shopping centers, as the population reached 6,700. By 1980 it topped 30,000. The same story was repeated throughout western and central Suffolk County. Brookhaven Township, the county's largest, jumped from 44,000 residents in 1950 to 365,000 two decades later. Huntington, Babylon, and Islip all quadrupled in size. Smithtown grew by 475 percent in twenty years.

In contrast to Nassau, where space was the only factor limiting construction, Suffolk's red-hot expansion was cooled by man-made events. The 1973-75 recession and inflation caused high interest rates and slow economic growth, consequently ending the era of cheap mortgages and homes. OPEC's oil embargo and the resulting high gasoline prices also made long-distance commuting prohibitively expensive. Bank foreclosures mounted; Suffolk's impres-

sive growth rate skidded from 10 percent annually in the 1960s to only 1.5 percent in the 1970s.

Holding the burgeoning communities together, indeed, making so much of the growth possible at all, was the tremendous expansion of Long Island's transportation network. Whereas Long Island's first land boom in the early twentieth century was based on the railroad, the suburbs of the 1950s and 1960s depended entirely on the automobile.

Well into the mid-century, many of Long Island's principal thoroughfares were tree-lined, two-lane affairs. Adequate for the traffic of the 1920s when they were first paved, they became increasingly overburdened with each passing year, however. State parkways on the North and South shore counted only two lanes in either direction, excluded commercial traffic, and barely penetrated Suffolk County. Yet, the volume of vehicles soared without precedent. Nassau auto registrations jumped from 210,000 in 1950 to 700,000 in 1970; Suffolk experienced identical growth. And so construction of new roads and improvements of old ones commenced. A Suffolk extension of the Southern State Parkway opened in 1946. Nine years later the route was widened to six lanes, invigorating older South Shore villages like Islip, Patchogue, and Bay Shore. New roads, including the Sagtikos Parkway, Meadow-

*Opposite page: Southampton is one of the most famous and fashionable summer resort villages in the United States. Surrounded by summer cottages, exceptional recrea-* *tional facilities, and natural beauty, this small village attracts hundreds of thousands of visitors each year. Photo by Joseph Adams. (SPLIA)*

*Above: During World War II women comprised more than 40 percent of the production force in Long Island's busy aviation and military support industries. At Grumman Air-* *craft, women worked as draftsmen, riveters, sheet metal workers, and mechanics. Courtesy, Grumman Aerospace Corporation*

*Left: Built in 1930-1931, The Big Duck in Flanders is a Long Island architectural landmark. For many years the huge duck contained a poultry store. Today, it is a historical landmark and sells T-shirts not poultry. Photo by Harvey A. Weber. Courtesy, SPLIA*

*Opposite Page: Nassau County's school age population greatly expanded in the 1950s and Suffolk County experienced the same growth a decade later. These schoolchildren are walking home from Lloyd Harbor Elementary School. Photo by Harry Haralambou.*

brook Parkway extension, and Seaford Expressway, improved north-south access. The old Sunrise Highway was enlarged as an expressway all the way to Southampton.

But of all the transportation projects, the most important was the (in)famous Long Island Expressway, a new six-lane concrete spine running down the center of the Island. Construction of the region's first high-speed commercial highway began in 1955, intending to facilitate commuter traffic into New York City and service Long Island's expanding industries. Road crews reached central Nassau in 1958, touched the Suffolk border in 1962, and pressed on to Riverhead in 1972. The new road lured commuters and businesses ever deeper into Nassau and Suffolk counties. In fact, it proved so popular that almost from the start, huge traffic jams developed. "The Longest Parking Lot in the World" often seemed the kindest epithet uttered by frustrated motorists.

Almost as important to Long Island's growth as the construction of modern highways was the emergence of the aerospace industry. Looking back over recent history, a local newspaper observed in 1965, "When Long Island's economy was in its prime in the 1940s and 1950s, the base of the boom was high-paying employment at five giant defense contractors." Clearly the growth of the aerospace industry contributed to the Island's transformation into a

heavily settled region of urban and suburban areas supporting a diversified manufacturing complex. Yet such a result was by no means preordained, since Long Island aircraft manufacturers had earlier endured decades of frustration and defeat.

Shops building one- or two-seater airplanes appeared during aviation's pioneer days, but fared poorly in securing investment capital and adequate sales. World War I altered the picture and a number of modern factories emerged: LWF and Chance Vought in Queens, Curtiss in Garden City, Breese in Farmingdale. Despite such progress and glittering growth prospects, the Armistice in 1918 triggered the near-complete collapse of American military aviation. Government contracts evaporated and surplus aircraft flooded the market.

The reviving civilian economy in the 1920s and epic achievements like Lindbergh's great flight rekindled interest in the industry. A new crop of inventors and manufacturers led by Igor Sikorsky and Sherman Fairchild entered the field. Their plans received a sharp setback with the onset of the Great Depression, however. Soon Sikorsky, Vought, Fairchild, and Curtiss moved away, and despite the Island's topographic advantages and nearby New York City's financial and industrial strengths, aviation's overall impact remained quite limited.

Gathering war clouds in Europe and the Orient changed all that, with firms like Grumman, Repub-

lic, and Sperry spearheading the shift to military production. Grumman began operating in a rented garage, but soon moved to larger quarters in Valley Stream and then Bethpage, where workers specialized in building fast, tough fighters for the Navy. The guiding spirit at the Seversky (later Republic) Aircraft Corporation was Major Alexander DeSeversky, an expatriate Russian naval officer who dreamed of building the world's fastest, strongest fighters. Many of his 1930s creations were flown to racing victories by aviatrix Jackie Cochran. Sperry, founded in Brooklyn at the turn of the century to produce naval navigation systems, entered aviation in a big way during World War I and thereafter became a world leader in aircraft instrumentation.

America's prewar rearmament effort led to rapidly rising employment and production levels, and Pearl Harbor triggered full-scale mobilization. Long Island's growing aviation industry responded heroically. Grumman increased its workforce from 1,500 to 25,000 and produced more than 17,000 airplanes. Bethpage-produced Wildcats and Hellcats played a dominant role in America's Pacific victory. Republic at Farmingdale exerted similar efforts, as a work-

force of 23,000 manufactured 16,000 aircraft, most notably the rough, tough P-47 Thunderbolt. Moving to Nassau in 1942, Sperry employed 32,000 men and women who turned out mountains of navigation and guidance equipment. Every Long Island garage and factory seemed to resound with the chatter of riveting hammers.

Victory in World War II led to temporary disaster on the shop floor. Washington cancelled most contracts and 80 percent of the 100,000 wartime workers were laid off. It appeared likely that the dismal post-World War I story would be repeated again. But aviation had become too important a part of national defense planning, and Long Island's firms were now too large to languish for long. Introduction of jet aircraft, especially Republic's F-84 Thunderjet and Grumman's F9F Panther, revived local industry. With the outbreak of fighting in Korea, new orders skyrocketed and employment jumped again. Republic hired hundreds weekly; the workforce peaked at 30,000 in 1954. Grumman, Sperry, Fairchild, and Arma enjoyed a similar upsurge, at the very moment the Long Island real estate boom was in full swing. As some of the largest employers in the New York metropolitan area, local aerospace firms provided high-paying jobs for thousands, subcontracts for hundreds of smaller firms, and an enormous ripple effect throughout the civilian economy. Within a few more years these same firms would be building guided missiles, satellites, and lunar landers. Suburbia armed was suburbia transformed.

The frantic postwar construction boom, while creating new homes, communities, and employment opportunities, spelled the final demise of Nassau agriculture and greatly altered the course of Suffolk farming. A socio-economic activity which dated back to the Indian era and the first days of colonial settlement was drawing to a close. Predictably, the impact was most severe in Nassau, where any available land sold at a premium. As late as 1945, the county retained 650 farms on 27,000 acres of cropland. Villages like Plainview, Woodbury, and Jericho remained overwhelmingly rural. But by 1954, with housing growing in the potato fields, cropland had already dropped to 13,000 acres. Small agricultural hamlets like Syosset, in the words of a local guidebook, "felt the pressure of home development . . . large tracts of farmland are reluctantly giving

# LEROY R. GRUMMAN

Leroy Randle Grumman was one of aviation's early pioneers in America and founded an aircraft company that grew and expanded into one of the nation's largest. This company was to become world famous as the designer of the Apollo Lunar Module.

Leroy Grumman was born on January 4, 1895, and was raised in Huntington, Long Island, attending Huntington High School where he graduated second in his class. His father, Tyson Grumman, was a carriage shop owner and later a postal clerk. As a youth, Grumman

developed a fascination for the budding field of aviation by watching early Long Island aviators take off and land on the dirt strips near his home. Long Island, in the early days of aviation, was an exciting and stimulating place generating an abundant cross-pollination of ideas. Most of the early pioneers flew their experimental biplanes, monoplanes, and pusher planes from the flat plains of Hempstead. In 1910 the first international Aviation Tournament was held at Belmont Park, where speed and altitude records were set. Glen

Curtiss, the aviator and inventor, thrilled thousands with his exhibitions of aerial feats in his "Gold Bug," an early pusher plane. Curtiss operated an aviation school near Mineola in the early teens and eventually headed the Curtiss Aeroplane and Motor Company. From 1909 to 1929, the activities of experimental fliers on Long Island fields made the Island world famous as "the cradle of aviation," culminating in the famous Charles Lindbergh flight across the Atlantic in the *Spirit of St. Louis.*

When Grumman left Huntington, he went to Cornell to study engineering, graduating in 1916. During World War I he became a Navy test pilot. After the war he worked in a Philadelphia Naval aircraft factory and then with Loening as general manager of its Long Island plant.

Grumman Aircraft Engineering Corporation got its start on January 2, 1930, in a Baldwin garage. Leroy Grumman, Jake Swirbul, and Bill Schwendler, along with former colleagues from Loening, opened the small company with a lot of ideas and spunk, but little capital. However, in the 1930s Grumman forged a strong relationship with the Navy developing naval aircraft, fighter biplanes, and amphibious aircraft. In 1937 the company constructed its first civilian aircraft, the twin-engine Grey Goose amphibian. The company was soon selling amphibians to a clientele that included Marshall Field, Henry S. Morgan, and Lord Beaverbrook. With war looming in 1939, the production of military aircraft became a priority. The fighter planes that Grumman designed during World War II were revered by pilots and were reported to have shot down more than 60 percent of the enemy aircraft destroyed in the Pacific. Vice Admiral John McCain said that "the name Grumman on a plane or a part is like sterling on silver."

Leroy Grumman's talents were legendary around the company. His sight had been damaged due to an allergic reaction to penicillin and he relinquished the role of president in 1946, but remained as chairman of the board for the next twenty years. A quiet man who did not go in for the showier side of

business, he steered his company to success with a combination of exceptional executive leadership and an outstanding staff. In 1968 he was awarded the first Hunsacker Medal from the National Academy of Sciences for his contributions to aeronautical sciences. Grumman died in 1982 and the flags at the Grumman plants were lowered to half-staff.

From his boyhood days watching the daring pilots take off from local dirt strips to the engineering genius who led the development of the Lunar Module used in the 1969 Apollo 11 moon landing, Leroy Randle Grumman was a major force in developing Long Island into the "cradle of aviation."

Tim O'Brien

*Opposite page: Leroy R. Grumman sits at his desk at the Grumman Aerospace Corporation. Courtesy, Grumman Aerospace Corporation*

*Above: Grumman's main plant at Bethpage features an air strip used for experiments. Courtesy, Grumman Aerospace Corporation*

FINE ARTS CENTER

way to the march of the homeseeker." Barely 7,500 acres of open land remained in 1960, just 1,500 by 1980, mostly located on scattered North Shore estates. Only a dozen small vegetable farms survived.

Suffolk agriculture rested on a firmer foundation and for a time successfully resisted suburban encroachment. The county's 2,100 farms contained 120,000 acres in 1950 and produced 15,000,000 bushels of potatoes and 5,000,000 ducks. A Long Island Rail Road brochure called the region an "Agricultural Paradise." But soon there was trouble in this agricultural haven, too. Financial pressures mounted and within a generation extensive residential and commercial construction nearly ended farming in Suffolk's western towns. The populations of formerly rural villages like Medford, South Huntington, and Hauppauge leaped from a few hundred to 15,000 or 20,000. Total county cropland fell by a quarter. Presented with the opportunity to sell out at high prices, many growers turned off the tractor and retired. Hundreds of farms were converted to homes and shopping malls, and by 1980 only 160 acres of cropland remained in Islip and just 74 acres were left in Babylon.

Further east, development proved less intense

and farming persisted, even flourished. Brookhaven, Riverhead, Southampton, and Southold continued producing potatoes, vegetables, and fruit. When older staples like potatoes and ducks declined, new ones, including fine wine grapes, replaced them. Surprisingly, with 50,000 acres in production and its 1980 crops valued at $100 million, heavily-settled Suffolk still stood first among New York's agricultural counties.

Realizing the great changes taking place in land use patterns, and hoping to preserve open, agricultural spaces, Suffolk's Planning Commission in 1960 recommended that at least 30,000 acres be saved from the bulldozer. As the problem grew even more acute, the county legislature responded in the early 1970s by enacting a fifty-five-million-dollar program to acquire farmland development rights, thus preserving the countryside's pastoral character. By 1980 about 7,500 acres had been reserved under this and a related New York State Agricultural Districts Law. Whether these programs could maintain additional amounts of open space, especially as demand for summer homes soared and the price of land rocketed upward on the vacation-oriented East End, remained to be seen.

*Opposite page: Established on land donated by philanthropist Ward Melville, The State University of New York at Stony Brook is considered one of the nation's best state universities. Its Fine Arts Center offers residents and visitors an extensive schedule of performances. Courtesy, SUNY at Stony Brook*

*Above: The Health Science Center at the State University of New York at Stony Brook is one of the world's most sophisticated medical centers. Its schools of medicine, dentistry, nursing, allied health professions, and social welfare are all linked to the dark glass towers of the 540-bed University Hospital. Courtesy, SUNY at Stony Brook*

*Above: Jones Beach was opened in 1929 and has received worldwide recognition for its beauty and outstanding recreational facilities. In the background is Jones Beach Theater, constructed in 1952 and known for the music concerts once conducted there by band leader Guy Lombardo. Courtesy, Long Island State Park Commission*

*Opposite page: Eaton's Neck Lighthouse and Coast Guard Station is one of many lighthouses guiding ships away from Long Island Sound's coastline. Photo by Robert V. Fuschetto*

*Above: Father and son feed the ducks at Heckscher Park in Huntington Village. Photo by Robert V. Fuschetto*

*Left: A mute swan and her cygnets glide through the waters of Connetquot River State Park. Photo by Barbara C. Harrison*

*Below: Freshwater fishing is a popular Long Island pastime for young and old alike. Photo by Paul J. Oresky*

*Right: Bicyclists enjoy the beauty and breeze of Cold Spring Harbor. The harbor town, with its impressive whaling museum, is listed on the National Register of Historic Places. Photo by Robert V. Fuschetto*

*Left: Children enjoy horseback riding at West Hills County Park in South Huntington. Photo by Robert V. Fuschetto*

*The Sherwood-Jayne House,
an East Setauket farm complex, is under the auspices of
the Society for the Preservation
of Long Island Antiquities.
Courtesy, SPLIA*

*Opposite: Long Island tree-lined
country lanes turn to gold
during autumn. Photo by Harry
Haralambou*

*Above: Scenic wetlands display their autumn colors around Huntington. Photo by Harry Haralambou*

*Right: Long Island has had considerable fishing, oystering, and clamming industries since its first settlements appeared more than 300 years ago. (SPLIA)*

*Beautiful, untouched vegeta-*
*tion can still be found in Long*
*Island's state parks. Photo by*
*Paul J. Oresky*

*A Huntington pond begins to show signs of autumn. Photo by Harry Haralambou*

*One of Long Island's many modern recreational facilities, the Nassau Veterans Memorial Coliseum opened in 1971 and features a wide range of events. It is the home of Long Island's major league hockey team, the Islanders. Discussions are underway to replace it with a newer, structure. Courtesy, Nassau Veterans Memorial Colliseum*

Long Island in the days of the great land rush and corresponding baby boom saw much more than just home construction and the disappearance of ancient farmland. An entirely new society was taking form, a family-oriented community larger than all but a handful of American cities. Young, affluent, mobile residents demanded services and amenities to fit their lifestyle, and nowhere was this more obvious than in public education. Nassau's school age population leaped from 70,000 in 1947 to about 330,000 in 1964, while Suffolk's crested about a decade later. Hundreds of new schools were built, tens of thousands of teachers were hired, and property taxes were raised again and again. No matter how high the cost, Long Island's parents seemed willing to pay it. However, in the '80s and '90s increased taxes faced resistance.

Nor was education expected to cease after high school graduation, for the Island's middle-class population placed great emphasis on college, as well. In the early years, returning veterans provided the bulk of new students. Adelphi College, a school for women in Garden City, became coed after the war. Within a few years, however, the children of the suburbs added to the collegiate throngs. Hofstra University in Hempstead had 3,500 students in 1950 and more than 12,000 two decades

later. C.W. Post College opened in 1955 with 121 undergraduates on a site donated by heiress Marjorie Merriweather Post. Over 15,000 attended classes a generation later. C.W. Post later became the anchor of Long Island University which also includes a campus in Brooklyn and Southhampton College on the East End. Nassau County organized a community college from scratch and eventually enrolled over 16,000 young men and women, while the state university built or expanded campuses at Farmingdale and Old Westbury. As Suffolk County grew and matured, it too received new facilities, notably the large community college at Selden, and even more significantly, the State University at Stony Brook which held its first classes in 1962. One of New York State's four university centers, Stony Brook attracted thousands of students, and within a decade a major teaching hospital was under construction there.

Retail services were a prime consideration of local residents, also. It often seemed that land not covered with homes, schools, or parks supported the new suburban mecca, the shopping mall. The first mall opened in Manhasset in 1945 and eventually grew to encompass 182 stores. During the next decades, huge retail complexes followed at Roosevelt Field in Garden City (148 stores), Green Acres in Valley Stream (100 stores), Mid-Island in Hicksville (159 stores), Wait Whitman in Huntington (125 stores), and Smithaven on the Smithtown-Brookhaven line (127 stores). Situated near the highway and designed to accommodate auto shoppers, these re-

*Above: The H. Lee Dennison Building (center) in Hauppauge was named after Suffolk County's first executive and houses the district courts and the traffic courts. Courtesy, Aero Graphics Corporation. Opposite Page: Grumman was Long Island's largest private employer from the '50s to the '80s. Best known as a manufacturer of mil-itary aircraft and aerospace systems, its other products included computer services, boats, truck bodies, and emergency vehicles. Courtesy, Grumman Aerospace Corporation.*

tailing palaces utilized generous parking, air conditioning, and tremendous variety to draw customers away from the older village centers.

Still another component of the suburban dream was sufficient recreational facilities for the growing crowds. During the 1920s and 1930s the Long Island Park Commission, headed by Robert Moses, had given the region a fine start with recreational facilities at Jones Beach, Fire Island, Bethpage, and Orient Point. Visitation at existing installations increased rapidly after 1945, and several layers of government actively intervened to develop additional parks. Nassau County created a large recreational complex at Salisbury Park and later constructed a modern indoor arena for basketball and hockey. Nature preserves were set aside in Massapequa and Roslyn. Local governments developed beaches and built pools and playgrounds.

Suffolk County, with 75,000 acres of recreational lands, actively participated in this movement, too. State, county, and town parks were established at Captree, Wildwood, Nicolls Point, Smith Point, Sunken Meadow, Shinnecock Inlet, and Hither

Hills. The magnificent beaches and open lands that had attracted so many excursioners in years past were thus preserved for future generations, despite the fantastic development pressures all around them.

Modern suburban life also required important changes in the political and governmental system. Nassau first came to terms with the processes of centralized management through its charter reforms of 1938. More rural Suffolk did not fully address the issue for another generation. Instead, the somewhat rustic county remained a rather loosely governed confederation of towns and incorporated villages, overseen by a Board of Supervisors. The challenge of coordinating the unprecedented regional growth of the 1950s called for expert and permanent leadership, however. In 1958 Suffolk followed Nassau's example with a major governmental overhaul. Lee Dennison, a Democrat in a largely Republican electorate, became the first County Executive. Also created were effective county agencies and a unified police force for the five heavily populated western towns. Hauppauge, located closer to emerging popu-

# ALICIA PATTERSON GUGGENHEIM

*The wealthy and socially prominent Alicia Patterson Guggenheim, founder and editor of* Newsday, *was the driving force behind what was to become one of the nation's largest evening newspapers. Courtesy, Newsday, Inc.*

Few newspaper ventures in modern history have succeeded as well as *Newsday*. Started in a drafty Hempstead garage in 1940, *Newsday* is now the nation's largest evening newspaper and tenth largest overall, with 539,000 copies circulated daily and 602,000 on Sunday. Its profit statements are envied throughout journalism. Both the birth and growth of *Newsday* bear the mark of one woman, Alicia Patterson. Miss Patterson began her undertaking with $70,000 from her third husband, millionaire Harry F. Guggenheim, the major benefactor of the Guggenheim Museum in New York City. The first day's sales on September 3, 1940, were 15,000 copies of a thirty-two-page tabloid printed on second-hand presses. With what she called sheer guts, Miss Patterson built the paper into a lively, irreverent, prize-winning venture of national reputation. Perhaps the pinnacle of her career came on September 13, 1954, when she appeared on the cover of *Time* magazine with the caption "Publisher Patterson. On Long Island, big city ways."

Born in 1906 into a fifth-generation newspaper family, Alicia Patterson did not have to work for a living. Her father, Joseph Medill Patterson, owner of the New York *Daily News,* was the grandson of the publisher of the *Chicago Tribune.* She spent her early years on an isolated Libertyville, Illinois, farm, her teenage years at a succession of private schools, and her leisure time at society parties in Manhattan and at Long Island's "Gold Coast" mansions. She also spent time big game hunting, riding to hounds, and setting an aviation speed record flying solo from

New York to London. After two marriages, she wed Harry Guggenheim and in 1940 started her own newspaper, holding a contest to name the new paper. She commuted to Hempstead from "Falaise," the thirty-room mansion she shared with her husband at Sands Point, now a museum owned by Nassau County. Despite her earlier, rather aimless life, Patterson had always wanted to be a newspaperwoman. "I have been in love with newspapers since I first learned to read," she said. "I've always had a passion for having a paper. I don't want to make money. I don't want political power. I just want a good newspaper." Guggenheim was *Newsday*'s president, owning 51 percent of the stock; Miss Patterson, called "Miss P" by the staff, was the editor and publisher. They frequently disagreed on editorials: Guggenheim was much more conservative, resulting in signed editorials. *Newsday* grew along with Long Island, with Levittown and the Long Island Expressway, with the young families and the shopping centers and the problems of a burgeoning suburb. By 1957 *Newsday*'s daily circulation was 130,000, as the paper mixed readable animal and crime stories with tough investigations. Miss Patterson's maxim was "Never let go, once you have sunk your teeth into a good story." "We have never succumbed to the stuffed-shirt approach to life; we have never been scared of

a fight," Miss Patterson wrote in 1959, as the paper crusaded against local real estate and political corruption that won it fame while it occasionally lost subscribers. "The paper is like me, for I am a temperamental person, with violent likes and dislikes." Her fervent support of President Franklin D. Roosevelt, in fact, led to an estrangement from her father, who changed his will in 1946 to leave control of the *Daily News* to his widow in trust for his son, James.

When she died at age fifty-six on July 2, 1963, following surgery for a stomach ailment, the paper's circulation had reached 370,000 daily, its weekly ad lineage topped every other New York newspaper, and *Newsday* had a Pulitzer Prize and four Polk Awards to its credit. Letters of condolence arrived from all over the country, including one from President John F. Kennedy, who praised her "initiative and leadership." Perhaps the most eloquent eulogy came from Adlai Stevenson, her childhood friend, who said: "Her memory will refresh and liven and stimulate. . . . The newspaper she created was a reflection of a genius that she inherited and enlarged . . . this remarkably vital woman who thought and lived with purpose, conviction and courage."

Kimberly Greer
Stuart Diamond

*Above: Brookhaven National Laboratory is considered one of the world's foremost institutions for research in the fields* *of physical, biomedical, and environmental sciences. Courtesy, Brookhaven National Laboratory*

*Opposite page: Local art leagues offer classes and workshops for adults and children in addition to lectures, symposiums, demonstra-* *tions, and exhibitions. Photo by Lisa Lewicki. Courtesy, Huntington Township Art League, Inc.*

lation centers, became an important hub of government activity. In 1965 the Long Island Regional Planning Board was established, and a few years later Suffolk created a countywide legislature.

Increased governmental capabilities and sophistication soon proved vital as the suburban experience took an unpleasant detour. By the early 1970s the Long Island Regional Planning Board was chronicling the impact of two decades of unrestrained growth: crowded beaches and parks, polluted waters, declining village centers, frustrating travel on clogged highways, and undependable trains. Suddenly, the suburban dream seemed in grave peril. The passing of the baby boom in the late 1960s and early 1970s, coupled with a dramatic decline in the

number of young families moving to the bi-county region, created problems that officials rarely contemplated in earlier, expansionary times.

But growth did end. The society which blossomed overnight now began to age, a process first reflected in Nassau County, which witnessed a decline in elementary school enrollments in the 1960s. The number of births fell by half and the average age for the entire populace rose sharply. In fact, significant out-migration commenced in the 1970s, as Nassau's population fell by 100,000 (8 percent), the first decline ever recorded.

Suffolk felt the same forces, but a decade later, reflecting its more recent suburban boom. Births decreased by 20 percent, while the proportion of

children in the community fell at twice that rate. Residential construction expenditures dropped by two-thirds, and the number of building permits fell by 90 percent. Only on the East End, where second homeownership gained strength, did earlier growth patterns persist.

The great slowdown spawned a host of new problems for governments, businessmen, and local residents. The prevalent boom psychology gave way to pronouncements of limited choices and scarce resources. No longer were neighborhoods concerned about where schools should be built, but rather which ones to close in the face of declining enrollments. In many cases education budgets were defeated and austerity measures imposed. The question of teacher layoffs divided many communities. Some schools, built at great cost in the 1950s and 1960s, were converted to alternate community uses. Others were boarded up or torn down, even before the mortgages had been paid off.

A shortage of affordable housing developed, proving especially troublesome to young couples just starting out and to retired citizens who no longer required the large homes they had purchased twenty or thirty years earlier. Many suburban villages

exacerbated the problem by opposing construction of multiple dwellings and two-family houses. Yet high costs and even higher interest rates demanded modification of established patterns. Between 1945 and 1956, fewer than 7,000 apartments were built in Nassau, yet the Levitts alone constructed more than 17,400 homes. During the 1960s, however, the balance began to shift. For the entire decade, apartment starts outnumbered detached home permits. By 1980 Nassau's 90,000 rental units comprised one-fifth of the local housing stock. Suffolk also increasingly turned to rental housing, and during the 1970s built about 30,000 new apartments. Despite intense opposition by many property owners, several towns eventually accepted the presence of two-family homes, as well.

The aerospace industry which achieved such prominence in the 1950s and early 1960s could not carry the Long Island economy alone. Despite their size, corporations like Grumman, Republic, and Sperry remained subject to the ebb and flow of Pentagon procurement policies. When Republic failed to secure a follow-on contract to the successful F-105 "Thunderchief" fighter-bomber, its fortunes rapidly turned downward. Thousands of

*Left: The Island's own philharmonic orchestra, seen here in a 1982 performance of Handel's* Messiah, *joins a host of other notable cultural institutions that offer a wide range of performances and exhibits throughout the year. Photo by Charles Abbott. Courtesy, Long Island Philharmonic*

*Pages 218-219: One of Long Island's major challenges is to balance its expansion and growth while preserving aspects of its history and architectural heritage for future generations. Here, the 1767 Joseph Lloyd Manor House, now preserved as a museum, provides the background for a colonial muster and encampment performed by the Huntington Militia, Queen's Rangers, and the 3rd New York Regiment. Photo by Joseph Adams. (SPLIA)*

employees were laid off, and the company was eventually sold to Fairchild-Hiller. After the firm proved unable to receive a contract for a new Air Force trainer, the company closed its doors and sold off its Farmingdale property.

In an effort to avoid a similar fate and reduce the overwhelming dependence on military orders, state and local officials backed programs leading to the construction of industrial parks specializing in diversified, non-defense, precision manufactures. Private industry also branched out into many technology-oriented fields: computers, guidance systems, communications, space exploration, radar. Though the Island's industrial sector remained heavily committed to military production, civilian efforts gained importance. Between 1964 and 1976, Nassau and Suffolk counties added 45,000 new manufacturing jobs and thirty-two million square feet of plant space, as Long Island industry acquired a marked high-technology orientation.

Equally important in sustaining the local economy as the 1970s progressed was the increased impact of white collar employment and related office construction. As late as 1965, Nassau contained less than two million square feet of commercial office

space in only fifty large buildings, while Suffolk supported barely half that amount. Most white collar workers still commuted to New York City. In the next few years, however, the rate of local construction increased, and by 1970 the volume of available office space had doubled. This was only a prelude to the 1970s, when New York banks, insurance companies, and brokerage houses finally discovered Long Island. The region's emerging computer and research firms also augmented the demand for commercial space. Major new office centers soon emerged at Melville, Lake Success, Jericho, and Garden City. Construction totalling over 3.5 million square feet was proposed for Mitchell Field in central Nassau, and a single complex containing over one million square feet arose adjacent to Hofstra University. By 1980 over twenty million square feet had been built, with much more underway. The result was a marked re-orientation of working patterns. In both Nassau and Suffolk, the number of locally employed workers increased rapidly, while the proportion of railroad commuters dropped sharply.

The growth of economic independence, the passage of time, experience with community-based organizations, and a growing appreciation of the region's unique past all combined to create a new sense of Long Island identity. Designation as a federally recognized metropolitan area in its own right aided the process. Despite their urban origins, local residents grew more distant from their New York City roots with each passing year. A new generation was raised on Long Island and knew no other home. More regional employment meant fewer commuters and greater interest in local economic affairs. Actively promoting a separate Long Island spirit were giant corporations like Long Island Lighting Company and Grumman; universities like Hofstra, Adelphi, the State University of New York, and C.W. Post; and a vigorous community press. These efforts often found expression in cultural groups like the Eglevsky Ballet, or athletic teams like the Islanders hockey club, both of which played to packed houses during the '80s.

As development engulfed many vestiges of local history, preservation and museum groups moved to save and interpret what remained. A major outdoor historical museum opened at Old Bethpage, while a growing collection of vintage airplanes at Mitchell

Field saluted the Island's aviation heritage. Several Gold Coast mansions have been preserved as museums, schools, or conference centers, including properties once belonging to the Vanderbilts, Coes, Guggenheims, Chryslers, Pratts, Posts, and Phippses. Preservation societies have restored architectural landmarks, while maritime museums at Sag Harbor, Cold Spring Harbor, Sayville, and Amagansett highlight the Island's fishing and whaling past. In some cases entire downtown districts have been refurbished, as in Sea Cliff, Roslyn, Sag Harbor, and Greenport.

And so, more frequently and more insistently than at any time since the colonial era, Long Islanders of the seventies and early eighties viewed their communities as something special and apart from the surrounding cities. Slowly at first, and then with accelerating vigor, a new society of 2.6 million

inhabitants took shape. The colonial outpost, the vital breadbasket, the urban playground, and the bedroom suburb had all come of age.

Long Islanders at the beginning of the 1980s look both to their past and to the uncertain future. Faded downtowns were being revived, older homes renovated, historic sites preserved, and some farmland saved. Residents were attempting in many different ways to reach out to those who had passed before. At the same time, planners, business people, officials, and ordinary citizens addressed the evolving and troubling questions of modern suburban life: a dearth of clean water, affordable housing, adequate social services, effective transportation, rational planning, and good schools. The dual focus of preservation and development should come as no surprise, however, for Long Island society has always accommodated a generous measure of tradi-

tion and growth, steady habits and social revolution.

In more than three and one-half centuries, the area has seen a world of change crowded onto its finite acres. The Island has borne the tread of Indian hunters and warriors. It has hosted settlers from other continents, and witnessed religious conflict and the clash of empires. In the compressed space of a few generations, Long Island experienced the political upheaval of the American Revolution, followed quickly by the social transformation of the Industrial Revolution. The post 1945 suburban explosion swept away many relics of earlier times, reshaping the landscape to suit its fancy.

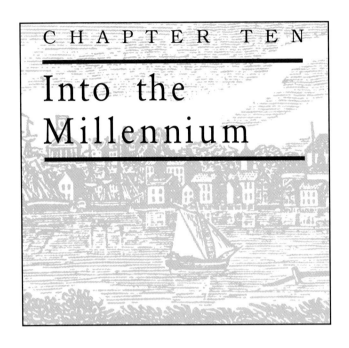

# CHAPTER TEN

# Into the Millennium

The forces of change at work on Long Island since the end of the Second World War shifted directions and intensified during the last decade and a half of the twentieth century. The resulting in transformations would have stunned anyone observing the Island from the vantage point of 1980. Demographically, the permutations affecting Long Island were rooted in conditions already forming by 1975. In contrast, between 1985-95 the economic foundations of the Island underwent a period of unexpected volatility. The result was a radical shift in the Island the structure of the Island's economy which was unforeseen previously. The changes in both population and business dynamics fed, and were themselves influenced, by social and political change.

While the winds of change blew strongly, countervailing forces struggled to hold fast to the Island's character and identity. Perhaps in reaction to the full torque transformations which buffeted the Island's people and economy, organizations and groups active in historic preservation and environmental protection became increasingly energetic in their efforts to preserve the essence of Long Island. Ironically, in the midst of a period of economic and demographic shifts, Long Islanders marked a number of significant anniversaries in the last two years of the '90s. In 1999 Nassau County marked the 100th anniversary of its creation out of the three easternmost towns of Queens County. In a more low-key way, Kings and Queens noted their incorporation into the City of Greater New York. Farther east, East Hampton Town looked back on 350 years of history, and special events were held at Montauk to commemorate the arrival of American troops from Cuba at the end of the Spanish American War. The celebrations, speeches, lectures and publications connected with these events gave Long Islanders much to ponder as they prepared to enter the new millennium.

*Among the many historical buildings on the Island are the Mulford and Payne Houses and windmill near the village green in East Hampton, circa 17th-18th century. Courtesy, Richard F. Welch*

*Long Island farmland is under continuous pressure from real estate developers. Here one of the last large farms in Western*

*Suffolk (Melville) succumbs to the bulldozer. Courtesy, Richard F. Welch*

Long Island's overall population growth slowed dramatically after the turbo charged increases of the '50s and '60s. In the decade of the '50s, the number of people living in the two non-city Counties rose by one million. The following decade saw lower but still heavy population growth with Nassau and Suffolk adding 589,000 persons, a 29.9 percent advance over the previous decade. The situation changed in the 1970s, with Nassau's population declining a little over 100,000 people while Suffolk maintained modest growth.

The reversal of the earlier massive population increases is partly ascribable to the fact that Nassau was already highly developed and moderately priced land for new houses was becoming scarce by the 1970s. Consequently, home prices escalated dramatically, a phenomenon that was also influenced by both the heavy inflation of the '70s as well as the County's extremely high property taxes. High housing costs may have made Nassau unaffordable to many young people just starting their careers, and led to the first calls for solutions to the housing crunch. With more developable land Suffolk avoided the losses incurred by Nassau, though the rate of growth remained modest. Nevertheless, suburbanization rolled relentlessly eastward through Brookhaven Town and into the retentively undeveloped East End Towns. The demographic situation remained static

during the 1980s, with only about 3,500 people being added to the bi-county region.

In the 1990s, both counties experienced a steady rise in population, though the rate of growth remains moderate compared to the post-war years. Western and central Suffolk are now almost as heavily built up as Nassau and real estate values have risen accordingly. In 1999, Nassau and Suffolk had a combined total of 2,665,115 people, up about 55,506 inhabitants from the beginning of the decade. Due to their much earlier extensive development, Kings and Queens, the Island's westernmost counties which are politically a part of New York City, have seen their populations level off at about two an one half million and two million and a half respectively.

Driven by the revival of the Island's economy after 1994, and reflecting the overall prosperous times, real estate prices, which had moderated somewhat in the '80s shot up again during the ensuing half-decade. With available land at a premium, new housing has been unable to keep up with demand. This has resulted in keen competition among buyers for both old and new homes. Virtually all neighborhoods have seen housing values soar with the median price of a house in Nassau and Suffolk now reaching $200,000. Concerns about the high cost of housing have been voiced since the 1970s, and the recent sharp spike in housing costs have fanned fears that the middle class may soon be priced out of Nassau and Suffolk. This was reflected in a February 2000 poll conducted by *Newsday* in which 73 percent of respondents declared the lack of affordable housing a major problem  East End real estate, which has been trendy for decades, has become even pricier as the number of year round residents continues to swell.  In particular, the South Fork, containing the Towns of Southampton and East Hampton, has seen an enormous boom in the upscale market.  Much of this reflects the desire of recently successful individuals and families to own a home, part or year round, in one of the nation's most prestigious neighborhoods.

A major national change, which has had a highly visible and profound effect on Long Island, has been the growth of the Hispanic and Asian populations.  The increase in the number of people from these areas is traceable to alterations in immigration policy enacted in 1965. While the influx of Asians, both from the Indian subcontinent and East Asia (China, Taiwan, Korea, Philippines, Vietnam and Japan), and Latinos was already underway in the 1970s, immigration from those areas exploded in the 1980s and 1990s.  During the period of the '80s and '90s the white population in Nassau fell ten percent to 79 percent of the total number of inhabitants while the white population of Suffolk dropped six per cent to 82 percent of the total.   Although the black population, the traditional minority, has grown about fifteen per cent in both counties in the last ten years, the

greatest increases among minorities have come from these immigrant groups.  For example, in both Nassau and Suffolk the government categories of Asian and Pacific Islander jumped 54 percent.  Demographic analysts divide Hispanics into "White Hispanic" and "Hispanic" which confuses things somewhat, but the combined categories reveal that the Hispanic population of Nassau increased almost ninety per cent in the past ten years and rose almost one hundred per cent in Suffolk.

The exponential growth of non-European descended residents since the 1970s has had a major effect on almost all areas of society and economy.  The political impact of these newer people has not yet been felt.  Nevertheless, especially since the Federal government has shown little inclination to reduce legal and suppress illegal immigration, the new immigrants are likely to evolve into an important political factor as the new century unfolds.

While arriving at almost the same time, the Asian and Hispanic immigrants have not followed the same paths.  Although both groups are highly diverse within themselves, the Asian community contains a higher percentage of professionals and business people than the Hispanic.  Asian immigrants have become a significant presence among small business owners operating such enterprises as stationary stores, fruit and vegetable markets, dry cleaning establishments, and computer stores.  Their presence is felt across the entire length and breadth of the Island, but seems especially vibrant in Flushing, Queens where Asians make up over half the population.  The Main Street—Northern Boulevard business section is now dominated by signs in Chinese and Korean.  In response, the Queens

*A sign of the times: East Asians are now the largest demographic group in the business district of Flushing. Korean and Chinese language signs and advertising signal this major ethnic trend. Courtesy, Richard F. Welch*

Historical Society now offers pamphlets in three Asian languages to meet the needs of the surrounding population. The three candidates in the 2000 race for the New York City Council seat from Flushing are all Asian—one Korean and two Chinese. Regardless of the victor, the area's representation by a person of Asian ancestry will be a first for Flushing and the City.

While the Asian presence may be most readily discernable in small businesses, Long Island is the beneficiary of a brain drain from the Asian continent. Large numbers of Indians and East Asians work in high technology areas especially those dealing with computers. Perhaps the best example of this is Charles Wang, president of Computer Associates which is now the largest manufacturing firm on Long Island. Wang has recently funded an Asian Center at the State University at Stony Brook, which now ranks second in the eastern United States, and third in the nation, among research institutions. The Asian Center, while an important educational asset in its own right, symbolizes the growing importance of the Asian community to the Island.

Looming larger in numbers than the Asians are the Hispanic immigrants who come from virtually every country in Latin America but who are dominated by immigrants from Central America and the Carribean Islands. Hispanic immigrants have generally not contained as high a percentage of professionals and business people as the Asians. Additionally, there are a greater number of illegal immigrants from Latin America. The Latino immigrants have become an important segment of the workforce and are involved in everything from basic manufacturing to the service sector. Restaurants in all price ranges are highly dependent upon workers from Latin America or their immediate descendants. Along with the overall prosperity which the Island has enjoyed since 1982, Hispanic workers have made possible the proliferation of landscaping and cleaning services used by numerous Long Island households.

While Asian immigrants have generally integrated well into the Island's population, the

The number 7 subway which runs through northwestern Queens from Times Square to flushing serves an area of unusual ethnic diversity. This painting, Ride on the Flushing Train, by Esteban Najarro, provides an artistic impression of the variety of people who might be encountered on a ride. Courtesy, The Museums of Stony Brook

Hispanic record is mixed. The increasing prevalence of Spanish in business and government has led to concerns about the centrality of English and its role as a unifying force for all Americans. In Suffolk County, this led to an attempt to have English declared the County's official language in 1996. Proponents touted the language's importance in assimilation and unity. Opponents charged that the measure was racist or an example of immigrant bashing. In the end, County Executive Robert Gaffney vetoed the measure, denying the County's citizens the opportunity to vote for it.

The presence of large numbers of unskilled young men, unknown numbers of whom may be illegal, who congregate in areas seeking day work from landscapers and contractors has led to friction with residents in some areas. Disputes have arisen over illegal housing since many immigrants live in badly overcrowded quarters.

The more bitter controversies erupted in localities such as Manorhaven, Glen Cove and Farming-ville where area residents complained that the crowds of young Hispanic immigrants were causing significant littering, vandalism, public indecency, petty crime and harassment of local women. In Glen Cove, one of Long Island's two Class B cities, local government responded by designating places for the immigrants to meet and look for work while providing better police supervision. The approach alleviated the situation though it remains a source of contention.

The dispute in Farmingville became even more acrimonious. In the central Suffolk hamlet, safety issues, including a drive by shooting, were added to the general apprehension regarding harassment of women and rowdiness. Upon investigation, concerned citizens discovered that their area was home to approximately 1,000 illegal aliens. In 1999, a committee calling itself the "Sachem Quality of Life" was organized to pressure local government to address the situation. Its objective was to prevent the community from being destroyed by what vice president Terry Sherwood described as a nexus of "illegal immigrants, greedy contractors and unscrupulous landlords." The resident's hopes for support from local government were dashed when a modest measure to regulate the places where the immigrants congregated for work was voted down in the Suffolk County legislature. The Farmingville situation remains unresolved, and such disputes, which simmer beneath the surface elsewhere, contain the potential for bursting into major social-political conflicts in the future.

Along with a growing population from the Third World, Long Island also mirrors national trends with a rising number of senior citizens. The segment of the population over 60, which will be swelled in the next few years by the huge "baby boomer" cohort has expanded enormously. For example, while the number of Nassau-Suffolk residents between five and nineteen shrunk by 146,177 between 1980 and 1998, the number of people over sixty grew by 93,707. The presence of so many elderly residents has

already affected governmental operations. Both Nassau and Suffolk County governments maintain agencies dedicated to senior citizens issues. Additionally, many of the Island's Towns such as Huntington, Brookhaven, and Hempstead operate their own senior centers, which offer a variety of programs and usually meals to the elderly. Transportation services are also provided for those unable to drive or obtain a ride from friends or relatives. In the private sector, churches and synagogues are the main providers of senior services.

The increasing presence of retirees and senior citizens has led to a rapid increase in the number of retirement villages, assisted living communities and nursing homes. While these have provided a source of employment for large numbers of people, some have wondered if it is not possible to have too much of one kind of service facility.

*Robert Gaffney, Suffolk County Executive (R) elected in 1991. Courtesy, Suffolk County Executive's office*

For example, Glen Cove in northern Nassau has an unusually large number of assisted living and nursing homes, which some younger residents blame for the defeat of school budgets.

If many of the demographic changes, which are now hurtling along at full speed, could be discerned in 1985, the Long Island economy has been transformed in ways few would have predicted fifteen years earlier. The virtual extinction of the aerospace industry is the most dramatic of the economic changes effecting Long Island. As late as 1980, Long Island still boasted two aircraft manufacturers, Fairchild-Republic and Grumman. These two large firms were joined by several smaller but important firms, which produced vital parts and components such as Eaton and Randtron. Fairchild Republic was the more vulnerable of the two mainframe corporations. Although it had turned out thousands of planes between World War II and Vietnam, its inability to secure contracts in the 1970s eroded its position. The failure to obtain another government contract after the A-10 "Warthog" doomed the facility, and it was totally out of business by early 1988.

Most surprising was the fate of the Grumman Aircraft Corporation headquartered at Bethpage.

Grumman had been a mainstay of Naval Aviation since World War II and, unlike Fairchild Republic, continued to win contracts throughout the 1980s. Additionally, Grumman supplied the lunar modules for the Apollo program and sold its aircraft to various Allied and friendly nations. The corporation seemed to be entering a golden age in the '80s as the Reagan Administration's defense buildup led to a greater demand for Grumman products. A-6 "Intruder" bombers, E-5 "Hawkeye" reconnaissance aircraft, and especially the F-14 "Tomcat" fighter rolled off the assembly lines at Bethpage. At night, when traffic on the heavily used Long Island Expressway is lighter, the planes were trucked to the Navy testing range at Calverton on eastern Long Island where they were put through their paces before being turned over to the Navy.

*The Indian population of Nassau County has grown exponentially over the past two decades. This is the Siku Temple in Glen Cove. Courtesy, Richard F. Welch*

The implosion of the Soviet Union and the presumptive end of the Cold War had an immediate effect on Grumman. With a vastly diminished demand for military aircraft only the strongest of the defense contractors would survive. Though a major player in the field, Grumman proved unable to compete against better-capitalized firms such as General Dynamics, Boeing or McDonnell-Douglas. In 1984, at the peak of production, Grumman employed about 22,500 people. The number of workers fell sharply as the "Tomcat" contract neared its end and remaining work was confined largely to spare parts and retrofitting. In 1994, Northrop Aircraft bought out Grumman creating another hyphenated corporation.

The new Northrop-Grumman Corporation soon phased out most of its Long Island operations. The bulk of the Bethpage property was sold for office space, paralleling the situation at the old Republic complex in Farmingdale, which is now a huge mall. About 3,000 workers remain at the diminished Bethpage plant engineering the upgrades on the radar systems for the E-2 "Hawkeye." The Navy test range at Calverton, which was used almost exclusively by Grumman, and where the TWA Flight 800 was reassembled for investigation after its mysterious crash, was given to the Town of Riverhead. Environmentalists and developers are locked into a debate over its future disposition.

Ironically, just as aircraft production was dying as a viable industry on the Island, Nassau County initiated plans for "The Cradle of Aviation Museum". This state of the art complex, rising on the site of the old Mitchell Field Air Force base in Garden City, is scheduled to open in 2001. The Museum has benefited greatly from the expertise, time, and labor of scores of former Republic and Grumman employees, many of whom originally built the planes they are restoring for exhibit. Containing vintage aircraft, artifacts, displays, photograph and an Imax theater, it is intended to celebrate the major role Long Island played in twentieth century aviation. With Grumman's prominence fast receding into memory, the "Cradle of Aviation Museum" will be a thoroughly historical institution

The recession of 1991-92 was the shortest in the post-World War II era and was effectively over by the end of spring, 1992. On Long Island, however, the rapid extinction of aerospace resulted in a sluggish business climate for another two years. In 1994, the Long Island Association, a business organization organized the Long Island Summit to address the needs of the Island's economy. Participants at the Summit drafted plans to deal with the specific problems facing the Island and drew up the "Long Island Action Plan" which addressed the Island's needs. The economy which emerged from the *sturm und drang* of the early '90s was noticeably different from that which preceded it. Computer Associates, owned by Charles Wang, emerged as the Island's leading manufacturing firm. Computer Associates continues to thrive and in 2000 purchased Sterling Software one of the top twenty firms in its field. Following national trends, additional computer-software firms have sprouted across the Island. Other advanced technology industries which show great potential are the biotechnology industry, now employing 10,000 people and already fourth in size nationally. Electronics, badly hurt by the demise of defense sector, has revived and employs about 20,000 workers. In order to facilitate the expansion of these hi tech industries the Long Island Technological Center was established at Great River on the south shore of Suffolk. Another tech center is planned for Lake Success in Nassau close to the Queens border. Long Island City, just across the East River from Manhattan has begun to attract some firms from Manhattan's "Silicon Alley" seeking cheaper office space.

Long Island boasts a number of superb institutions of higher education and research. The State University at Stony Brook is now recognized as one of the nation's premier research institutions. Indeed, recent reports estimate that the University's various activities pump one billion dollars into the Island's economy. Brookhaven National Laboratory and the internationally celebrated Cold Spring Harbor Laboratories lead the way in nuclear physics and DNA-genetic research respectively.

*The Cold Spring Harbor Laboratories operate the DNA Learning Center at this separate facility in the village. The Learning Center offers programs explaining genetics and DNA research to high school and college students. Courtesy, Richard F. Welch*

*Thomas Gulotta, Nassau County Executive (R) who found himself under fire from both Republican and Democratic members of the County Legislature as a result of Nassau's financial crisis. Courtesy, Nassau County Executive's Office*

The work of these facilities augurs well for the further development of biotech enterprises on the Island, though some business leaders have called for greater coordination and cooperation among these hi tech leaders.

Such observers also point out that despite the growth of the fast forward industries, the currently hot economy is driven primarily by the traditional service sector industries, which accounted for 87 percent of the job growth between 1992 and 1998.[17] Indeed, the top twenty private sector employers on Long Island are all engaged in services of one sort or another. Whether or not Long Island develops into another Silicon Valley or Route 128 corridor is impossible to predict though much of the foundation has been laid.

Politically, Long Island remains highly fragmented. Kings and Queens are boroughs of New York City and the City Council and mayor represent their residents. Suffolk County elected its first County Executive, H. Lee Dennison, in 1960 and ten years later replaced the Board of

Supervisors with a County Legislature form of government. In 1991, in the face of financial difficulties and a property tax increase, County Executive Patrick Halpin was defeated by Robert Gaffney who has held the position ever since. Gaffney succeeded in getting a hold over Suffolk's finances and the County was in a healthy position to take advantage of the economic expansion of the 1990s. Although the official County seat remains in Riverhead, the legislative offices in Hauppauge and the court complex in nearby Central Islip have combined to make the central Suffolk area the County's true nerve center.

Nassau entered the '90s with its circa1945 form of government still intact. Like Suffolk, Nassau has a county executive who runs independently for that position. Until recently, however, the other major component in the County government was the Board of Supervisors. This consisted of the town supervisors and the mayors of the two Class B cities, Glen Cove and Long Beach. The Supervisors' votes were weighted to reflect the differences in the population they represented. This system came under increasing criticism as undemocratic and exclusionary to minorities. Consequently, in 1994 Nassau also adopted the County legislature form of government. The County was divided into nineteen legislative districts which send a representative to the county seat at Mineola. Though the system was new the political balance of power remained the same. Republicans dominated the legislature in the same manner as they had controlled Nassau County, with one short interlude, since its creation in 1899. In 1999, however, the credit rating of Nassau's bonds fell to a grade barely above junk level. Though one of the most— some say *the* most—heavily taxed areas in the country, Nassau was deeply in debt. Spending more than it took in, and providing some of the most expensive services in the nation, the County government ran up deficits which ultimately lowered the jurisdiction's credit rating. The financial debacle, and the real possibility of tax increases, precipitated a voter's revolt. For the first time in the County's history voters returned a majority of Democrats to County government. With the County Executive still in Republican hands, however, the ability of the Democrats to force change was difficult. Nevertheless, for the

*The Heckscher Art Museum in Huntington is one of the most active of the Island's art institutions, mounting several exhibitions a year. Courtesy, Richard F. Welch*

County to return to a sound fiscal footing, both parties must cooperate. How Nassau weathers this storm is yet to be decided.

From as early as the 1960s, the economic, political and social lives of the residents of Nassau and Suffolk have been increasingly independent of New York City. Eighty-seven percent of Suffolk County residents find it unnecessary to travel outside the County for work. Only 12 percent of Suffolk residents commute into the City although thirty-two percent still travel from Nassau into the City for their livelihood. Kings and Queens, politically part of the City, are totally integrated with the other three boroughs by the City's public transportation system, though even there, centuries old traditions of local identity linger on.

While a minority of Long Islanders still work in the City, many more enjoy the cultural, entertainment, and recreational opportunities offered by the City. Yet, Long Island now provides an increasing array of such activities that many Long Islanders seldom visit the City except to catch a plane from La Guardia or JFK airport—both of which are in Queens.

Long Island's cultural and entertainment facilities and institutions are numerous and diverse. Many television programs which emanate from New York are taped at the Kaufman Studios in Astoria and the Silvercup studios in Long Island City. Major motion picture companies also use the studio sound stages. Long Island has its own cable system, Cablevision, a multi million-dollar enterprise owned by the Dolan family whose interests have stretched to encompass Madison Square Garden. Theater lovers can see first-rate productions at the Gray Wig Theater on the Hofstra University campus or at Bellport and the East Hampton Guild Hall. Concerts involving all types of music and entertainers are presented at numerous venues. The most unique of these is the Jones Beach Marine Theater on Zach's Bay which hosts a full summer schedule of major rock and pop acts.

The Island's cultural and entertainment scene offers an increasing number of diverse, prestigious institutions and facilities. While very little can compare with Manhattan's Metropolitan Museum of Art, the Brooklyn Museum has become an

Top: The Parrish Art Museum in Southampton is the leading institution in an area famous for its active arts scene. Courtesy, Richard F. Welch

Bottom: Among the newer museum's relating to Long Island's History is the Hallockville Museum Farm on the North Fork. Courtesy, Richard F. Welch

increasingly active host for visiting shows and possesses a superb permanent collection of art and antiquities which is being rediscovered by a new generation of Long Islanders and Manhattanites. The Nassau County Fine Arts Museum on the former Frick Estate in Roslyn mounts several exhibitions a year spotlighting a diverse body of artists and artistic styles. The Heckscher Museum in Huntington, the Parrish Art Museum in Southampton and the Guild Hall in East

When New York State announced it was shutting down its fish hatchery at Cold Spring Harbor a volunteer organization, now called The Cold Spring Harbor Fish Hatchery & Aquarium expanded its exhibits & programs and refurbished the buildings. This is the institution's main turtle pond. Courtesy, Richard F. Welch

Island. Both private and public courses are available and new facilities have been laid out on the East End in recent years. Indeed, over the past decade Suffolk County has been averaging one to two new courses per year. The 2001 US Open Gold Championship will be held at Bethpage State Park's formidable "Black Course" which is being specially prepared for the event. This major event in the golf world will shift to the venerable Shinnecock Hills course a few years after it is hosted by Bethpage.

Surrounded by water, Long Island boasts some of the finest beaches in the world. The barrier islands off the south shore contain over sixty miles of Federal, state, town, village-owned, private Atlantic Ocean beach facilities. The world famous Jones Beach State Park is the

Hampton are all active members of the energetic Long Island art community. The Society for the Preservation of Long Island Antiquities' Gallery in Cold Spring Harbor, the Museums at Stony Brook, and the Suffolk County Historical Society proudly feature the work of Long Island artists and craftsmen throughout the Island's history. Almost all of the Island's colleges and universities feature art galleries and the number of private galleries is high.

The sports scene on Long Island continues to thrive. While The New York Islanders have yet to return to the halcyon days of the early '80s when they won four Stanley Cup championships in a row, they still play thrill packed ice hockey games at the Nassau Coliseum in Uniondale. With the recently completed acquisition of the team by Charles Wang and his Computer Associates partner, Sanjay Kumar, sports lovers are hopeful that local ownership will result in better management and a rejuvenated team. A minor league baseball club, the Long Island Ducks opens its season at Central Islip stadium and, of course, the New York Mets pursue the dream of another World's Series win at Shea Stadium in Flushing Meadows. For tennis fans, the US Open Tennis championship is held at a recently built tennis complex within walking distance of Shea. Golf has an avid and growing following on Long

Dancing at the Polish American Fair in Riverhead, 1990. Photo by Audrey Gottlieb. Courtesy, The Museums at Stony Brook

most famous of these, but Robert Moses State Park and Fire Island National Seashore also attract tens of thousands of sand and sea lovers through-out the warmer months. Despite heavy and continuing development, virtually every sport from polo, to hunting, to bocce can be found on the Island.

The shopping mall revolutionized merchant activities on Long Island and in some cases has replaced long established villages as the hub of commercial activity. Most Long Island malls were well established before 1990, though several such as Roosevelt Field in Garden City and the Walt Whitman Mall in Huntington have received extensive renovations and upgrades over the past decade. In the face of this new competition, some villages have suffered declines and are characterized by unimpressive stores offering only necessities or cheaper items. However, many other have met the challenge of the malls and superstores, and have thrived by modernizing the premises and offering attractive, high quality merchandize and specialty items. Roslyn, Oyster Bay, Cold Spring Harbor, Huntington, Stony Brook, Port Jefferson and Bellport are among the many Long Island villages which

*Heading into East Hampton on Main Street, looking east. Summer traffic is frequently bumper to bumper. Courtesy, Richard F. Welch*

*Long Island's only bridge and tunnel connections to the mainland are located in Kings and Queens Counties. Ferry service from Orient Point or Port Jefferson provides the only other public conveyance from the Island to Connecticut. Here the* Grand Republic *loads at Port Jefferson as the P.T. Barnum arrives from Bridgeport, Connecticut. Courtesy, Richard F. Welch*

have retained their viability through the preservation of their historic character and prescience of smart, modern business establishments.

Many of the most successful villages have become meccas for diners and entertainment seekers. Long Island restaurants commonly range from the modestly priced to the extremely expensive and offer everything from traditional American cuisine to Chinese, Italian, and French. Reflecting the growing ethnic diversity, and more adventurous palates, Afghan, Thai, Indian, Vietnamese and Caribbean establishments have multiplies over the past fifteen years. Pubs, clubs, and bars combine food with entertainment and conviviality. Some villages like Bayside in Queens and Huntington in Suffolk are centers of an active nightlife scene with a panoply of diverse pubs, restaurants, marinas and clubs which draw a heavily college age crowd, especially in summer. And then, of course, there's the East End.

The term "East End is slightly ambiguous. It can refer to the five eastern Towns (often called Townships in other states), but is frequently applied only for the Towns and villages on Long Island's two forks. While the East End remains the least heavily developed part of Long Island, the forces of suburbanization have become well entrenched, especially since 1970. For well

*The end of the line: the Long Island Rail Road station at Montauk. The new diesels and double-decker cars were introduced in 1999. Courtesy, Richard F. Welch*

over a century, the area has been famed as a summer paradise drawing a large number of people in the arts, as well as wealthy families seeking attractive locales for their leisure time. With the Atlantic Ocean to the south, Long Island Sound to the north and Gardiner's and Peconic Bays dividing them, water related activities are available almost everywhere on both the North and South Forks. The presence of so much surrounding water is sometimes credited with creating "Hampton Light," a condition which initially lured artists to the then isolated and sleepy area in the 1890s. No longer isolated and sleepy, the Hamptons have become the trendiest area in New York State outside of Manhattan. Galleries, film festivals, vacationing or resident entertainment and media personalities, chic parties, the frenetic beach and summer culture, and the still picturesque historic villages combine to exert an irresistible force on a huge number of tourists, day-trippers and summer people. With only a two-lane blacktop as the main road between Southampton and Montauk, the swelling popularity of the Hamptons has resulted in horrendous traffic and frequent congestion—a situation that is the norm during the summer season between Memorial Day and Labor Day.

While best know for its art colony or art/ cultural or wealthy/celebrity scene, The East

*Shelter Island is the largest of Long Island's Islands. It can be reached by ferries, which run from early morning until 1:50AM. Ferries leave from Greenport on the North Fork and North Haven, near Sag Harbor, on the south fork. Here motorists at North Haven load on the ferry that will take them to Shelter Island (in the background). Courtesy, Richard F. Welch*

*Announcing a new Long Island enterprise on Sound Avenue near Northville. Courtesy, Richard F. Welch*

End remains the last stronghold of two traditional Long Island pastimes—agriculture and commercial fishing. The overall western pattern of development led to the extinction of agriculture in Queens, Kings, and Nassau. Today, farming and baymen activities—lobstering, shell fishing and commercial fin fishing—are relict occupations in western Suffolk. Despite the voracious appetite for East End land, which has driven prices so high that many farmers continually sell off their holdings, Suffolk County remains New York State's number one County in terms of the value of its products. However, there has been a marked shift within Suffolk farming. The number of establishments devoted to potatoes and cauliflower, mainstays since the nineteenth century, has continually declined while the acreage devoted to sod, nursery farming and—on the North Fork—grapes, has risen. The sod and nursery farms serve the needs of both suburban style developments as well as the mini-estates, which are relentlessly gouged out of the potato farms and woodlands.

The vineyards are a result of the establishment of a now thriving winery network on the North Fork. The modern Long Island wine industry was created by Alex and Louisa Hargrave who set up the first vineyard and winery in Cutchogue in 1975. Soon other entrepreneurs were attracted to the rich loamy soil and the mild sea girted climate of the North Fork. At present, the North Fork is home to eighteen wineries or vineyards while the South Fork claims three. Long Island wines have come into their own and are now rated among the best in the nation, regularly winning competitions with better known, and longer established labels from California and Europe.

Despite its productivity, the number of acres devoted to agriculture declines yearly as farmers are forced to concede the logic of selling off land whose value as real estate far exceeds that of several years of crop yields. A similar situation exits in sea related activities. The number of Long Islanders engaged in full-time fishing, shell fishing and lobstering has plummeted since 1960. The decline of commercial fishing is a direct consequence of population growth, which has polluted some of the most productive shell fishing waters in the world. Additionally, the mysterious red tide has wiped out the formerly lucrative scallop industry for several years, and the decline of formerly abundant "money fish" like striped bass and cod has led the

A commercial fishing vessel returning to Montauk harbor. Recently, friction between the beleaguered East End fishermen and state Department of Environmental Conservation officials led to vandalism of DEC cars and charges that the state police and DEC were harassing the fishermen. Courtesy, Richard F. Welch

government to limit the number which may now be taken. Beginning in the summer of 1999, Long Island Sound lobsters have been dying in large numbers from some as yet unidentified cause, further diminishing prospects for the Island's baymen. While commercial fishing vessels still ply the waters off the East End, the docks at Montauk and Greenport are now dominated by "party boats" and sportsmen's vessels. In 1986, Peter Mathiessen, naturalist, natural history writer, novelist, and Sagaponack resident wrote *Men's Lives*, a powerful and moving account of the South Fork's seine fishermen and their current plight. Ten years later, Steve Wick, a *Newsday* reporter, published *Heaven and Earth* which did for the North Fork's farming community what Mathiessen had done for the fishermen. Both writers chronicled traditional pastimes pushed to the wall by socio-economic pressures. In many ways the books are an elegy to a vanishing way of life.

While the North Fork is closing in on its

southern counterpart in housing costs, the Hamptons is still the address of choice among writers, artists, actors, celebrities, assorted "glitterati" and upscale wannabes. The Hamptons art colony was established by late nineteenth century painters such as William Merritt Chase and Thomas Moran. In the post-World War II years, many modern artists settled in what was still an under populated and generally inexpensive area. Jackson Pollack, Lee Krassner and Willem de Kooning founded the area's thriving modern art community. They were joined by writers such as James Jones, Willie Morris, John Steinbeck and Joseph Heller. The attractive colonial villages, swelling uplands and miles of beaches soon lured the wealthy from media and entertainment, as well as more prosaic fields such as electronics and cosmetics. But the artsy/entertainment crowd and their imitators tended to set the tone for the "new" society, even if they were a shrinking part of it. Today, day trippers and tourists drive up and down the Montauk Highway from Shinnecock to Amagansett, but especially East Hampton, which may be the nations' leading trophy village, searching for a glimpse of Christy Brinkley, Steven Spielberg, Peter Jennings, Kim Bassinger, Martha Stewart or Puff Daddy and his current squeeze, Jennifer Lopez. They are usually disappointed.

The South Fork, and especially East Hampton's, burgeoning reputation as a playground of the hip and affluent, enticed a growing upscale crowd driving up real estate values and setting off yet another major building boom. Aside from some townhouses, condominiums and developments, most of the new construction has been based on the axiom that "more is more." structures of 10,000 to 12,000 square feet are no longer unusual in the Hamptons and the proliferation of enormous, architecturally pretentious houses blighting the natural landscape finally forced Southampton to pass a zoning ordinance limiting new construction to 20,000 feet. Southampton's action was triggered by the construction of a 57,000 square foot, "residence" containing twenty-five bedrooms, and thirty-nine-bathrooms in Sagaponack. The building is such an insult to the landscape it was satirized by James Brady in his novel *The House That Ate the Hamptons.*

The rampant, poorly controlled growth has diminished the Hamptons desirability for some residents. The crowded roads and shops have recently induced rock'n'roll Hall of Famer Billy Joel to sell his ten a half acre estate on Further Lane—the epicenter of East Hampton chic—to Jerry Seinfeld for a reputed thirty-five million dollars. Joel, who regrets his public support for the local baymen had no effect on their continual decline, is moving back closer to his roots in Nassau, but not to his old hometown of Hicksville. Instead he's relocating along the old "Gold Coast" of Nassau's North Shore which is enjoying a new era of desirability for those with large wallets who don't want to drive the additional two hours further east.

A major concern for Long Islanders everywhere, ranking among such concerns as housing costs and property taxes, is the environment. This includes worries about toxic wastes in water, the high rate of breast cancer in some areas, and the location of landfills. Environmental concerns are inextricably linked with development issues. With so much of the Island heavily suburbanized, Long Islanders are generally sensitive to proposals to consume more space. The City was slow to set aside land for parks and preserves and what little open space remains in King and Queens is heavily utilized. Nassau was quicker to see the need to set aside land and has been helped by the willingness of some of the early estate owners to donate their property to the County, local village or Town. A similar situation prevailed in Suffolk, and for a time, the East End's distance from the centers of population protected it from heavy development pressures.

Today, the forces of development and the forces of conservation face each other uneasily, existing in an uneasy equilibrium which tilts one way and then the other. The president of the Long Island Association is concerned that the Island will not have enough people for its workforce needs and the construction trades have a vested interest in transforming space into buildings. The Island's geographical and topographical nature makes it especially vulnerable to such pressures. One hundred twenty miles long and about twenty-five miles wide at its greatest width, space can, and has, become a premium. While most Long Islanders recognize the need for economic growth and development, they are equally concerned not to destroy the very qualities, which have made the Island so desirable in the first place. Fears are also voiced about the safety and quality of the Island's water supply which is drawn exclusively from underground aquifers. These are highly vulnerable to contamination. Under the circumstances it is not surprising that environmentalist-developer disputes arise frequently.

Both permanent and ad hoc citizens groups actively promote the preservation of key areas for esthetic, environmental or historical reasons. In 1999 the citizens of Cold Spring Harbor prevented the New York State Department of Transportation from totally obliterating the scenic qualities of the Harbor by turning Route 25A into a virtual service road for the Long Island Expressway.   Land acquisition is a major objective of both the Long Island and South-Fork-Shelter Island chapters of the Nature Conservancy which are active in purchasing land for wildlife refuges and soft-use human activities.  Over the past ten years the Long Island Pine Barrens Society worked successfully to preserve the core of the unique Pine Barrens ecosystem in central east Suffolk from total development.  Attempts to extend the preserve onto the South Fork collapsed amid mutual recriminations with advocates charging Southampton Town officials with capitulating to developers while Town officials countered that the Pine Barrens supporters were interfering with local prerogatives and engaging in a de facto land grab.  Despite the unpleasant nature of the Pine Barrens debate, both Southampton and East Hampton have instituted temporary moratoriums on building permits while they

*The Frank Flower Shellfish company began business in 1887. They hatch out seedling oysters and deposit them in Oyster Bay for future harvesting. Here the main structures of the company dominate the harbor at Bayville. The floating frames in center rear curtain seedling oysters waiting to be taken to the oyster beds for "planting." Courtesy, Richard F. Welch*

assess the effects of recent heavy development and seek ways to maintain both the beauty and prosperity of their areas.

As Long Island enters the 21st century, it can look back on a half century of warp speed change, which shows little sign of slowing. Many of the changes have improved and enhanced the lives of its vastly increased population.  On the other hand, much of Long Island's natural uniqueness and historic character has been lost. In many areas the Island is up against the limit of its carrying capacity. Long Islanders, and especially their political, economic and civic leaders must recognize that if the Island is to retain the features which have made it such an attractive home to so many, they will have to carefully weigh the gains and losses of preservation and development.  Growth must be "smart" and preservation must be intelligent. The future is open, but it begins now.

# CHAPTER ELEVEN

# Chronicles of Leadership

As perhaps the definitive suburb, Long Island is the product of meshed contradictions. Increasingly self-sufficient in its professions and service industries, yet as dependent on international markets as on New York for its major industries, it is actually more city-state than suburb.

The Indians were Long Island's first baymen, harvesting rich bundles of scallops and clams from inland waterways, from coves along the Sound facing Connecticut, and from the Great South Bay at the edge of the Atlantic. They ventured into the vast ocean to hunt great whales, which seventeenth-century English explorers dubbed "royale fish."

But if raging ocean shore and swelling leeward pools attracted Dutch and English explorers in the 1600s, Long Island's acres of sunken meadows, wooded hills lush with game, and rolling farmland kept them coming shipload after shipload from Europe. Farming remains a staple of Long Island commerce, though cabbages, potatoes, pumpkins, and sod acres gave way to horses and vineyards.

As Long Island fishing and farming prospered into the nineteenth century, shipbuilding, banking, publishing, and spectacular feats of engineering appeared at its westernmost end in Brooklyn and Queens. In 1834 the railroad came. Today the Long Island Rail Road, America's oldest operating under its original name, is the nation's largest business commuter line.

The twentieth century dawned, and Long Island was the cradle of American aviation. However, real cowboys were still driving herds from Montauk to the Riverhead rail junction.

Suddenly, Long Island was the home of major military suppliers even as the Depression began.

The world grew smaller, and the universe closer, as the technology that revolutionized communications, and sent Americans to the moon, was born and developed on Long Island.

Today Long Island ranks with "Route 128" in Massachusetts and with the "Silicon Valley" in California as a seminal high-technology center.

Still, Long Island remains synonymous with the terms "bedroom community" and Manhattan "satellite." The ubiquitous 1955 Levitt home is still many people's idea of the place. Ironically, British occupying forces, bivouacked on Long Island's western shore to hold Manhattan against George Washington's Continental Army, were even earlier commuters. Old notions die hard.

The organizations whose stories are detailed on the following pages have chosen to support this important literary and civic project. They illustrate the variety of ways in which individuals and their businesses have contributed to the area's growth and development. The civic involvement of Long Island's businesses, institutions of learning, and local government, in cooperation with its citizens, has made the community an excellent place to live and work.

*During the latter part of the nineteenth century Brooklyn's docks absorbed Manhattan's expanding trade, benefitting local industry and providing jobs for workers such as these at the Lawrence Paper Box Company on Atlantic Avenue. Courtesy, The Long Island Historical Society*

# AAA TRANSPORTATION GROUP, LTD.

From humble beginnings in Franklin Square, Jack Meehan built the AAA Transportation Group "...$10 at a time, one delivery at a time." In 1970 Jack, then age 24, founded "AAA Messenger Service." Initially, Jack started by making his own parcel deliveries with his car, establishing himself with local companies and custom-house brokers. Jack's first Fortune 500 customer was American Express Company. American Express originally hired Jack to transport accounting documents between its operating centers in New York City and Miami, Florida. However, it soon expanded Jack's services to Phoenix, Arizona and for international shipments to and from Haywards Heath, England, ultimately requiring service to their offices world-wide.

As the business grew, so did the client list and client demands. To meet those increasing needs, the company hired additional employees and branched out into various transportation-related services. Soon AAA Transportation was shipping everything from documents to aircraft equipment. When American Express began to use AAA Transportation to ship their traveller's cheques and credit cards, the company incorporated security measures to enhance its dependable delivery service of sensitive materials. In

*Pro-Service Forwarding, Co., Inc., Valley Stream operation.*

the mid-'80s, the United States Postal Service underwent deregulation and AAA Transportation expanded into shipping and distributing international mail. In 1990, the Postal Service allowed postage discounts for pre-sorted mail and AAA Transportation capitalized on the opportunity by opening a mail pre-sorting company.

Today, AAA Transportation is comprised of several companies that conduct business worldwide. AAA Transportation's affiliated operating companies engage in specialized global mail processing/distribution, security, courier, and international freight forwarding services. The companies are: International Mail Express, Inc.; Pro-Service Forwarding, Co., Inc.; P.S. Clearance Co., Inc.; Pro Security Services, Inc.; AAA Air Express and Super Sort Corporation. AAA Transportation is headquartered in New Hyde Park, New York, and has locations throughout the United States and Canada.

Founded in 1975, AAA Air Express (the progeny of AAA Messenger Service) is a domes-

tic and international courier/messenger service that picks up, ships and delivers mail and financial documents 24-hours a day, 7 days a week, through its global network of offices and agents. AAA Air Express custom designs complete air freight systems to enhance and stream-line any organization's shipping objectives. Services include onboard courier service for "hands on" control of freight security and timelines.

Pro-Service Forwarding Co, Inc. (PSF) is an international freight forwarding company that was founded in 1979. While PSF arranges the ocean or air shipment of various commodities,

*CEO Jack Meehan.*

*IMEX, College Point location, showing mail being sorted for locations throughout the world.*

it specializes in handling aerospace shipments for large and mid-size international airlines. From a 747 jet engine to a 10-ounce roller bearing, PSF arranges door-to-door, and door-to-airport, transportation between the equipment manufacturer and airline customer. PSF also helps airlines minimize costly downtime by quickly delivering replacement parts in emergency situations. PSF is a member of the International Air Transportation Association (IATA), licensed by the Federal Maritime Commission (FMC), and a Non-Vessel Operating Common Carrier (NVOCC). PSF concentrates on large U.S. gateways including: New York, Los Angeles, Seattle, Chicago, Miami, Houston, San Francisco; and Canadian gateways, including Montreal and Toronto.

P.S. Clearance Co., Inc. (PSC) is AAA Transportation's custom house brokerage company. Licensed by the U.S. Treasury Department, PSC is located at most PSF locations to clear imported items with U.S. Customs. Originally customs' entries were hand filed, but with the technology boom, "paperless" entries are now made through a computerized, automated clearing house system.

International Mail Express, Inc. (IMEX), founded in 1986, is a full-service international mail company. IMEX sorts, routes and distributes bulk literature from the U.S. to worldwide mail hubs via direct injection into foreign post offices, United States Postal Service consolidations, and value-added services. IMEX picks up mail from customers through out the United States and brings it to one of their mail hubs, where it is sorted for delivery to foreign and domestic post offices or to the ultimate addressee. IMEX sends large mail volumes to countries such as Great Britain, Canada, Mexico, France, Germany and Spain.

Pro Security Services Inc. (PSS) is a security transportation company with a present and growing nationwide network of over 170 security agents that are mostly comprised of current and former law enforcement officials. Founded in 1980, PSS specializes in domestic and international shipping of valuable security items, including credit cards, travelers cheques and securities. PSS does business with major banks and financial institutions in more than 30 states and over 100 metropolitan areas nationwide.

Super Sort Corporation is an automated pre-sort mailing

company located in Hicksville, NY. Super Sort, founded in 1990, is one of the first automated pre-sort mailing companies on Long Island and is one of the first to become a Certified Combined Mailer by the United States Postal Service. Super Sort serves on the Board of Postal Customer Councils (PCCs) for New York City and Westchester County, and is also a member of the Long Island PCC, the Long Island Association (LIA) and Long Island Software & Technology Network (LISTNET). Super Sort combines the mail of many different clients and sorts the mail by zip code via state-of-the-art computerized machinery and software. As a result, clients achieve significant postage rate discounts.

AAA Transportation believes that e-commerce and technology will continue to grow, as will the world's need for transportation-related services. While AAA Transportation grows with this demand, its philosophy and culture remain consistent. Handshakes and commitments will be honored, as embodied in the corporate slogan, "Delivering on our promises since 1970."

*A panoramic view of the Super Sort facility operations area.*

# AVIS GROUP

Avis' famous advertising campaign slogan, "We Try Harder" became a household phrase in the 1960s. The "We Try Harder" slogan not only strengthened Avis' foothold in the car rental industry, but it completely revolutionized corporate advertising. It also defined the service ethic of the Company and the dedication of its employees to provide customers with individualized attention and services.

This service ethic has enabled Avis to thrive and change to constantly meet the demands of a world that has become increasingly more mobile. The Company has been transformed numerous times as it has grown. Today, Avis Group Holdings, Inc. encompasses not only the second largest general use car rental business in the world, but it is also one of the world's leading providers of comprehensive automotive transportation and vehicle management solutions through its Vehicle Management Services Group, consisting of PHH and Wright Express. Wright Express is also the world's largest fleet card provider.

The history of Avis began in Detroit in 1946, when Warren Avis realized the potential for a car rental business linked with airline travel. He established his car rental counter at the airport there and called it, "Avis Airlines Rent A Car System." This was the first car rental counter in America located in an airport. By 1948, Avis began franchising the rental operations, which provided for additional openings of Avis Rent A Car System in downtown locations as well as in airports.

In 1954, Warren Avis sold his interest of the Company to Richard S. Robie. This was the first of several changes in the Company's ownership. The Company adapted to these changes and continued to grow. For example, in March 1962, Avis was a $25 million, 7,500-vehicle company and was acquired by Lazard Freres and Company. Within three years, Avis expanded its corporate locations as far as Mexico, Italy and France while its corporate sales climbed to $74.5 million. By 1975, Avis Rent A Car System, Inc. was valued at $433 million.

Avis Rent A Car was constantly an innovator. During the 1970s, Avis revolutionized the travel industry with the introduction of "Wizard," the first fully-computerized, real-time reservation and rental processing system. The Company continued to set industry trends through the 1980s with the introduction of "Roving Rapid Return." In that same decade the Company also became employee-owned.

*Avis Rent A Car at Long Island's MacArthur Airport. Avis has over 1,000 car rental locations in the United States and Canada.*

In October 1996, the Company was acquired by HFS, Inc., which a year later took the Company public. On the day of the initial public offering, Avis stock, which trades under the symbol AVI, was the most heavily traded issue on a percentage basis in the 205-year history of the New York Stock Exchange. As a public company, Avis Rent A Car began to acquire major franchisees to ensure consistent delivery of customer service.

In May 1999, Avis announced the acquisition of PHH Vehicle Management Services and Wright Express, positioning the Company as a comprehensive provider of vehicle management solutions through its rent a car unit and the fleet management and fuel card businesses of PHH and Wright Express. In March 2000, Avis Rent A Car changed its legal name to Avis Group Holdings, Inc. to signify the diverse services it provides by combining the strengths of Avis Rent A Car, PHH and Wright Express, enabling other companies to thrive in the mobile world.

*Wright Express, a member of Avis Group Holdings, Inc., is the world's largest fleet card provider.*

# BAE SYSTEMS ADVANCED SYSTEMS

Alan Hazeltine announced his concept of the Neutrodyne circuit to the engineering community in a paper presented at a meeting of the Radio Club of America, at Columbia University on March 2, 1923. The Neutrodyne circuit's higher sensitivity and ease of tuning made it the first to achieve wide household acceptance and commercial success. On February 1, 1924, Hazeltine Corporation was formed as a public corporation to manage licensing of patents for the Neutrodyne and of subsequent inventions.

Since then, the company has been on a progressive path of innovation and technological development. Currently, the facility in Greenlawn, New York, is known as BAE SYSTEMS Advanced Systems, a business unit in the second-largest global systems, defense, and aerospace company. Chief Executive John Weston stated, "I believe BAE SYSTEMS, with our North American presence, as well as the U.K. and seven other home markets, is well positioned for success in this emerging global defense environment."

During the 1930s, the company designed commercial electronics that were applied successfully to radio, monochrome and color

*Its design looks simple, but the impact of the Neutrodyne circuit radio was felt worldwide when it became the first commercial, successful radio, and the reason for the company's existence.*

*Originally located in Professor Hazeltine's home in Hoboken, NJ, Long Islanders recognize this sleek, symmetrical building as the home of BAE SYSTEMS Advanced Systems, formerly known as Hazeltine.*

television, medical photography, transportation, and oil exploration equipment industries. By the 1940s, the company had developed a television studio and transmitter, and provided electronic defense systems and frequency radio tuners, aircraft heat radiation detectors and Identification Friend or Foe (IFF) systems for the U.S. government. Post-war developments included military radar displays and sonobuoys to detect and transmit signals from underwater to surface to air. Commercial success was established through technological innovations that improved color television receivers dramatically.

As sonobuoy technology was updated for nuclear submarines and satellite communication, and the Mark XII IFF system progressed, a display system for the Airborne Early Warning Radar System was developed—a forerunner of the current AWACS (Airborne Warning and Control System). The 1950s were marked with progress in innovative distance-measurement equipment for the Federal Aviation Administration, as well as microwave landing systems for airports.

The company moved some of its attention from air to space during the 1960s and its display systems served NASA's monitor-

ing and control networks for spacecraft launching as well as manned and unmanned flight. Its imaging equipment helped convert signals from the Viking II space probe for the world to see the first pictures of Mars. However, the company remained committed to ground, sea, and air-related innovations as well, such as the Combined Interrogator/Transponder (CIT), installed on the F-16 and F/A-18 fighter aircraft. New IFF technologies kept the company in a leadership position in air defense and ground combat battlefield applications. During the 1980s and 1990s, the company continued to make great strides in development of its IFF, Display Systems, antenna design, and marine-related products. As of November 30, 1999, it officially became part of the global corporation, BAE SYSTEMS, and is poised to enter the 21$^{st}$ century as a benchmark aerospace and defense company.

BAE SYSTEMS Advanced Systems also includes a facility in Mt. Vernon, New York and Braintree, Massachusetts.

# BLUMLEIN ASSOCIATES, INC.

In 1914 the construction of a new house on the Flushing and North Hempstead Turnpike was finished. Aloysius Huwer had built this structure as a new home for his daughter, Louisa, her husband, Frederick J. Blumlein and their children, Frederick R. and Elizabeth. The house was located next to his own home on the Turnpike and his landmark hotel. Aloysius was born in Alsace/Lorraine in 1843, came to America as a young man, fought in the Civil War, owned a glass factory in Brooklyn and was the last owner/operator of the Bull's Head Hotel.

Built before the turn of the last century (and located at the contemporary intersection of Northern Boulevard [Route 25A] and Glen Cove Road in Greenvale), the hotel was a major refreshment stop for farmers who drove wagon loads of produce along the Turnpike to markets in western Queens. According to Alison Cornish, a Long Island antiquities specialist, "the construction of the new roadway in 1837, by the North Hempstead-Flushing Turnpike Company, was a response to the opening of the Erie Canal in upstate New York. Long Island's farmers, no longer able to compete with the

*A visitor-interactive map designed by BAI for the Off To Arctic Grounds exhibit, The Whaling Museum, Cold Spring Harbor, Long Island, NY.*

*Aloysius Huwer (second from left) with family and friends on the porch of the Bull's Head Hotel, circa 1910.*

quantity and price of Midwest grain, sought ways of moving their perishable produce to the city more quickly."

In the early 1900s, President Theodore Roosevelt was known to have tied his horse up at the front porch of the Bull's Head Hotel after riding from his summer White House in Oyster Bay. The porch was also a favorite spot to pull up a rocker and view the Vanderbilt Cup automobile racers as they sped pell-mell along the Turnpike.

Today, Northern Boulevard remains a major North Shore route of automobile and truck transportation to and from New York City, and Greenvale remains one of this roadway's major commercial hubs. Of the original Huwer family homestead structures, only the 1914 building remains...it is now the home of Blumlein Associates, Inc.

Blumlein Associates, Inc. (BAI) is an environmental and graphic design firm that specializes in the design of interpretive

exhibitions, retail stores, and entertainment-related interiors. Fred Blumlein, a great-grandson of Aloysius Huwer, established BAI and manages its ongoing design activities.

For many years Blumlein was a daily commuter from Long Island to Manhattan and to a teaching position as a professor in the School of Art and Design at Pratt Institute in Brooklyn. In the 1970s he decided to throw away the commute, continue teaching and open a design firm on the Island. His goals for the new office were (and are to this day) to work on meaningful projects, empower his staff with creative freedom, and be financially responsible and fair to BAI's clients, sub-contractors and staff. Raised in the 1914 house and a life-long resident of Long Island, he was well aware of the Island's impressive history,

*An exhibition for Sony Electronics, Inc. at PC Expo, Jacob Javits Convention Center, New York, NY.*

beauty, strong community spirit and the availability of the technical support that BAI needed to flourish. With an office on the Island, the BAI staff could put in the long hours needed to work on design commissions and, on most occasions, enjoy life with families and friends. Over the years, the advances in computer and telecommunications technology have allowed BAI to remain at its unique location and, at the same time, to quickly and easily communicate its design concepts to its national clientele.

BAI's work has appeared at The Museum of Modern Art, Massachusetts Institute of Technology, Indiana University, Lincoln Center, EPCOT Center, Cirque du Soleil and Universal Studios in Hollywood and Orlando. BAI is a major supplier of environmental design and management services to Sony Electronics, Inc. and Sirius Satellite Radio, with commis-

sions appearing at major technology-related trade shows in the U.S. In 1996, BAI designed all of AT&T's Customer-Calling Centers at the Summer Olympics in Atlanta. On Long Island, its design commissions include work for The Friends for Long Island's Heritage, The Reckson Visitor Center at the Cradle of Aviation Museum, the Nassau County Museum, The Museums at Stony Brook and many local historical societies.

The continued success of BAI's work is attributable to its ability to listen very carefully to its clients' concerns and design requirements, and its ongoing invitation to them to become part of the designing process. In addition, during the development of projects, its staff of enormously talented individuals has been guided by the creative ingenuity of Bill Arbizu and Chris Leonardi, both award-winning designers. Through these people and this proven process, BAI has continued to discover new ways of conceptualizing exciting physical spaces

and matching them with the addition of powerful environmental and print graphics. Through the years, in museums, theme parks, and historical societies, millions of individuals have visited, enjoyed and remembered the unique environments created by Blumlein Associates, Inc.

The legacy of Aloysius Huwer is much more than an historic building that still stands on the "Turnpike." It is about stories... stories concerning people and places and how they live and change through time. Following this notion, the people at Blumlein Associates, Inc. have become master storytellers about the world and painting them in the medium of environmental design.

*"The Sound Cameraman"-The Dawn of Sound traveling exhibition by BAI for AT&T.*

# BEATTY, HARVEY & ASSOCIATES, ARCHITECTS

Beatty, Harvey & Associates is Long Island's oldest architectural firm. Founded in 1880 by Francis Berlenbach and John Beatty, the firm has provided continuous service to a wide range of clients for over 120 years. John's son George Edward Beatty took over the firm in 1931 and was joined by his son George Beatty Jr. in 1969, when the firm took on the name of Beatty & Beatty. The death of George E. Beatty Jr. in February 2000 marked the end of three generations of involvement by the Beatty family. Today, under the direction of Todd Harvey and new partners Pat Fusco and Michael Tortorice, the multi-disciplined, 35-person firm continues to grow and expand. Beatty Harvey & Associates thrives as a company with an excellent reputation in the design of educational, library, healthcare, corporate and governmental facilities.

The firm started out at a time when architects were referred to as "master-builders." Most of their early work was for the archdiocese in Brooklyn, New York, designing many of the churches and cathedrals across Long Island. In the 1950s the firm expanded into educational work, designing numerous public schools and colleges including the entire campus for Molloy College in Rockville Center.

*Center for Behavioral Neuroscience, SUNY Stony Brook.*

*Sachem Public Library, Holbrook.*

As Long Island grew and expanded so did the firm, designing a wide range of prominent projects including the Suffolk County Correctional Facility in Riverhead; St. Charles Hospital in Port Jefferson; and the recently-completed EAB stadium in Islip, home of the Long Island Ducks. Through the '70s, '80s, and '90s the firm continued to diversify, developing specialties in the design and planning of laboratories, libraries, historic renovation, hospitality and housing.

They have been the regional architects for the U.S. Environmental Protection Agency since 1993, designing laboratory projects throughout the country. Over the last 10 years they have planned and designed over 40 public and private libraries in the metropolitan region including the new Kumar-Wang Library at Friends Academy in Locust Valley, the Rogers Memorial Library in Southampton and the Suffern Library in Suffern, NY.

Expanding their reach beyond Long Island, Beatty Harvey & Associates is currently working on a mixed-use development called Inner Harbor East in Baltimore, MD. The project includes a 750-room Marriott waterfront hotel, a 350-room Marriott suite hotel, two apartment buildings, two office towers, and a multiplex theater—all built over street front retail spaces and underground parking.

The firm has achieved its success and longevity by offering a high level of personal service and by creating a highly-collaborative design process. Their designs have won numerous awards, including several from the Long Island Chapter of the American Institute of Architects.

As the firm moves into the next century they continue to "push the envelope" on their designs, and to explore better ways to integrate technology and broaden their experience.

# BROOKHAVEN NATIONAL LABORATORY

Established in 1947 on the grounds of a former U.S. Army camp as the nation's first peacetime federal laboratory, Brookhaven National Laboratory operates large-scale facilities for studies in physics, chemistry, biology, medicine, applied science and advanced technology.

Located on a 5,300-acre campus in central Suffolk County in Long Island, Brookhaven is primarily funded by the U.S. Department of Energy and managed by Brookhaven Science Associates, a company founded by the Battelle Memorial Institute and the Research Foundation of the State University of New York (SUNY) for SUNY Stony Brook.

Each year, Brookhaven's 3,000 scientists, engineers and support staff are joined by more than 4,000 visiting scientists from around the world who use its "big science" facilities for research as diverse as understanding the nature of matter to unraveling the secrets of DNA.

Brookhaven has a rich history and a bright future in scientific achievement. The Laboratory is the home of four

*Brookhaven is a world leader in brain research, including how drugs, mental illness, and even normal aging affect the brain. A Brookhaven collaboration was the first to discover that a drug used to control epilepsy stops cocaine's addictive effects in animals.*

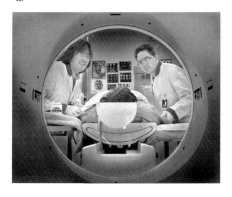

*Aerial view of Brookhaven National Laboratory. The Relativistic Heavy Ion Collider (top center) is 2.4 miles in circumference and dominates Brookhaven's 5,300-acre campus.*

Nobel Prize-winning discoveries in physics. Three of these, awarded in 1976, 1980 and 1988, were made using Brookhaven's Alternating Gradient Synchrotron, one of the world's premiere particle accelerators. The 1957 Nobel Prize was awarded for a discovery in theoretical physics.

Today, Brookhaven is home to the Relativistic Heavy Ion Collider, the world's newest and biggest particle accelerator for studies in nuclear physics. Physicists working at the Collider aim to recreate the conditions of the early Universe, just moments after the Big Bang, to gain insights into the fundamental nature of matter and extend the boundaries of scientific understanding through the 21st century and beyond.

One of the world's premiere facilities for research using X-rays and ultraviolet and infrared light, Brookhaven's National Synchrotron Light Source has been used to decipher the molecular structures of proteins and viruses, to investigate nanotechnology and fabrication processes, and to study magnetism, supercon-

ductivity and other properties of materials. Each year, some 2,400 scientists from around the world use the NSLS to perform research in a wide variety of fields.

In the medical arena, Brookhaven scientists use an imaging technique called positron emission tomography to probe the brain chemistry of addiction, mental illness and aging, in search of effective treatments.

Whether partnering with industry on a specific invention or performing basic research, Brookhaven's researchers have made scientific breakthroughs that have led to improvements in everyday life, such as:

• L-dopa as a treatment for Parkinson's disease

• Technetium-99m, used annually in 24 million nuclear medicine procedures worldwide

• Zinc-phosphate coating that dramatically cuts corrosion of steel surfaces

• Pollution-eating bacteria

• Asbestos-digesting foam

• World's first video game

Brookhaven strives to be a scientific resource for the world and a good neighbor to Long Islanders. The Laboratory is Long Island's fourth largest high-tech employer and spends tens of millions of dollars annually on goods and services in the area. Each year, thousands of students take advantage of learning and research opportunities at the Laboratory, and community participation in many of its outreach programs is encouraged. For more information on Brookhaven National Laboratory, visit their Web site at www.bnl.gov.

# COMPUTER ASSOCIATES INTERNATIONAL, INC.

The quietly spectacular growth that has made Computer Associates the world's leading provider of eBusiness solutions began nearly 25 years ago when Charles B. Wang, his college friend Russ Artzt and Judy Cedeno began selling a single software program, CA-Sort, from a small office in midtown Manhattan. Since 1976, CA has grown into a technology giant, serving the Global 2000 marketplace, with revenues over $6 billion and 20,000 employees operating in more than 100 countries. What has never changed, however, is a dedication to practicality, nimbleness, and the belief that technology must, above all other things, serve a client's business needs.

Money was tight during those first few frantic years, as the company turned a "boot-strap operation" into a corporate virtue. With growth sometimes outpacing hiring, employees were encouraged to pitch in and do whatever was required to get the job done.

*From right to left: Computer Associates Chairman Charles B. Wang and CEO and President Sanjay Kumar.*

*Computer Associates' world headquarters in Islandia, Long Island, New York.*

The words "Sorry, it's not my department" are not in the CA corporate lexicon.

What began as a ritual of bringing donuts to a handful of employees has grown to a policy of free daily breakfasts for its 20,000 employees. This caring attitude has since expanded to in-house day care and physical fitness centers, and benefits programs that are honored and widely-imitated. And the informal, family feeling remains an essential part of the CA culture.

CA moved to Long Island in 1979 and went public in 1981. In 1986, when CA moved its headquarters to Garden City, the company was producing revenues of $191 million by following a strategy of internal software development, acquisition and integration. In 1989, CA became the first software company to reach $1 billion in annual sales.

Acquisition also proved a good way to secure technical talent. The 1987 purchase of UCCEL Corp. not only increased CA's technology base and market scope, but also brought on board a young development manager named Sanjay Kumar, who is now CA's president and chief executive officer.

Throughout the 1990s, CA strengthened its position as the leading, independent business software provider with a steady flow of innovative solutions and services. Today, a major reason

*Computer Associates and its employees continue their commitment to helping those less fortunate through volunteer efforts such as Habitat for Humanity.*

for CA's continuing leadership is a clear understanding of the clients' evolving eBusiness needs.

CA's award-winning Unicenter TNG provides the platform to manage processes and transactions at every point in the business-to-business and business-to-consumer marketplaces. CA's unique Jasmine ii software delivers the first comprehensive platform for enabling intelligent eBusiness. Neugents, CA's patented neural network-based technology, provides predictive intelligence to eBusiness applications. CA is also the world's largest provider of storage management and security software.

To ensure that its products reflect the most advanced technology, CA partners with virtually every leading hardware and software supplier, including Cisco, Compaq, Dell, Fujitsu, Hewlett-Packard, IBM, Intel, Microsoft and Sun Microsystems.

With tens of thousands of enterprises around the world relying on CA solutions to run eBusiness, CA continues to outpace other software providers while setting industry standards in enterprise computing. CA provides more software running on more computers to more businesses than any other company.

The nature of eBusiness is changing rapidly. The traditional use of the Internet to communicate and distribute information has quickly shifted to finding new customers, marketing and selling. And today it's shifting again with a focus on integration—business-to-business integration, business-to-consumer integration, integration within the enterprise, and integration with existing systems. CA delivers the solutions that enable customers to create eBusiness systems with the security and reliability required for success in the marketplace.

Approaching age 25, CA is still learning and it's still fast on its feet. It is a company supremely aware that its focus on the business needs of its clients is as much a key to the future as it is a proud legacy from the past.

With CA's standing as a major, multi-national corporation, one that could do business just about anywhere in the world, the question is frequently asked, "Why Long Island?" The answer lies both in the attractiveness of Long Island's highly-educated, high-tech work force, and in the commitment of CA's leaders to the Long Island community.

CA believes interaction between all employees creates a breeding ground for fresh ideas—for CA believes its employees are the key to its tremendous growth. At CA, employees come first. CA allows each person to realize his/her potential through individual contributions and collective efforts as part of a team.

Attracting and retaining talent is a CA priority, one that is reflected throughout the company headquarters and in the its guiding philosophy that, "If you want to attract the best people on the globe, you have to have the

*CA chairman Charles B. Wang and New York Governor George Pataki outside CA's newly-expanded headquarters in Islandia, Long Island, New York.*

facilities for them." CA provides an award-winning, extremely progressive work environment that is designed to help employees balance their personal and professional lives. The company offers many opportunities for ongoing career development by offering interesting and challenging work on groundbreaking technology. CA also provides a healthy and supportive culture, with a host of progressive policies and benefits to help employees succeed and grow.

CA continues to win industry-wide acclaim for a progressive work environment that encourages teamwork while recognizing individual contributions. In its annual survey of leading information technology companies, *ComputerWorld* magazine recently cited CA as one of the "100 Best Places to Work in IT" for the sixth consecutive year.

*CA Chairman Charles B. Wang and CEO and President Sanjay Kumar at the Smile Train booth at CA World 2000. The Smile Train is a non-profit organization committed to eradicating the problem of cleft lips and palates by empowering local surgeons and medical professionals in developing countries to perform the surgery themselves.*

Recognized as a world leader in innovative management strategies, CA has been named one of *IndustryWeek*'s 100 Best-Managed Companies for three consecutive years. *Fortune* magazine also named CA one of America's "most admired companies." CA was the second highest ranked software company and was rated number one in social responsibility.

CA received the 2000 Dale Carnegie Training Leadership Award for its continuous dem-

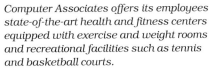

*Computer Associates offers its employees state-of-the-art health and fitness centers equipped with exercise and weight rooms and recreational facilities such as tennis and basketball courts.*

onstration of superior leadership in human resources development, in alignment with its dedication to promoting people-friendly, family-friendly and environmentally-friendly corporate policies.

Employee growth at CA is bolstered through distance learning programs, special training events, on-site courses, and a twice-a-year Boot Camp for newly-hired computer science graduates from around the world. Once assigned a particular job, the company encourages employees to try many different positions. These job shifts often serve to bring fresh outlooks to each CA department and provide excellent opportunities for individual career growth and advancement.

In line with its commitment to foster a progressive work environment, CA recently announced a 400,000-square foot expansion of its state-of-the-art corporate headquarters

in Islandia, which opened in 1992. The expansion, dubbed Project Acorn, features new office and research-and-development facilities, a state-of-the-art technical training center, and an enlarged indoor/outdoor fitness center. CA has also expanded its award-winning, Montessori-based child development center, making it one of the largest in the Northeast. Within the next 10 years, CA expects to have more than 8,000 employees on Long Island. CA's existing 720,000-square foot facility currently houses more 3,000 employees, a three-fold increase since 1992.

CA is also expanding software training classes for both staff and clients by adding an innovative training center that will provide the network and desktop tools necessary to keep up with changing technology.

A major new food service area will feature aerial views of southern Long Island, indoor and outdoor dining areas and a roof top garden. In keeping with CA's multi-national employee population and global market reach, the restaurant will also feature international cuisine.

CA and its employees are involved in a variety of charitable programs and philanthropic activities. The company's ongoing humanitarian efforts are far reaching— from a generous, company-sponsored Matching Charitable Gifts program and private contributions from CA officers and employees, to millions of dollars in corporate donations. The company designed and is hosting Web sites for Missing and Exploited Children in the United States, Europe and Asia, and also actively supports The

Smile Train to provide surgery for children with cleft lips and palates, and the Make-A-Wish Foundation to grant wishes to terminally ill children.

Closer to home, CA support extends to the Nassau County Sports Commission, a non-profit organization that promotes and enhances the quality of life for area residents while improving the economy of the region through sports. CA also supports local and national chapters of Habitat for

Humanity, which seeks to eliminate homelessness from the world, KaBoom!, which builds safe playgrounds in local neighborhoods across the country, Christa House, which focuses on hospice care for AIDS sufferers and the poor, and Junior Achievement.

---

*Computer Associates' on-site, Montessori-based Child Develement Centers boast spacious, colorful classrooms and large outdoor and indoor playgrounds for children ages six weeks to six years.*

# CROSSTEX INTERNATIONAL

As one of the world's most rapidly growing healthcare product manufacturers, Crosstex International is a company grounded by its successful roots in an entrepreneurial family tree.

Founded by Frank Allen Orofino in 1938, Crosstex has become a business where both fathers and sons know best, with three generations guiding the company into the year 2000. Richard Allen Orofino, Mitchell Steinberg and Gary Steinberg operate the company today with a deep respect for its history, as it is too, their heritage and legacy.

Orofino's vision began simply —with the first storefront-type dental laboratory in New York City. His strategy, however, was of a budding entrepreneur. He located his laboratory next to the NYU Dental College knowing the value of location—as well as of a captive audience of students and faculty.

After years of experimentation, he introduced the division of labor to the science of denture technology and he perfected the process of mass-producing dentures. This marriage of industrialism with healthcare was revolutionary and paved the way for expansion.

Seizing the opportunity for diversification and growth, he formed a partnership with his accountant, Norman Steinberg, creating the Cross Country Paper Products Corporation in 1953. As with most great evolutions, the beginnings were humble, at best. Utilizing a 25-year-old towel machine and locating it in the back of a gas station, they began manufacturing disposable towels made of paper for use in the

*Crosstex Corporate Headquarters, Long Island, New York.*

healthcare, beauty and barber markets.

In 1957, the company welcomed the first of its second generation with Richard Allen Orofino, Frank's son. In the vein of his father and Steinberg, Richard was ready to create his own mark of success by doing things differently. With his primary focus on the laboratory he pioneered new methods of sales while Steinberg focused his attention to Cross Country Paper Products.

In 1962 Cross Country Paper Products developed the first plastic-backed paper towel to be worn by patients during their dental visits. Over the next several years the company surpassed many of its original expectations, with annual sales exceeding $1,000,000.

Steinberg's oldest son, Mitchell, joined Cross Country Paper Products in 1980, inter-

jecting a new enthusiasm, as well as fresh ideas. He quickly launched an expansion and the name Crosstex was born. The product line was broadened to include more disposable dental products including plastic cups, tray covers, sponges and cotton rolls.

As the awareness and focus of infection control in the dental practice became more prominent, the product line was further expanded to include gloves, sterilization packaging, face masks and disinfectants, to name a few.

The length of the family lines within the company continued to grow. Steinberg's youngest son, Gary, joined the company

*Left to right: Richard Allen Orofino, Gary Steinberg, Mitchell Steinberg, and Richard Orofino, Jr.*

business, focusing on the laboratory with Richard. In 1988, the Orofino-Steinberg team sold the laboratory and joined Mitchell at Cross Country Paper Products. Within a year the company's first off-site distribution center was opened. Located in Los Angeles, California, the facility allowed the company to maintain pace with their growing demand, but with reduced costs for both the company and their distributors.

As the '90s came into focus, so did their tact to steer the company successfully towards the new millennium. They increased their ownership in the products they sold by manufacturing more of them in-house. This allowed the company to maintain control of both quality and cost.

To complement their thriving West Coast facility, a second distribution center was opened in Atlanta, Georgia in 1994, bringing support to the southeastern part of the country as well as Latin America and the Caribbean.

Richard Orofino, Jr. ushered in the third generation of the longtime family business affair in 1995. In 1996 the company improved on its initial product, the patient towel, by patenting and manufacturing the first

Frank Allen Orofino, left, and Norman Steinberg, right, circa 1956.

patient towel with adhesive tabs, eliminating the need for bib clips or chains. Since its introduction, the product has allowed the company to expand into new markets—infants and geriatrics.

The company, still located in Long Island, New York, found strength, not strain, from its rapid growth in the '80s and '90s. Becoming public was an option, however the principals agreed to maintain the business under the tradition from which it was born—keeping it private and family owned.

A senior management team was formed to help drive the business under the guidance of the fathers and sons. This dynamic team comprised of Sheldon Fisher, vice president in California; Ron Psimas, vice president in Georgia; Les Gershon, vice president for the northern region; and Andrew

Whitehead, vice president of sales and marketing, brought many decades of experience to the family's company table.

The late 1990s introduced international expansion. The company established its first overseas distribution center in The Netherlands in 1998. They were now able to more efficiently service Europe and increased their European sales with positive results. In 1999, the second overseas distribution center was opened in Buenos Aires for their South American business expansion.

Shortly following in 2000, another international distribution center was opened in Osaka, Japan. This new facility helped round out the company's worldwide reach, with their products now sold in over 60 countries.

The new millennium brought yet another change; the company's name became Crosstex International. With their proud and impressive history, the company was honored as a finalist for Ernst & Young's Entrepreneur of the Year 2000 on Long Island and as recipient of the Hauppauge Industrial Association's (HIA) Small Business Achievement Award for 2000.

The company has come far, with their new name and logo; worldwide representation as an industry leader; and a diverse senior management team. Two things, however, still remain: the desire to produce the most innovative and highest quality products possible and to maintain a faith in family to create a reality from a dream—just as Frank Orofino and Norman Steinberg did so many years ago.

Left to right: Les Gershon, Ron Psimas, Andy Whitehead, and Sheldon Fisher.

# BOWNE
## SIDNEY B. BOWNE & SON, LLP
## BOWNE MANAGEMENT SYSTEMS, INC.
## ROUTESMART TECHNOLOGIES, INC.

Over one hundred years ago, engineering excellence was firmly established by Sidney & William Bowne. Today, with three affiliated companies, the multi-disciplined, 125-person organization continues to provide exceptional service.

BOWNE is at the forefront of developing innovative engineering and information technology solutions for federal, municipal, and private clients. One of the reasons for the firm's great success is its dedicated staff which includes individuals with the firm for over 57 years. Whether working for a small Long Island community to solve a drainage problem or a large hi-tech firm on an imaging project, each client receives technical expertise and personal attention.

The following reflects the chronological timeline of Bowne's growth on Long Island.

c. 1895-William H. Bowne opens a surveying firm in Mineola, NY.

c. 1904-Sidney Bowne begins his career working with his uncle, William H. Bowne.

c. 1922-The firm of Sidney B. Bowne is established.

*Engineering design for the new Hempstead Bus Terminal successfully completed in 1993.*

*The Bowne Team in 1908.*

c. 1930-Bowne expands its corporate office, maintaining a presence in the Mineola community.

c. 1952-With offices in Italy and Iran, international work begins for Bowne. They form a joint venture known as Litchfield, Whiting, Bowne, Panero, and Severud.

c. 1960s-Design and surveying continues to increase as more and more roadway projects are completed. Bowne works on large-scale projects such as Jones Beach, Old Bethpage Village Restoration, and LIRR commuter stations.

c. 1970s-Bowne plans, designs, and manages the construction of the largest commuter parking structure in Hicksville, under budget and in record time.

c. 1982-Bowne Management Systems is established as clients' move forward with computerization. Information Technology (IT) solutions include geographic information systems, custom applications, and systems integration.

c. 1985-A delegation from the Beijing Research Institute and Energy Ministry of the People's Republic of China meets with Bowne to develop a computerized energy distribution system.

c. 1986-Bowne develops RouteSmart software to manage business and transportation logistics. An affiliated company, Bowne Distinct, is established to create and market Route-Smart which today operates under the auspices of Route-Smart Technologies.

c. 1990s-Bowne's engineering and IT services take off! Bowne continues to successfully complete civil, environmental, and IT projects for municipalities, high tech companies, state and federal agencies.

The firm looks forward to meeting its clients' challenges in the new millennium.

# DIONICS, INC.

*....against all odds.*

Dionics, Inc., founded in December 1968, has done some very unusual things during its corporate history. Most of these involve technical developments in the company's chosen field of semiconductors and micro-electronics. Perhaps the most unusual thing it has done is to survive "against all odds." And even more unusual, it has done so twice.

Most new companies fail. They fail during their first few years, frequently due to insufficient funding and some-times just due to poor management. Eighteen months after Dionics' relatively under-funded beginnings, however, the company was self-support-ing on a cash-flow basis. Its unusual Dielectric Isolation (DI) technology gave rise to superior electronic perfor-mance, which made Dionics' chip components very desirable for the emerging hybrid-circuit market. Dionics was well on the way to its first survival "against all odds," a new small under-funded company that did *not* fail in its first few years.

But while Dionics was pursu-ing its slow and steady growth, the semiconductor industry was

*Cleanroom assembly station where Dionics SSRs are made.*

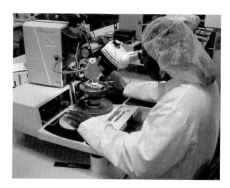

changing dramatically. Soon the relatively new Dionics factory, equipped with state-of-the-art machinery when the company started, was unable to process the newer, large, raw material silicon wafers. Lacking the financial means to re-equip itself, the company shifted its strategy to the only other viable one—supplying niche products on smaller wafers. Here the value would stem from the product's performance, not the size of the wafer used to make it.

The niche strategy succeeded for a number of years, and resulted in Dionics developing

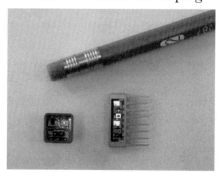

*Uncovered Dionics SSRs near pencil for size reference.*

many specialized products. One of these, used by a gas pump manufacturer, grew into a very high-volume applica-tion. Year after year, the quanti-ties grew and Dionics soon found itself in the troubling position of having a single, dominant customer who repre-sented close to half its $3 million sales volume. New products intended to dilute the impact of this large customer took too long to reach meaning-ful sales levels, and one day the inevitable happened. After eight years of production, the customer did a redesign and no longer needed the Dionics

*AIRBUS flight-controls use Dionics Solid State Relays.*

high-voltage Integrated Circuit. Within 18-months, sales vol-ume had dropped by 50 percent. Disaster loomed.

Cutting back on every con-ceivable expenditure, the company went into survival mode. It was soon drained of cash, and all out of borrowing power. Forced by its bank to sell one of its two buildings, the company consolidated oper-ations into its one remaining building.

Shunning the protection of Chapter 11 bankruptcy, how-ever, the company and its loyal employees, under the leadership of one of its founders, president Bernard Kravitz, began the long march back. This time, the new prod-uct line that clicked was a family of Solid State Relays (SSRs) that were designed into the flight-control systems of the AIRBUS aircraft.

At the time of this writing, 32 years after its founding, the company has again, appar-ently survived "against all odds." Nothing is forever, and no one can predict the future, but Kravitz, in reviewing the company's "near-death" experi-ence, likes to quote Winston Churchill: "Never, never, NEVER give up!"

# LONG ISLAND UNIVERSITY

No history of Long Island, particularly one that delves into its explosive population growth since World War II, could be complete without the substantial contributions of Long Island University, the Island's largest private institution of higher learning. In much the same way, no history of the university would be complete without the development of the Island: university and island grew up together. Founded in 1926, Long Island University marks its 75th anniversary in the year 2001.

The story begins where the island does, geographically speaking—in downtown Brooklyn, a place in the early 20th century of industry, optimism and a burgeoning population ranging from socialites to stevedores. Rising expectations called for institutions of higher education; prejudice excluded many groups from the institutions that existed.

Long Island University was established to open doors and

*The refurbished lobby of Brooklyn's former Paramount Theater symbolizes the first campus of a University open solely to merit and promise.*

*As the suburbs grew, the University's C.W. Post campus created new uses for the distinguished mansion of Marjorie Merriweather Post.*

minds solely on the basis of merit and promise—a university of access to the American dream. As the Island's population moved eastward so did the university, and today it meets educational, cultural and economic needs not only in New York City, but in Nassau and Suffolk counties and points beyond.

After the war the university established three more campuses—C.W. Post, Brentwood and Southampton College. At first, expansion into Nassau County, with the C.W. Post Campus in Brookville in 1954, was a response to the needs of returning veterans. The Brentwood "branch" in Suffolk County was a further commitment to an expanding suburbia and its legions of working or homemaking adults. Southampton College, founded in 1963, responded to the East End's desire for a higher education catalyst of its own. The University created the Arnold and Marie Schwartz College of Pharmacy and Health Sciences in 1979 (renaming and expanding the Brooklyn College of Pharmacy, founded in 1886). Also established were the graduate campuses, for adult learners seeking Masters' degrees, north of New York City in Westchester

County (1965) and Rockland County (1980). The Friends World Program joined the University at Southampton College in 1991.

While each unit has a distinct character and curriculum, at the same time they give Long Island and its New York neighbors one of the most diverse private institutions in America—and the country's eighth largest. Enrollments total nearly 30,000 undergraduate, graduate and non-credit students. Thanks to growing financial support from corporations and private donors, between 1985 and 2000 the University completed more than $175 million worth of construction and modernization, added two Ph.D. programs, enhanced scholarships, introduced a large information technology initiative, and witnessed a tenfold increase in its endowment.

Through the decades Long Island University has educated a vast proportion of Long Island's teachers, librarians and public servants; it has prepared countless men and women for entry into professional schools of law and medicine.

*"The Lincoln Center of Long Island," Tilles Center for the Performing Arts created a cultural hub for the evolving region.*

Its programs in business and accounting, as well as its offerings in the arts, communications, humanities and the sciences, are respected nationally for the quality of their graduates. Between 1975 and 2000, 35 Southampton College graduates won Fulbright awards for advanced study. Celebrated University alumni include Gary Winnick, founder, chairman and chief executive officer of Pacific Capital Group, the investment banking firm that started Global Crossing, one of the most successful new firms in global telecommunications; Terry Semel, former chairman and co-CEO of Warner Brothers and Warner Music Group; Louis Lemberger, a leader of the pharmaceutical team that developed Prozac; the novelist and screenwriter Nicholas Pileggi ("Goodfellas," "Casino"); and marine biologist Sandra Shumway.

Since its earliest days, the University has extended its ser-vices to the entire community. It was the first institution in the region to open its regularly scheduled classes to adults, paving the way for one of the nation's first "Weekend Colleges," and for its present cornucopia of continuing education offerings. The University's WPBX-FM 88.3 in Southampton brought public radio to Long Island in 1993; the Long Island University Public Radio Network, featuring jazz and news, later grew to include WCWP-FM 88.1 in Brookville.

As a cultural center for all of Long Island the University is a recognized leader. Tilles Center for the Performing Arts, on the C.W. Post Campus, is the Island's premier concert facility, with a seating capacity of 2,200 in the main hall for world-class presentations in music, dance and theater. The Brooklyn Campus's Salena and Nathan Resnik Galleries, the Hillwood Art Museum at C.W. Post and the Avram Gallery at Southampton College are among the many spaces given to exhibition, lecture and research

for student and community.

As the new century opened, the campus-community relationship reached a new and logical level: C.W. Post became a center for the study of Long Island history. Adding to special collections aready in place, in 1999 the library received two important archives of primary material.

Fittingly, one of those is the papers and memorabilia of Arthur T. Roth, an innovative banker who made banking approachable and mortgages readily available, changing the scope of banking and the face of the Island. The other is the Cedar Swamp Historical Society Collection, a trove of documents, memorabilia and books illuminating Long Island history since pre-Revolutionary War days. The new donations testify once again to the community's faith in Long Island University, and to the University's dedication to Long Island.

*The ambience of the University's Southampton College is captured in the evocative colonial windmill that stands on one of the site's rolling hills.*

# MARDERS

Marders Nursery was established by Charles (Charlie) and Kathleen Marder in the living room of Charlie's mother's home in 1977. Always self-employed, Charles and Kathleen began their career in the Green Industry after they graduated college by raking lawns, cutting firewood, and providing a tree transplanting service to residents in the towns of Easthampton and Southampton. Charlie was one of the first landscapers in the Hamptons to employ a "tree spade" (a Vermeer "Big John") in transplanting large red cedars (Juniperus virginiana) from local horse and cattle pastures to new estates in the seaside communities of Sagaponack, Georgica, and Wickapogue. A tree spade is a mechanically-operated shovel, and this unique invention transformed what was once a costly, seasonal, and weather dependent activity into a year-round business. As Charlie once commented, "the tree spade was the personal computer of landscaping" and his use of such cutting-edge equipment added credibility and authority to their newly-established venture.

Charlie and Kathleen met while they attented Ripon College, a small liberal arts school in Wisconsin. Kathleen (nee Foran) was born in Michigan and was raised in the suburban communities of Bloomfield Hills (near Detroit) and Westport (Connecticut). Charles Marder was one of three children and is an 11th generation East Ender. He was born in Flushing in 1953, but was raised in his parents' household (Norma Edwards Marder) in the hamlet of Springs. Springs is one of

several small communities that dot the South Fork and the Edwards were one of the first European families to settle the area in the 1600s. The hamlet was named after fresh-water springs and those who lived in and around the brooks that flow into Accabonac Creek were known, somewhat derisively, as "Bonackers" because they were self-employed, independent, and

produced a living from such maritime activities as fishing, claming, and harvesting salt hay.

Although the Edwards' were not were not Bonackers, their entrepreneurial and independent spirit influenced Charles during his early childhood and formative years in school. He excelled at sports, became captain of the Bonackers, the local football team, and was elected class president of East Hampton High

School three years out of four. Along with leadership skills, Charlie honed his social and entrepreneurial skills by vending hot dogs at horse shows sponsored by his sister, collecting copper, iron, and other scrap metals, and by doing yard work for the actors, artists, and novelists that summered in Springs and the adjacent communities. Charlie received a scholarship to play football at Ripon but was injured during his sophomore year and went on to become a Fine Arts major specializing in sculpting. He and Kathleen met while attending a class in Art History. Erwin Breithaupt, the professor who taught this and a series of related classes, had a profound affect on Charles and Kathleen. The late Professor Breithaupt was influenced by the Swiss architect Charles-Edouard Le Corbusier and the American Frank Lloyd Wright and he instilled in both a way and means of approaching and resolving problems and they took this model with them when they graduated. Charles and Kathleen married in 1976 and they returned to Charlie's mother's house where they decided to start their own business.

As in his childhood, Charles and Kathleen began providing a service to summertime and the growing community of year-round residents by doing yard work and designing and planting flower, herb, and vegetable gardens. Ever perceptive, Charlie found a niche for his business in the influx of new homeowners and the expanding market for large, specimen, and unusual materials. Recognizing the authority and credibility equipment gave to a fledging business, he rented a tree spade and set in motion a business plan whereby he would provide large, mature trees for homeowners who did not want to wait for smaller-sized material to mature. He scouted local pastures, removed large unwanted trees (for a nominal fee), and transplanted them to the yards and gardens of new homeowners. Landscaping in the Hamptons is competitive, and Charlie offered a two-year guarantee and replaced free of charge all plants that failed to survive in a friendly and judicious manner. He was applauded for his honesty and reliability.

It was during these early and in many ways formative years (1977-1982) that Charlie and Kathleen learned through their experience the creativity associated with horticulture and landscape design. Charlie soon realized that their competition, a number of long-established landscape contractors, had a rather superficial approach to aesthetics, planting a tree here and a shrub there in repetitious, cookie-cutter-like designs. Rather than using run-of-the mill material and creating superficial designs, they began to employ non-standard varieties that were hardy to Long Island but were rarely employed. Unlike other industries, trees and shrubs are not manufactured on an assembly line but are nurtured over decades, and Charlie's use of large, unusual, and specimen materials mandated hiring a tree and shrub buyer to search the country for nurseries and rare-plant growers who specialized in such materials.

Every business has a "big break" and Charlie's was no exception. As his reputation spread, Charlie was contacted by the artist and sugar magnate Alfonso A. Ossorio. Ossorio had purchased a 60-acre estate known as the Creeks and set about transforming it into a world-class arboretum. Ossorio contacted Charlie to aid and assist him in his quest for rare and specimen material and they quickly became friends sharing a mutual interest in rare plants, horticulture, and the principles of design. Their relationship matured and developed over the course of the decade it took to complete the million dollar project. It was through referrals by Ossorio that Charlie was contacted by fellow artists, gallery-owners, and plant collectors like Louis K. Meisel and Eric Lustbader.

In 1982 Charlie and Kathleen rented a barn on Montauk Highway in the village of Bridgehampton, and Marders became a retail nursery. As with landscape design, the garden shop, soon to be known as the "Landscape Store," specialized in rare and unusual annuals and perennials along with trees and shrubs, and provided an opportunity for Charlie and Kathleen to bring their artistic background to bear on a retail nursery. As Charlie commented in a recent interview (cf. *The East Hampton Star*, March 1999), "People are much more educated and sophisticated about gardening today than they were a decade ago and want something more than 14 varieties of day-glow impatiens." In many ways their retail operation is directly responsible for this education. They staged a series of public events in which rare and unusual plants like Japanese maples (Acer palmatum), European beeches (Fagus sylvatica), and weeping hemlocks (Tsuga canadensis "sargenti") were treated, not as sterile objects, but living subjects to be cultivated for a lifetime. Their ideas and sensibilities struck a responsive chord, and along with the older clients who frequented their shop they attracted new clients like Martha Stewart and Stephen Spielberg. Their business grew and expanded throughout the 1980s. They soon outgrew the location on Montauk Highway and purchased an 18-acre parcel on Snake Hollow Road in 1992, enabling them to realize a vision. Charlie and Kathleen purchased a post and beam barn in Pennsylvania and reconstructed it on the new site. They expanded the array of goods and services they offered to include lawn maintenance and irrigation, a potscaping service, distinctive garden ornaments and statuary, and most recently, an assortment of antiques imported directly from Europe.

Suffice it to say that what began 20-odd years ago in the living room of Charlie's mother has blossomed into a premier landscape design firm employing 200 people in a unique, arboretum-like setting. Customers here can meander through what may be one of the largest selections of rare, unusual, and specimen trees and shrubs to be found in the Northeast.

But the story does not end there. As part of their commitment to the quality of life on Long Island, Charlie and Kathleen have removed all chemical pesticides, herbicides, fungicides and fertilizers from their shelves and have replaced them with eco-friendly organic and natural products, making Marders a truly 21st-century corporation.

# NORTH SHORE-LONG ISLAND JEWISH HEALTH SYSTEM

*The North Shore-Long Island Jewish Health System's mission is to improve the health of the communities it serves by providing the highest quality clinical care; educating current and future generations of health care professionals; searching for new advances in medicine through biomedical research; promoting health education; and caring for the entire community regardless of ability to pay.*

In the early 1950s, Long Island was in the midst of a post-war baby boom. Farms were replaced by new houses, and to meet the health care needs of the new residents, hospitals were built, foremost among them North Shore University Hospital in Manhasset and Long Island Jewish Hospital (LIJ) in New Hyde Park. Located just a mile-and-a-half apart, each was dedicated to quality—in health care, scientific research, medical education and community involvement.

Over the years, each became a premier provider of health care in the region. North Shore grew into a 10-hospital health system and

*Researchers at the North Shore-Long Island Jewish Health System focus on disease-oriented investigations to develop new and more effective therapies for patients.*

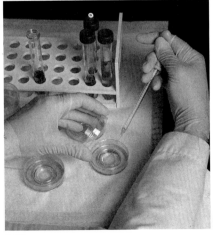

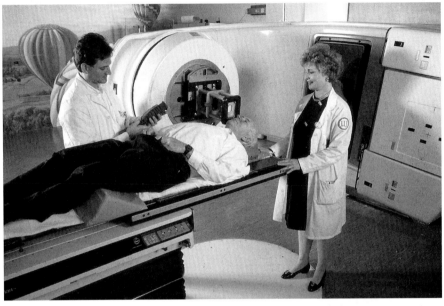

*Medical care provided at North Shore-LIJ is enhanced by state-of-the -art technology. For example, the system's linear accelerators and three-dimensional planning systems are the ultimate in radiation treatment.*

LIJ became a medical center with a free-standing children's hospital and an internationally-renowned psychiatric facility. These developments were hallmarks of progress; the commitment to quality remained steadfast.

As the population on Long Island grew, so too did its health care needs. Meeting those changing needs required innovative and bold leadership. In 1996, a group of Trustees representing LIJ and North Shore met to discuss a solution. Their answer was a daring one: to merge the North Shore Health System and Long Island Jewish Hospital, creating a health care system of national size and quality.

Today, the North Shore-Long Island Jewish Health System has a $3 billion budget, with 29,000 employees, 6,500 physicians and 7,500 nurses. Its 14 hospitals include North Shore University Hospital-Manhasset; Long Island Jewish Medical Center; Franklin Hospital Medical Center; Hillside Hospital; Huntington Hospital; North Shore University Hospitals at Forest Hills, Glen

Cove, Plainview, and Syosset; Schneider Children's Hospital; Southside Hospital; and Staten Island University Hospital-North, South & Doctors Hospital.

Its Hospice Care Network is the largest in the region. The System also includes five home health agencies, a 40-vehicle Emergency Medical Services and Transport Department; two long-term care facilities—the Center for Extended Care and Rehabilitation and the Franklin Hospital Geriatric Division—and more than 100 specialty and primary ambulatory care facilities. Its extensive affiliations include the Association for Adults and Children with Developmental and Learning Disabilities and Sterling Glen Communities, senior housing communities.

But the true story of North Shore-LIJ is told by different numbers: two million ambula-

*Saul B. Katz, left, and Roy J. Zuckerberg, then co-chairmen of the North Shore-Long Island Jewish Health System, sign the documents merging the two systems in October 1997. David R. Dantzker, M.D., left, and John S.T. Gallagher, then co-presidents and CEOs, look on.*

tory and clinic visits; 110,000 ambulatory surgical procedures; 575,000 home health visits; 200,000 inpatient discharges; 385,000 emergency room visits; and 22,000 newborn deliveries! The Health System touches virtually every member of the community.

Despite its large size, the medical staff, management team and volunteer corps work as one to care for the sick, to serve the poor and to make the community well, every day of the year.

The merger of North Shore and LIJ changed the way health care is delivered throughout Long Island, and its benefits will be seen for years to come. For the first time, a health network has made strengthening the quality of care at each of its hospitals and facilities its most important goal. The Health System's maxim, "*setting new standards in health care*" reflects this commitment. Its success was recognized when it made history as the first health care network to receive the Joint Commission on Healthcare Accreditation's prestigious Codman Award for outcomes measurement to achieve health care quality.

The Health System's mission goes beyond providing excellent care. It includes training the next generation of health professionals. Accordingly, North Shore-LIJ provides professional education and training each year to more than 1,100 residents and fellows in 55 accredited programs and teaches over 1,300 medical students from five affiliated medical schools. It also provides current practitioners with an extensive continuing medical education program.

It especially means being a good neighbor. Its physicians, nurses and staff generously give of their time to help improve the health of their neighbors. With more than 850 free community education programs, a mobile pediatric health van, a widespread professional speakers bureau and participation at health fairs throughout Long Island, to name just a few of its programs, the Health System is truly a part of the community.

Finally, medical research is also an important component of the Health System's mission. Each year, the North Shore-Long Island Jewish Research Institute receives nearly $30 million in research grants, making it one of the premier institutes of its kind. The Institute has special expertise in neuroscience; psychiatry and movement disorders; inflammatory and infectious diseases; molecular and cell biology; human genetics; and in the development of viral vectors for gene therapy and oncology.

As North Shore-LIJ grows and evolves, its goal will be to expand each of these initiatives and to continue reaching out to all those who have never had access to the kind and quality of programs and services it provides. Only then can it say that it is truly *setting new standards in health care.*

*Patient-centered is the word that best describes the treatment services provided by a team of empathetic professionals at the North Shore-Long Island Jewish Health System.*

# NU HORIZONS ELECTRONICS CORPORATION

In the early '50s, after the Korean War, the Lower East Side of New York City was home to many of the original distributors of electronic components. The military establishment, spurred on by the Cold War, needed components for the latest in electronic warfare. Manufacturers of radar, guidance systems, communication equipment and instrumentation for weaponry were scouring the market for suppliers of the latest technologies. At the same time, the nascent television industry was taking off and the telephone, radio and "hi fi" makers were also growing at a steady pace. Distribution was needed to supply not only the major manufacturers, but also the hundreds of new entries springing up all over the country. Distributors in the City began moving to the suburbs of Long Island for more economical space and a higher standard of living for their employees. Industry leaders such as Hamilton/Avnet, Arrow Electronics, Schweber, Milgray, Diplomat and Jaco all called Long Island home. In the '60s and '70s the electronics distribution industry saw dramatic expansion and

*New Nu Horizons Building.*

many of these companies opened branches throughout the country. Hundreds of small distributors were started and many failed or were purchased by the larger distributors. The early-'80s brought a new era to the electronics industry as the personal computer started its pervasive takeover of technology in everyday life.

In 1982 three veterans with a vision and a strong motivation for success founded Nu Horizons Electronics Corporation. The industry didn't really need another distributor of electronic components, and many critics predicted an early demise. With a private placement of $500,000 collected mostly from friends and relatives, the company entered the arena of selling semiconductors and related electronic components. Started with nine employees and a 2,500 square foot office and warehouse, Nu Horizons shipped nearly $18 million in its first full year in business. Thinking back, Arthur Nadata, president and CEO says, "We had a lot of friends in the industry who trusted us and supported us with their business." Irving Lubman, chairman of the board remembers

the early days when he was a combination salesman, shipping clerk and janitor. "We did everything from opening the boxes of components to cleaning the bathrooms, but it was always fun." Richard Schuster, president of the NIC Components subsidiary says, "To this day the three founders are hands-on and have an open door policy to all of our employees." Concentrating on the New York Metropolitan region and selling mainly to makers of military electronic products, the company relied on limited suppliers and a relatively small customer list.

Almost 18 years later the company will have revenues of over $600 million, more than 10,000 customers, approximately 500 employees, and sales offices throughout the United States and most recently in England, Singapore, Hong Kong and Malaysia. However, even as a global player in the dynamic electronics industry, Nu Horizons is still rooted in Long Island. Headquarters, encompassing top management, finance, training, engineering and

*Left to right: Richard Schuster, vice president, secretary and director; Arthur Nadata, president and CEO; and Irving Lubman, chairman of the board and COO.*

the major portion of its inventory still resides on "the Island."

Nine months after its inception Nu Horizons did its initial public offering and was listed on the NASDAQ national market (NUHC). The capital raised was used for opening new sales offices and increasing inventories. One year later the company did another equity offering, again using the proceeds for expansion. While the market slowed down in the mid-'80s, Nu Horizons continued to invest in its infrastructure and became the youngest company to ever be listed on the American Stock Exchange. In 1992 the company decided to return to a listing on NASDAQ where it continues to be listed today. In the late-'80s Nu Horizons made a critical decision affecting its sales and marketing strategy for years to come. The electronics distribution industry encompasses quite a few large, diversified entities selling everything from advanced microprocessors to wire and cable to switches and batteries. There are also numerous smaller distributors who are localized in their sales and limited in their product offering. Few of these distributors offered a high degree of engineering expertise, which was mostly left to the manufacturer of the components and their independent sales representatives. Nu Horizons decided to become the leading engineering distributor of semiconductor products. "Demand creation" became their motto and philosophy: add value to the customer by bringing him the latest technologies and helping him design his products so they would be more successful in their market. Add value to the supplier as a conduit for their latest technologies to the emerging growth

customer base. Nu Horizons has the highest engineer to sales ratio per capita in the industry today. Its sales people are trained to understand the product they sell and offer a level of service to customers that is not available from its competitors.

This is why Nu Horizons represents a limited number of suppliers. Nu Horizons' sales people are more knowledgeable and at the same time give more attention to the vendor than others. Nu Horizons represents such industry leading companies as Sun Microsystems, Xilinx, Hyundai, ST Microelectronics, Maxim, NEC passives and Hitachi. With over 300 sales people around the world they are now selling such industry giants as Cisco, Nortel, Motorola, Dell Computer, Symbol Technologies, Ademco, SCI, Solectron, and others.

In the late-'80s Nu Horizons went back to the NASDAQ National Market and recently has been one of its top performers. The company has been recognized as one of the top 50 Long Island public companies for the last five years. In October 1999, Nu Horizons was recognized by Electronic Buyers News as one of the Best Managed companies in the Electronics Industry. Arthur Nadata, the president and CEO has been named Entrepreneur of the Year on two separate occasions. The company is also involved in many community activities and charities. Recently Nu Horizons sponsored a golf outing with proceeds going to the Ronald McDonald House Foundation. In the past, the company has sponsored baseball game outings for homeless children and contributed to the

Henry Viscardi School for the physically challenged.

Looking around, one can see the pervasive use of electronics in every walk of life. Cell phones, laptop computers, PDAs, video games and CD players are on the streets, in restaurants, on trains and planes, and of course in places of business. Driving in the car people listen to radio and CD players, talk on car phones and program directions on their navigation system. Under the hood are a host of microprocessors controlling ignition, braking, diagnostics, air bags, temperature controls and suspension. Homes have the latest in video and audio technologies, smart appliances, security and alarm systems, personal computers, phones and intercoms, toys and games and medical monitoring instruments. With the dramatic growth in usage of the internet more electronic components are needed to run the hardware. Nu Horizons Electronics is supplying state-of-the-art components and engineering expertise for all the above applications and many more in the business and industrial world. Demand will grow and so will the Nu Horizons organization, to service the electronics market of the future.

---

*Nu Horizons' investment in a 50,000 square foot sophisticated, state-of-the-art, material handling and distribution facility further positions the company as a world class electronic component distributor.*

# PEOPLE'S ALLIANCE FEDERAL CREDIT UNION

Looking for the best place to take care of your finances? Well, look no further. People's Alliance Federal Credit Union (PAFCU) is a not-for-profit financial organization dedicated to offering exceptional service to its members. With headquarters conveniently located on Wireless Boulevard in the middle of the Hauppauge Industrial Park, the credit union makes the needs of its membership their top priority.

It all began in Baltimore, Maryland. A group of Pan American employees thought it would be a great idea to form a credit union. They pooled together $25, the amount necessary to pay as a fee, and applied to the U.S. Farm Bureau Administration for a charter. Charter number 3633 was granted on January 29, 1940, and the credit union was born. It was named Pan American Airways Co. (Atlantic Division) Federal Credit Union.

In the early days, PAFCU was basically a one-man, out-of-pocket operation. Volunteer field collectors at various work locations accepted payments, which were then turned over to the treasurer. The first full-time employee was hired in 1942. The early one-man staff operated from a shared desk at the LaGuardia Airport Seaplane Hanger.

In the beginning passbooks were issued to each member and all transactions had to be recorded manually by a teller (cashier) in the office. Quarterly statements replaced the passbooks in 1954.

In 1990, People's Alliance's main office moved to Hauppauge and in 1993, the credit union changed its name to People's Alliance Federal Credit Union. PAFCU today has 93 employees of its own and serves 40,000 employees of over 300 different

companies, mostly from Long Island. At People's Alliance there are no customers—everyone is a member and owner of the credit union and receives friendly, respectful service from a dedicated, experienced and supportive staff.

President Nicholas M. Lacetera, for example, has been with the credit union for 36 years. "The biggest asset People's Alliance has is its members. They add to our strength simply by using the credit union on a regular basis," says Lacetera. "By doing so, they ensure that PAFCU's philosophy of "People's Helping People to a Better Quality of Life" will endure for many years to come."

A credit union is a cooperative financial institution organized to serve people who have a common bond of association, such as employment with a company or membership in an organization. People's Alliance is a federally-chartered credit union whose operations are supervised by a U.S. government agency,

*People's Alliance Federal Credit Union's headquarters in the Hauppauge Industrial Park.*

the National Credit Union Administration (NCUA), which also insures deposits up to $100,000.

Because it is a non-profit cooperative, PAFCU can offer a complete package of very consumer-friendly services at very favorable rates. For example, checking accounts are free, and even the checks themselves are free if a member uses automatic deposit into his or her account on payday. Loan rates are generally lower than at for-profit institutions, and dividends on savings accounts are higher. Members can purchase $500 Share Certificates to earn even higher rates.

Services including direct deposit, home banking, Bill Payer, Tel-Me 24-Hour Automated Telephone Service, and Loans by Phone were created to allow PAFCU members to handle their finances at any time, at any place. People's Alliance also offers various loans and mortgages designed to help its members live more comfortably. They even offer MEMBERS Financial Services which has an array of products and services such as mutual funds, stocks, bonds, tax deferred annuities, life insurance and other financial planning services.

People's Alliance has seven locations and over $132 million in assets. The NCUA has not only given People's Alliance a top rating for its financial performance, but has also granted PAFCU blanket approval to immediately enroll any company located within the Hauppauge Industrial Park.

The credit union takes its ties to the community very seriously.

PAFCU employees are your neighbors, and the local schools, companies and families are the credit union's neighbors. It is for this reason that they participate in many philanthropic endeavors, such as literacy programs and the Marty Lyons Foundation. They have implemented programs such as Groundhog Job Shadow Day, which gives local teenagers a chance to "shadow" a workplace mentor during a day on the job at PAFCU. It gives the student's real, up-close experience learning how the skills they learn at school are put into action in the workplace.

"We realize that our members *are* the credit union. Through effective management and con-

trolling expenses, we work hard to keep the fees charged to our members as low as possible," says Lacetera. "Through listening to our members, getting involved in the community, and introducing more and more services every year; we strive to fulfill all the financial needs of our membership. I give thanks for our strong relationship with our members who make it all possible."

*PAFCU executive staff, seated left to right: Nicholas M. Lacetera, president; Joanne Steigerwald, vp operations; Carol A. Allen, vp finance. Standing left to right: Walter M. O'Connell, vp internal controls; William O'Connell, Sr. vp operations; John A. Romanchek, executive vice president; Patricia A. O'Connell, vp human resources.*

# POLYTECHNIC UNIVERSITY

Founded in 1854, Polytechnic University, the nation's second oldest science and engineering school, has been an education leader on Long Island for four decades.

Today, Polytechnic is undergoing an extraordinary transformation on Long Island. It has strengthened and expanded its graduate programs by creating a Graduate Center for Professional Studies. The Center, conducting programs in strategic locations, offers trend-setting courses and degrees in cutting-edge disciplines, including wireless, e-commerce, telecommunications, computer science, software engineering and technology management. For the first time, the University is offering three executive-format masters programs on Long Island: the Master of Engineering in Wireless, the Master of Science in Management of Technology and the Master of Science in Telecommunications Information Management. These three

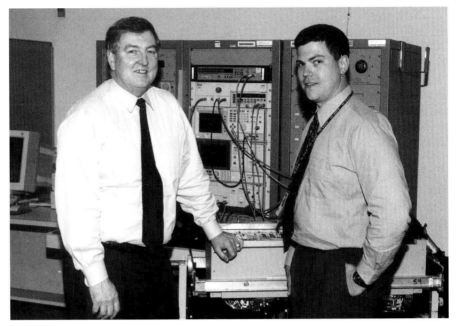

*Polytechnic produces leaders: James M. Smith, left, president and chief operating officer of AIL Systems Inc. in Deer Park, credits much of his success to a Polytechnic master's degree in electrical engineering, which he earned part time. David E. Fowler, an Engineer 3 at AIL, earned his B.S. in mechanical engineering from Polytechnic and is pursuing a master's degree at the school while working full time.*

*Graduate faculty at Polytechnic University on Long Island are expert teachers with real-world professional experience and have won prestigious professional and academic prizes.*

masters programs provide exceptional opportunities for mid-career professionals who prefer to continue working full time and attend school part time on a concentrated and accelerated basis on weekends.

"Long Island is a technology-based economy and society," says Dr. Ivan Frisch, Polytechnic's provost, executive vice president and director of the University's new Graduate Center. "We all face the challenge of upgrading our knowledge and skills, adapting to new markets and leading innovations for the rest of the country. The keystone to meeting this challenge is education, re-education and continuing education. That is our mission on Long Island."

Over the past 10 years, close to 900 students on Long Island have graduated from

Polytechnic's graduate programs in engineering, science and technology, and over 1,600 students have taken courses. Among the University's graduates are more than 200 top executives of Long Island firms.

One executive, James M. Smith, president and chief operating officer of AIL Systems Inc., a defense, electronics and aerospace company based in Deer Park, Long Island, took evening classes at Polytechnic's Long Island program to earn a masters of electrical engineering in 1971. "Polytechnic gave me a first-class engineering education," Smith says. "The strong fundamentals I got at Polytechnic helped me and countless others on Long Island solidify

*Students at Polytechnic University's Graduate Center for Professional Studies on Long Island have access to high-tech facilities, including state-of-the-art laboratories and programs in wireless, e-commerce, telecommunications, computer science, software engineering and management of technology.*

our careers in engineering and other technical fields."

Polytechnic's enduring relationships with business and industry were a unique draw for Smith. "Polytechnic has a big influence on Long Island's technical pre-eminence," he says. "Continuing my career while earning a graduate degree was possible only because of that relationship."

Polytechnic's transformation is made possible by the University's $275 million Campaign for Polytechnic Fulfilling the American Dream, including a $175 million bequest from the estates of Donald F. Othmer, a long-time Polytechnic professor of chemical engineering, and his wife, Mildred Topp Othmer. Their bequest is the

largest, private cash gift ever to an American university.

To guide the transformation, the University, led by President David C. Chang, has completed Strategic Planning 2000, a bold plan to expand graduate studies on Long Island while consolidating all undergraduate programs at a new world-class campus at MetroTech Center in Brooklyn. The transformation is well under way. The Graduate Center for Professional Studies has been established on Long Island, and more than $100 million is being invested in capital and intellectual improvements on the MetroTech campus.

One of the most important improvements at MetroTech is a $41 million, 16-story, 400-bed residence hall, a facility that allows Polytechnic to attract top students, not only from Long Island but also nationally, and to increase its undergraduate enrollment from 1,800 to 2,800. This enlarged pool of skilled and motivated students is a major source of talent for industry on Long Island.

Under Strategic Planning 2000, the university is building upon its stellar history as a leader in research and education and is the metropolitan area's pre-eminent resource in science and technology. Polytechnic's roster of historic figures includes Herman Mark, the "father of polymer chemistry," who established the Polymer Research Institute at the University in 1942, and Dr. Ernst Weber, former president of Polytechnic and a pioneer in microwave technology.

Today, Polytechnic faculty continue garnering honors and acclaim: six faculty, including Dr. Frisch, are members of the

prestigious National Academy of Engineering. Three are among the 11 winners of the IEEE's Heinrich Hertz Award, initiated in 1989 to recognize outstanding achievements in Hertizian (radio waves), and 11 are IEEE Fellows, an honor limited to one-tenth of one percent of the organization's membership.

Polytechnic boasts three Nobel Prize winners: two alumni, Martin L. Perl, who won the Prize in physics in 1955, and Gertrude Elion, who won the Prize in medicine in 1988, and a faculty member, Professor Rudolph Marcus, who won the prize in chemistry in 1992.

"The direction Polytechnic is taking in this new century is impressive," says Smith. "It should guarantee its standing as a first-rate school for a long time to come."

*Polytechnic University is at the frontier of research and has increased its commitment to provide part-time cutting-edge graduate courses on Long Island to allow professionals to advance their careers while working full time.*

# SCHEINE, FUSCO, BRANDENSTEIN & RADA PC

Edward R. Scheine and Victor Fusco, former classmates from Brooklyn Law School, founded the firm of Scheine, Fusco, Brandenstein & Rada, P.C. on October 16, 1978. They began in one small, shared office in another attorney's suite, and within a few short months, the practice moved into its own suite at 170 Broadway, New York City.

Both partners, having acquired experience working with clients with disabilities and serious injuries, chose to focus their efforts in helping working people maintain their lifestyle and dignity by obtaining financial and medical benefits from insurance companies and governmental agencies.

At the outset, the firm concentrated on Workers' Compensation and Social Security disability claims. It rapidly expanded. In 1979 it added an office in Hauppauge, Long Island. Later that year, Richard J. Brandenstein, another classmate, joined the firm to staff the Suffolk County office and assist

*Front view of the Scheine, Fusco, Brandenstein & Rada PC main office.*

with the growing practice. The firm's growth continued. An office was opened in Hempstead in 1980, at which time a Personal Injury Division was added. In 1982, Milan Rada joined the firm. In addition to his acumen in Social Security Law, he added expertise in the areas of Municipal Retirement Law and Appellate Law.

In 1993 the firm relocated and consolidated their headquarters in the center of Long Island. Choosing Woodbury as their main office, the firm purchased a 17,000 square foot facility. With a Long Island-based headquarters, the firm was able to attract many skilled workers, including technical experts furloughed from Grumman. Through upgrades

in their automation systems, the firm now controls six regional office locations with three more on the drawing board for 2001. The firm has represented over 50,000 clients and has appeared in over 300,000 hearings and court appearances.

When asked what makes his firm different from most, Edward Scheine quickly replies, "Our staff! We have always been blessed to find compassionate, family-oriented staff members whose core values mirror our own. Our clients have found empathetic service to support them through difficult times. We have made a positive difference in people's lives, and that is what our law firm is all about!"

Mr. Scheine mentions two anecdotes to illustrate the impact that a true, "people-caring" firm

*Conference Room at Scheine, Fusco, Brandenstein & Rada PC main office.*

*The Partners of Scheine, Fusco, Brandenstein & Rada PC.*

can provide: "Several years ago a young 21-year old woman came to our office with a minor neck injury she suffered after a box fell on her head while working for a fast food restaurant. During the interview I asked her why she looked so sad. She replied, 'my father died last week of a heart attack.' I then asked her how old her father was and what he had done for a living. She stated he was 41 years old and he had been an air conditioner mechanic. I asked her what her mom did for a living, to which she replied 'a housewife,' and had never worked. I then asked her how she thought they would be able to live. She stated that she was only making $6.50 an hour and that her father had been the sole support of their family. She said, 'we will probably lose our house and my mom is very scared of the future.' I told the young lady to bring her mom in to see me and I would do everything I could to help them. An interview with the mother revealed that the

husband's work activities might have contributed to his death. We filed a death claim on their behalf. Eventually the family received $27,000.00 in past due benefits and the widow received a $300.00 per week pension for the rest of her life. It is the positive feeling we derived from helping this family which keeps us in this business. We made a difference in their lives. We saved their home and helped them keep their dignity."

"In another case, we represented a hard-working man who was the most popular employee of his roofing company. In a freak accident, he sustained a horrific injury. He lost so much blood that he went into a coma, where he has remained for many years. The family was devastated and frightened. Through compassion and heart-felt empathy, we gained the confidence of the family. Because our firm's core values were very similar to theirs, a close relationship developed with this family. After much concern and effort, we obtained a $32,000,000 verdict for the family! We believe this result was due as much to our core value relationship as it was to the skill of our firm. The jury, under extreme hardship, (the trial lasted four months) stayed intact because their core values begged for justice, and justice was served. We emphasized that their social values and ours were the same. The jury was

empathetic with our client."

"Helping people is what Scheine, Fusco, Brandenstein & Rada is all about. Caring for people is who we are and is responsible for our success. Long Island is our home and we are honored to be part of its rich history of helping one another."

Mr. Scheine, in addition to his legal duties for the firm of Scheine, Fusco, Brandenstein & Rada, is currently serving as president of the New York Workers' Compensation Bar Association. He also participates as a chairman-facilitator for

*Edward R. Scheine.*

TEC, an organization of CEO's. Mr. Scheine serves in the capacity of a trusted business advisor for owners and heads of businesses in the Long Island region. When asked how this differs from his law practice, he responded, "not much. "The essence of any good advisor, no matter what the service, is good empathetic listening skills combined with strong core values, which equals making a difference in people's lives."

269

# PERIPHONICS

At Periphonics it's not just about the technology they produce, it's more about the people who use their interactive voice solutions. With a unique goal to remain, what the company refers to as, "customer-centric," Periphonics has focused on the user of their product since its beginnings in 1970.

With a dedication to development, marketing and support of products and professional services for call processing solutions used in computer telephony integration and telecom enhanced network services, the company offers many diversified products and services. The company's products use technologies such as Interactive Voice Response (IVR), speech input, messaging, fax and web browsers and automated call and transaction processing. Periphonics also focuses on call center operations allowing for increased agent productivity, in turn creating more revenue for their customers.

But their involvement does not end with the close of a sale; they believe in forming a long-term relationship with their customer. Periphonics uses a team approach to achieving first rate customer satisfaction, joining highly-accredited and experienced experts in their fields. In fact, 65 percent of

*Software Quality Assurance, extensive testing and analysis ensures unsurpassed quality.*

*Worldwide Corporate Headquarters office, Bohemia, NY.*

revenue is gained from business retention, supplying existing customers with additional telecom products, and expanding on their present Periphonics systems and services.

It is Periphonics' goal to identify the customers' needs early on, and to ultimately ensure that the customized solution proposed by the team is the best fit. It is a total-solution concept, which interfaces with customer specific network infrastructures, databases and service-creation environments.

With customers in more than 50 countries today, Periphonics addresses new market needs by remaining on the cutting edge and developing user-friendly products. The company is a global leader in supplying Interactive Voice Response systems which allow individuals to access information from a computer database using the buttons on a touch-tone telephone.

As a matter of fact, most consumers' lives have been made easier through Periphonics' technology. When dialing a Northwest or American Airlines toll-free number for flight-arrival times, inquiring about account

balances with American Express or Greenpoint Savings Bank, or confirming a closing stock price by phone with a Merrill Lynch or Charles Schwab brokerage firm, a caller is most likely using an Interactive Voice Response system developed by Periphonics.

The company sells its products and services to mid- and large-size companies in industries such as telecommunications, financial services, government, transportation, health care and higher education. They seek to solve the companies' advanced automated systems' needs through comprehensive packaging of technologically-advanced products, professional services and life-cycle maintenance and support.

The Bohemia, New York-based company also continues to grow because of their vision for the future. They recognize the changing needs which demand more powerful and versatile technologies from growing numbers of telecom service providers. The company easily keeps up with marketplace growth through varying network

*IVR Systems are designed, built and tested at Periphonics' headquarters in Bohemia, NY.*

elements including process-optimizing system solutions for wireline, wireless and packet network service providers.

In keeping pace with the expanding information age, Periphonics has experienced highly satisfactory results. In fiscal year 1999, compared to FY '98, the company increased total revenue by 21 percent resulting in $142.3 million; system sales 22.5 percent to $107.4 million; maintenance revenues by 17.6 percent to $34.9 million; gross profit to 27.3 percent to $72.4 million or 50.9 percent of total revenue; and, as every public company strives to do, increased earnings per diluted share 103 percent to $0.65.

Of course, the bottom line is very important, but at the top of Periphonics' goals are to produce a quality, cost-efficient product that can help its customers enhance their customer service offerings, increase caller satisfaction, reduce operating costs and often create new revenue opportunities by automating call and transaction processing.

The international market has been very receptive to the company's products and services. Today, Periphonics has a strong presence worldwide including Europe, the Middle East, Africa, Asia/Pacific, Latin America, the United Kingdom, Germany and Italy. Total international revenues for FY 1999 increased 32.1 percent to $50.7 million compared with the prior year. With the economic unification of Europe providing more opportunity as well as an enhanced competitive environment, Periphonics has become a market leader globally. In fact, international revenues have surpassed those of the overall

company's over the past several years.

Moving towards a bigger and better future, the opportunity for true growth developed when Nortel Networks acquired Periphonics on November 12, 1999. Nortel Networks issued approximately 8.4 million common shares in connection with the acquisition.

The merger has resulted in many new opportunities for the future. Today, as part of Nortel Networks, Periphonics is stronger than ever. Together with Periphonics, the technology leader in Interactive Voice Response, Web response and advanced speech recognition and Clarify, the first to deliver an integrated CRM and eBusiness suite, Nortel Networks is at the heart of the Internet Revolution—the global leader of communications, networking, and Internet protocol solutions.

Nortel Networks eBusiness portfolio of customer relationship solutions leverages the new, high-performance Internet to turn every point of customer interaction into an opportunity

for stronger, more profitable customer relationships. With Nortel's eBusiness solutions, businesses and service providers can integrate their customer service, marketing and sales capabilities to deliver a truly integrated customer experience.

Periphonics, Nortel Networks and Clarify are committed to providing integrated customer care solutions with the highest level of customer service possible. Together they will create a new generation of eBusiness that generates new revenue sources for customers by combining traditional call centers with the power of the Internet. With the strength and vision to pioneer the growth of a new generation of eBusiness services, Nortel Networks will redefine the meaning of "customer loyalty."

*Nortel Networks' unveiling celebration, August 2000.*

# ST. JOHN'S UNIVERSITY

St. John's University was founded in 1870, when a small group of Vincentian priests opened a day college on the corner of Lewis and Willoughby Avenues in Brooklyn. St. John's is an independent, not-for-profit institution of higher education chartered under the laws of the State of New York and is one of the largest Catholic Universities in the United States. Its four campuses are located in Queens, Staten Island, Eastern Long Island, N.Y., and Rome, Italy. The University, which has a total enrollment of more than 18,500 students, offers associate, baccalaureate, master's, doctoral and professional degrees.

With a mission that is Catholic, Vincentian, Metropolitan and Global, St. John's was established to provide a quality education to the children of immigrants and first generation Americans, grounded in Catholic teaching and moral values. Inspired by St. Vincent

*St. John's College circa 1868, Brooklyn.*

de Paul's compassion and zeal for service, St. John's continuously strives to provide excellent education for all people, especially those lacking in economic, physical or social advantages. The University benefits from the cultural diversity, intellectual and artistic resources, and unique professional and educational opportunities offered by its location.

Originally incorporated under the corporate name St. John's College, Brooklyn, on September 29, 1871, the University opened the doors of its first building in Brooklyn with an initial registration of 40 students. The first of the University's many professional departments was established in 1908, and in 1925 a new building in the Borough Hall section of Brooklyn provided space for four new educational units. During the next 25 years it became clear the University would need larger facilities to meet its ever-growing student population.

In 1953 ground was broken on an approximately 105-acre

tract of the University's Jamaica campus. Because of the University's expansion to Queens the corporate name was changed to St. John's University, New York, and the move to the new campus commenced two years later. The University experienced unprecedented growth in the '50s as several new buildings were completed.

In 1971, the University acquired the former Notre Dame College of Staten Island. As a result, all programs at the Brooklyn Center were transferred to the Queens or the Staten Island campuses. The '80s and '90s saw the further expansion and modernization of the Queens campus as several new buildings were completed and facilities were updated to meet the needs of students in the coming millennium.

September 1995 saw the inauguration of the University's Rome campus, its first international site. The campus is located

*St. Augustine Hall, the Library Building at the Queens campus.*

*St. John's Mansion at the eastern Long Island campus.*

in facilities provided by The Vatican, and offers master's level programs in Business Administration and International Relations, providing access to the network of libraries now available in Europe, including the European Union Depository.

In 1998 construction of on-campus housing for up to 2,800 resident students began, and the first facilities opened in time for the Fall 1999 semester to welcome nearly 800 students. The residence halls are part of a $300 million Master Space Plan now in progress at the Queens campus. This plan will affect every corner of the St. John's community, and is designed to give the University an enriched student body, strengthened academic and social offerings and a national reputation of increased stature.

In addition to residence halls the Plan calls for enhanced academic facilities; a modern

student center; redesigned parking; a new admissions/administration building; continuation of campus-wide improvements; and a new church. New athletic quarters, including expanded and improved women's facilities, state-of-the art health and fitness quarters, and a new soccer stadium incorporating enhanced facilities will also be added.

In the Summer of 1999, St. John's purchased the 175-acre LaSalle Center in Oakdale, a school encompassing grades Pre-K to 12, operated by the De La Salle Christian Brothers. The innovative partnership assures both the long-term continuation of the Christian Brothers' educational mission and the independent operation of the school. It also secures the property for use by St. John's to provide adult education programs, athletic activities, and a place to begin partnerships with Long Island businesses and Roman Catholic communities. Some 27,000

St. John's alumni live in Nassau and Suffolk counties.

Throughout its existence St. John's has provided countless individuals with the opportunity for a high-quality education. As St. John's has broadened its scope, becoming an international University, more students than ever before are able to access that tradition of academic strength and Vincentian spirit. Scholarship and academic excellence thrive at St. John's and continue to serve as the foundation for its future.

*New Residence Hall at Queens campus.*

# SUFFOLK CEMENT PRODUCTS, INC.

When Wilhelm Lohr stood proudly on the rich, sandy soil of Long Island in the late 1920s, little did he realize that his courageous footsteps would leave indelible tracks that generations would follow. From brick to block to bulk cement, Suffolk Cement Products, Inc. is truly a story of how raw initiative, focused determination and unwavering pride in performance can produce a company business that continues the pioneer spirit of its founder through children, grandchildren and into the future.

An emigrant from Germany, a young Wilhelm Lohr established himself as a bricklayer in the town of Riverhead, after arriving on American soil in 1925. Three years later, his wife Katherina and children William, Erna and Emmie arrived to celebrate Lohr's success in his new chosen hometown and built their first home on Raynor Avenue in Riverhead. Son William, or "Billy" as he was known to his new American friends, left school after the eighth grade to help his father who was now building brick homes and buildings in the township. Side by side, they made their reputation for their knowledge of bricks and cinder blocks.

*Mid to late 1940s. Founder Wilhelm K. Lohr & son William K. Lohr accepting one of their first new cement mixers. Original office background.*

*Mid to late 1940s Calverton plant site, looking West on Route 25.*

Suffolk Cement Products was about to be born.

Although the East End of Long Island was still farmland at this point in time, Lohr saw that the future held the vision of building and growth. Having purchased property in Calverton from which he could easily service both the north and south forks of Long Island, Lohr built an office at the west end of County Road 58, also known as Route 25 in Riverhead, in 1937. (Dun & Bradstreet has listed the company's start in 1930 although family history has a recorded date of 1937.) Here, the soil was rich in sand, the perfect ingredient for making block and ready-mix cement, and the perfect ingredient for making his business grow and prosper.

After accepting the project to supply block for the construction of Central Suffolk Hospital, Lohr was told by Harold Reeve of H.R. Reeve and Sons, Builder, "If you can locate a truck to mix some concrete, you can have

that part of the job, too." And, with that challenge, the ready-mix part of the business was born. Because automation was not yet part of production practice, manual labor ruled. Teenager Bill Lohr learned the industry with his muscles, cutting endless bags of bulk cement to empty into the silos, either to be cut to make blocks or to store as ready-mix. A few of Bill's school friends also worked for the growing company, one who would later play a major role in producing the products that helped shape the secure foundation for local schools, office buildings and hospitals.

Then came the 1940s and World War II. Bill Lohr was called and served his country overseas for three years in the Army Airforce. At last he returned safely to his family and the family business in Riverhead.

*The Calverton plant site looking east in 1998. In background, Suffolk Cement Precast, Inc. Established in 1975 by William Rusch, Alexander Koke and K. W. Lohr. Tanger Mall located on the South East side of the Long Island Expressway.*

In 1946, Bill married Eileen M. Kessler, and their three children Kenneth, Linda and Mark grew to become the next generation of family to spearhead Suffolk Cement Products, incorporated in 1965.

In 1969, oldest son Kenneth returned as a U.S. Army veteran of the Viet Nam War to work full time at the plant loading the ready mix trucks. More family came to support the flourishing company, with Emmie's son Billy in the block plant, Linda in 1971 to fill in for a vacationing secretary and Mark in 1980 after high school and mechanic's school graduation. In 1997 Mark was named president when brother Kenneth stepped down to fulfill his dreams of buffalo ranching; Linda is now vice president, responsible for administration of the company.

Through the 1970s, the business witnessed more growth on the south shore of Long Island. Under Kenny's direction, more property was obtained in East Hampton Township and a second ready mix plant was constructed. In 1990, Suffolk Cement Products purchased their own tractor trailers for hauling in their materials. That addition to the fleet of vehicles added employees, which helped the company to continue to expand in the community. In fact, from 15 employees in the early 1970s, the company grew to a roster of 48 in the 1990s.

The late 1990s hold vivid memories for the Lohr family. It was then that William Lohr, at age 78, got back on his bulldozer and, to his family's applause and cheers of encouragement, demolished the company's original block plant building—the very one he had helped create so many years before. In August 1998 this site welcomed the new state and county-approved block production plant, one that would house the most technologically advanced equipment for block plant automation, and a full wholesale and retail mason supply yard, as well as a space for the leadership of a whole future generation of the Lohr family. In 1999, a state-of-the-art, 5,000 square foot office building was built, the original, small building happily leveled by 80 year old Bill Lohr and his bulldozer.

Three generations—one vision—a proud member of the community, and a good friend to its people. Suffolk Cement Products, Inc. has brick-by-brick built its reputation for pride in an honest day's work and in the highest standard of performance. A company whose handshake is as good as its word, and who shares the trust and respect of long-time employees, clients, customers and colleagues, throughout New York State and, of course, Long Island.

For over six decades, the Lohr family has adhered to the discipline of hard work first set by patriarch Wilhem. They have, literally, built a tangible legacy that will stand the test of time, from the earliest Central Suffolk Hospital, and massive concrete pouring for Brookhaven National Labs to the most humble headstones in Calverton National Cemetery. They have followed in Wilhem's footsteps well, leaving a brilliant trail for future generations to follow.

*New office building in 2000.*

# WEBB INSTITUTE: AN EXCEPTIONAL COLLEGE

Webb Institute is the only four-year college devoted to naval architecture and marine engineering in the United States. Located in Glen Cove, on the picturesque north shore of Long Island about 30 miles from New York City, it seeks to attract able students who are interested in engineering. Graduates earn a B.S. in Naval Architecture and Marine Engineering while learning about the design and construction of ships of all types and their mode of power.

The aim of Webb is that of educating its students generally, while simultaneously providing professional competence in naval architecture and marine engineering. To this end, the curriculum is designed to be of such depth and quality that all graduates will be fully prepared to enter directly into the practice of their profession or to go forward into graduate work and research. Special effort is made to develop the student's capability for independent study and original thought, as well as to foster those work habits which contribute to professional excellence.

The Mission of the college is: "The provision of high quality engineering education with a strong professional education orientation to prepare young people for leading positions and successful careers in the maritime and associated industries." All students, 70 to 90 in all, have a four-year, renewable, full tuition scholarship after being selected by rigorous standards for a fast-paced academic program. The faculty to student ratio is 7:1.

*Stevenson Taylor Hall is the main academic building.*

The Institute is chartered by New York State Board of Regents, and is accredited by the Middle States Association of Colleges and Schools, and the Engineering Accreditation Commission of the Accreditation Board for Engineering and Technology, Inc. The school maintains close contact with the marine industry and assists graduates in their placement.

*Ship calculations in Robinson Model Basin.*

Webb graduates are in great demand in the marine field as well as in numerous other endeavors. Webb has a 100 percent job placement record, and most graduates have gone on to become leaders in their fields. They have been very successful in entering the graduate school of their choice and many continue on to the doctoral level. Webb's graduates rank fifth in the nation for the percentage who earn Ph.D.'s in science and the school ranks 17th out of 550 colleges nationwide as the source of U.S. corporate senior managers. Webb delivers these accomplishments as a result of its very selective admissions policy, rigorous academic program and select, dedicated faculty.

The story of Webb Institute begins with its founder William H. Webb, who was born in New York City in 1816, the son of Isaac and Phoebe Webb. Isaac, who had his own shipyard in the city, died suddenly in 1840, and at the age of 23 William, who had learned how to build ships as an apprentice at the age of 15, assumed responsibility for the shipyard.

From 1840 to 1872, William Webb and his shipyard were the premier shipbuilders in New York City, constructing a larger number and greater tonnage of vessels than any other American shipbuilder of that era. Technical change and low cost foreign competition, however, brought an end to that dominance. Iron and steel hulls replaced wooden hulled sail propelled vessels, and geography made it impossible for New York City to become a center of iron and steel ship construction.

In the 1880s, Mr. Webb began to form a vision for the future of American shipbuilding. Knowing that shipbuilding would revive and being aware that technological change necessitated a more formal education than the apprenticeship system allowed, he began to dream of a college that would provide world class engineering training for young Americans in both the art and science of ship design and construction. In 1888 he selected and purchased land in the Fordham Hill section of the Bronx and on April 2, 1889 the Governor of New York signed the Articles of Incorporation. Moving quickly ahead, by Fall 1890 a Board of Trustees had been established and had approved building plans. The first class of students arrived in the newly-constructed Webb school in Spring 1894.

Webb Institute was relocated in 1947 to its present site in Glen Cove in the former Herbert L. Pratt estate on Long Island's "Gold Coast." Subsequent construction added five more buildings to the campus, including a ship model basin, marine engineering laboratories, a private beach, boat house/yacht club, tennis courts, and a gymnasium.

The original endowment by Mr. Webb has significantly increased by wise investments and gifts from alumni, foundations, corporations and friends. Upon entering, each student is provided with a laptop computer loaded with the latest software packages needed for technical calculations.

One of the unique features of the educational system is the Winter work term during

---

*Professor and students in electrical engineering class.*

January through early March. During this period between academic semesters, each student is required to engage in eight weeks of practical work in a shipyard, aboard ship in the engine room, in a design office or in other course-related industries. This practical work period not only provides a break in the academic routine, but it gives the students opportunities to relate their classroom and laboratory work to actual commercial practice.

Webb Institute enters the 21st century with confidence and enthusiasm to continue Webb's vision, and to prepare its students for work and leadership in ever-changing technologies that its founder could never have imagined.

# THE SOCIETY FOR THE PRESERVATION OF LONG ISLAND ANTIQUITIES

The Society for the Preservation of Long Island Antiquities is a nonprofit organization devoted to the preservation and interpretation of Long Island's past. Since 1948, SPLIA has pursued this goal through several historic house museums and their collections, a gallery for changing exhibitions as well as numerous educational programs and publications devoted to Long Island's rich history and architecture.

Now in its 50th anniversary year, SPLIA continues to work with all levels of government, historical societies, museums and individuals to provide knowledge and insight into the cultural inheritance of every Long Islander and to further the goals of historic preservation.

SPLIA owns, or has under its auspices, historic house museums running the length of Long Island. These distinctive buildings, which portray different aspects of the region's history, include the Wycoff House, a 17th century Dutch farm house in East Flatbush; Rock Hall, a formal Georgian mansion in Lawrence;

*Long Island students at one of SPLIA's historic house museums.*

the Joseph Lloyd Manor, an 18th century manor house at Lloyd Neck; Sherwoood-Jayne, an East Setauket farm complex; the Thompson House, a late 17th century "saltbox" in Setauket; and the Custom House in Sag Harbor, home of the port's first Custom Master, Henry Packer Dering. The houses are furnished with one of the most important assemblages of Long Islandiana, comprising over 3,000 objects and including masterpieces of regional decorative arts and craftsmanship. The Society also possesses significant archival and photographic collections in addition to a wealth of textiles, fine arts and pottery, either owned or made on Long Island.

SPLIA's Gallery in Cold Spring Harbor opened in 1990. It provides a facility with flexible space for changing exhibitions and programming. The adaptively reused Carnegie-era library is open year round and features shows about Long Island's significant history and cultural heritage. The museum shop at the Gallery features an excellent collection of books and materials pertaining to Long Island's local and regional history.

A variety of innovative school discovery programs are held at SPLIA's historic house museums. These dynamic "hands-on" classes actively involve students in discovering and analyzing many aspects of Long Island history. Role-playing, object handling, house hunts, creative writing and art workshops are used to involve students in an exploration of the past. Each program includes extensive pre-visit kits

*The Custom House, Sag Harbor, New York.*

with activities, original documents and thoughtful questions. A detailed brochure and a signed pre-visit video are available for the programs at Lloyd Manor and the Thompson House.

The publication of studies and catalogues concerning salient aspects of Long Island's history and material culture is a long-standing tradition at the Society. Recently published studies include *Long Island Country Houses and their Architects*, 1860-1940; *Discovering the African-American Experience in Suffolk County*, 1620-1860; *AIA Architectural Guide to Nassau and Suffolk Counties, Long Island*; and *Between Ocean and Empire: An Illustrated History of Long Island*.

As advocates for historic preservation on Long Island, SPLIA has been actively involved since 1948 in extending a helping hand to those engaged in preserving our region's landmarks. Through its periodical *Preservation Notes*, workshops on preservation topics, hearing appearances and the stewardship of covenanced properties, SPLIA seeks to make a future for Long Island's past. Through these venues the Society acts as a resource for individuals and organizations engaged in the preservation of our cultural heritage.

# SWEET PRODUCTIONS LTD.

Helping people to eat healthy is the main mission of Sweet Productions, Ltd., located at 5100 New Horizons Boulevard in Amityville. And chances are, the average household in the United States probably has one of their nutritious snack items in the pantry. But when Paul Schacher and Ben Cohen co–founded their company, along with Joe Pizzo in 1982, it was with very little knowledge of the food business.

"My brother Glenn has a health food company," recalls Paul, "and he was looking for new snack items—that gave us our reason for starting." Sweet's first product was called "Glenny's Rice Treats," the forerunner of the popular rice cakes now sold in most super- markets. In 1982, the nutritious snacks were only made for a small niche market, and the food entrepreneurs had to learn by trial and error. "When we started, there was very little in nutritious snacks," notes Paul.

The company began in a home kitchen where the products were made by hand. With about 10 employees, Sweet Productions soon moved to a 1,500 square-

*Joseph Pizzo, vice president of operations.*

*Ben Cohen, executive vice president (left) and Paul Schacher, president (right).*

foot building in Copiague and started its long process of research and development to create its various low-fat, high-protein or low-carb snack bars. "We created ways for adults and children to relate to having a healthy snack," says Paul. "We get a lot of happiness from making something that is really contrib-uting to someone's health."

Their belief is that proper nutrition is the foundation of health. Success also followed, as the market for nutritious snack items grew from a niche market to a mass market. As the de-mand for nutritious snacks grew, Sweet Productions was faced with the decision to expand and find larger clients. The demand became so great that three years ago the company moved to a 40,000 square-foot facility and one year later added 35,000 square feet. Sweet modernized its operations when it relocated and now employs approximately 200 people.

"One of the things I'm most proud of," says Paul, "is our wonderful group of hardworking employees and the flexibility in which we've had to deal with our growth. We had to recreate the

infrastructure of the business to handle the tremendous growth." Sweet's products may be available in your local supermarket or discount store, but consumers won't see a "Sweet" label on the snack bar or sports nutrition item. That's because the company develops and creates the products for major brand names, who then market the products under their own label. Sweet Productions now manufactures about 50 products, which include many of the leading brands of nutritious, low-carb, high-protein and low-fat or fat-free bars.

Paul Schacher's goal is for Sweet Productions to become the number one producer of nutritious snack foods in the United States. "You have to keep seeing the vision of what you want to create, and also be willing to readjust the way you get there, and then you will achieve your dreams."

With this philosophy in place, Sweet Productions is well poised to continue its dramatic growth and accomodate the ever chang-ing needs of its market.

# MIDDLE COUNTRY PUBLIC LIBRARY

The Middle Country Public Library has evolved from a modest beginning to the largest public library on Long Island. Organized in the mid-1950s, the Middle Country Public Library was originally chartered as the Selden-Centereach Public Library on January 28, 1960. Throughout the 1960s, the library operated out of two small storefronts, one in Selden and one in Centereach. It relocated in 1972 to a newly constructed modern building on Eastwood Boulevard in Centereach, while maintaining a small branch in Selden.

In 1983 the library acquired an elementary school building from the school district. This building, now known as the Middle Country Public Library Cultural Center, houses a browsing collection of popular reading materials, an Early Childhood Room, the Computer Place and meeting rooms for community groups and library sponsored programs.

By the Fall of 1984, its level of service had simply outstripped the ability of its facilities. On October 9th, a bond issue to expand the Main Library in Centereach was overwhelmingly passed. On December 15, 1986, a completely renovated and enlarged 53,000 square foot library was opened to the public. In 1999, the Library passed a bond referendum for $12 million to again expand both buildings.

In 1985 the Middle Country Public Library was selected by an independent university study as one of the top 50 public libraries in the United States. The library, its collections and services, reflect the informational and cultural needs of the community. The Children's Services Department serves children from birth

through 8th grade, parents, and professionals working with children. The Adult Services Department is designed to serve patrons ages 14 and over. All patrons, including children, are accorded the same privileges.

The Middle Country Public Library is the community's center for information, culture, educational enrichment, and recreation. Committed to lifelong learning, it provides access to current, historical, and technological resources, programs, and services that reflect a wide range of views in a variety of formats. The Library is a welcoming, accessible, aesthetically pleasing environment with a well trained, congenial staff.

Honoring its tradition of excellent patron service, Middle Country Public Library invites continuous dialogue with the community by reaching out to individuals and families of all ages and abilities. Community support for outstanding public library service has created the impetus for Middle Country's development as a state-of-the-art institution. The Library is dedicated to a leadership role

*Artist rendering of the Main Library in Centereach.*

in library service, to provide a model for family-centered libraries, and to enhance the quality of life for the Middle Country community.

The population served by the Middle Country Public Library includes, but is not limited to, the 55,000 residents of the Middle Country Library district, a largely blue collar working class community located in the geographic center of Long Island comprised primarily of Selden, Centerreach and portions of Lake Grove and Coram. This community is largely white with an increasingly significant immigrant population from a variety of cultures (Hispanic, Asian, Middle Eastern and East Indian). Beyond the local community, the library also supports library initiatives that are developed as model programs in libraries serving populations in diverse racial and socioeconomic communities across Long Island as well as urban and rural settings around the country.

The Library is in a leadership role in the ongoing development of exemplary library programs and services and participates in networks to enhance its position in local, regional and national initiatives. It provides a leadership role in the Suffolk Coalition for Parents and Children, the Parent Educators Network, the Librarian's Alliance for Parents and Children, and the Library Business Connection. The Center for Business and Careers is working in partnership with the Hauppauge Industrial Association (HIA) to provide electronic business reference services. The Library has spearheaded the development of the Family Place Library Model and implemented the national Family Place Project in cooperation with Libraries for the Future. Middle Country continues to expand the Community Resource Database of Long Island in partnership with health and human service agencies in the development of its Long Island database.

In 1997, the Middle Country Library formed the Middle Country Library Foundation to raise funds and also direct restricted funds from a variety of sources to support the Library's Family Place Initiative, its Library Business Connection and the Community Resource Database of Long Island. The Foundation provides the governance structure for those activities and projects of the library and assists it in maintaining its leadership role in the broader library community. It encourages initiatives, which supplement, complement and augment the basic program of the Middle Country Public Library and encourages excellence and leadership in library service.

Known for its creativity, innovation and leadership, the Middle Country Public Library is a living laboratory for library-based services. Embracing the notion that public libraries add value and quality-of-life to local communities, the Library has infused its community with exemplary programs and serves as a model for libraries everywhere.

*Artist rendering of the Cultural Center in Seldon.*

# A Timeline of Long Island's History

**1524**—Giovanni Verazzano sails along the south shore of Long Island.

**1609**—crew members from Henry Hudson's *Half Moon* land on Coney Island.

**1614**—Adrian Block sails through Hellgate to Long Island Sound and maps a land mass he names *Lange Eilandt*.

**1624**—The first permanent Dutch settlements on Manhattan and Governor's Island.

**1636**—Dutch establish the first European settlements on Long Island in Gowanus and Nieuw Amerfoort (Flatlands.)

**1639**—Lion Gardiner purchases the island, which now bears his family name, lying between the north and south forks.

**1640**—Colonists from New England found the first English settlements on Long Island at Southold and Southampton.

**1643**—Lady Deborah Moody establish Gravesend, an English settlement in Dutch controlled western Long Island.

**1643-44**—Kieft's War, Dutch troops attack Indians on Long Island and the mainland.

**1645**—Vlissingen (Flushing) established.

**1645**—Breuklen established as a town.

**1648**—East Hampton settled.

**1650**—Treaty of Hartford divides English and Dutch territory on Long Island at approximately present day Nassau-Suffolk border.

**1656**—Rustdorp (Jamaica) receives a charter.

**1657**—Flushing Remonstrance, first major document in America arguing for religious freedom.

**1662**—John Bowne arrested for allowing Quakers to worship in his home, Bowne was acquitted after a trial in the

### A PROCLAMATION

By His Excellency the Honorable WILLIAM HOWE, General and Commander in Chief of all His Majesty's Forces within the Colonies lying on the Atlantic Ocean, from Nova-Scotia, to West-Florida, inclusive, &c. &c. &c.

WHEREAS it is represented, that many of the loyal Inhabitants of this Island have been compelled by the Leaders in Rebellion, to take up Arms against His Majesty's Government: Notice is hereby given to all Persons so forced into Rebellion, that on delivering themselves up at the HEAD QUARTERS of the Army, they will be received as faithful Subjects; have Permits to return peaceably to their respective Dwellings, and meet with full Protection for their Persons and Property.

All those who chuse to take up Arms for the Restoration of Order and good Government within this Island, shall be disposed of in the best Manner, and have every Encouragement that can be expected.

GIVEN under my HAND, at Head Quarters on Long Island, this 23d Day of August, 1776.           WILLIAM HOWE.

By His Excellency's Command.

ROBERT MACKENZIE, Secretary.

*Proclamation issued by British General William Howe at the onset of the British occupation of Long Island.*

Netherlands.

**1664**—Dutch surrender New Netherlands to England. Colon renamed New York for the King's brother, James, Duke of York.

**1665**—Duke's Laws proclaimed at a convention in Hempstead.

**1673**—Dutch recapture New York. English towns on East End refuse to submit. New York returned to England in peace settlement in exchange for Surinam in South America. (Super bad deal for Dutch).

**1683**—Kings, Queens and Suffolk Counties created on Long Island.

**1692**—New York Assembly officially names Long Island "Isle of Nassau" Name does not take hold, but is remembered.

**1703**—King's Highway, present day Jamaica Avenue, authorized by province.

**1711**—Jupiter Hammond, America's first black poet born on Lloyd's Neck.

**1737**—first nursery in America open by Prince family in Flushing.

**1766**—Sons of Liberty in Oyster Bay protest Stamp Tax.

**1774**—First Continental Congress in Philadelphia orders embargo on English goods. Generally supported on eastern Long Island, with considerable opposition on western section.

**1775**—Whigs in northern part of Town of Hempstead declare independence from loyalist leaning southern half. Division officially confirmed in 1784.

**1776**—June 22-23, skirmish between revolutionaries and Tories in Hempstead Swamp, now part of Tanglewood Preserve.

**1776**—William Floyd of Mastic, Francis Lewis of Whitestone and Robert Livingston who owned a country home on Brooklyn heights sign Declaration of Independence as representatives of New York.

**1776**—August 27-29, Battle of Long Island on Brooklyn Heights. Washington defeated, retreats to Manhattan and then to mainland.

**1776-1783.**—Long Island occupied by British during Revolution. Rebels and Tories raid each other across Long Island Sound. Many patriots flee for Connecticut.

**1777**—Battle of Sag Harbor, Colonel Return Jonathan Meigs leads successful commando style raid to destroy British supplies and shipping at Sag Harbor.

**1782-83**—Thousands of Long Island's Loyalists flee for Canada.

**1783**—December 4, last British troops leave Long Island.

**1784**—New York legislature levees fine on Long Island for passivity during Revolutionary War.

**1784**—Clinton Academy opens in East Hampton. First chartered academy in New York.

**1787**—Erasmus Hall in Flatbush and Clinton Academy receive state charters; become first incorporated secondary schools in New York.

**1788**—New York ratifies constitution.

**1789**—Federal government designates Sag Harbor an official port of entry.

**1791**—President George Washington tours Long Island.

**1791**—David Frothingham publishes *Long Island Herald* in Sag Harbor. First Long Island newspaper.

**1795-96**—Montauk lighthouse constructed at eastern terminus.

**1799**—New York begins gradual emancipation of slaves.

**1801**—Brooklyn Navy Yard established.

**1806**—First turnpikes built on Long Island connecting Jamaica and Rockaway.

**1812-13**—School districts established throughout New York State, each expected to provide tax-supported elementary schools.

**1812-15**—War of 1812, British Naval squadron anchors in Gardiner's Bay, raids Sag Harbor.

**1814**—Steam ferry service begins between Brooklyn and Manhattan.

**1814**—Jamaica becomes first village to incorporate on Long Island

**1816**—Village of Brooklyn is incorporated, becomes a city in 1834.

**1824**—lighthouse constructed at western tip of Fire Island.

**1827**—Hicksite schism roils Quakers, names for Jericho Quaker, Elias Hicks.

**1827**—slavery totally ended in New York.

**1830-67**—William Sidney Mount, Stony Brook artist and limner of Long Island scenes.

**1834**—Long Island Rail Road

Unknown Residence, *watercolor on paper by Edward Lange. Elwood, Suffolk County, NY. Collection of Valdemar Jacobsen, Courtesy, SPLIA*

charted. Reaches Hicksville in 1836, Greenport in 1844.

**1842**—First Queens County Agricultural Fair held in Hempstead.

**1842**—William Cullen Bryant, poet and editor of the *New York Post* buys land in Roslyn for country estate, *Cedarmere.*

**1845-1875**—whaling boom. Sag Harbor and Cold Spring Harbor active in the industry.

**1850**—"Modern Times" utopian communal village established by Joseph Warren in present-day Brentwood.

Observing the Seawanhaka Cup Races in the 1890s, *from "The Long Island Country House, 1860-1940, Part I: A Recreational Paradise" exhibit. Courtesy, SPLIA*

**1855**—Walt Whitman, son of West Hills family, publishes the first version of *Leaves of Grass,*

**1857**—Army establishes Fort Totten at Willet's Point.

**1859**—St. Francis Academy founded in Brooklyn, becomes a college in 1884.

**1861-65**—Camp Winfield Scott on the Hempstead Plains serves as major training grounds for Union soldiers.

**1862**—Ironclad *Monitor* launched at Brooklyn Navy Yard.

**1863**—Anti-Draft riot in Jamaica.

**1863**—Long Island Historical Society founded becomes Brooklyn Historical Society in 1985.

**1864**—Women's Relief Association sponsors Brooklyn and Long Island Sanitary Fair at the Brooklyn Academy of Music. $400,000 raised for medical supplies.

**1869**—Alexander T. Stewart purchase over 7,000acres of the Hempstead Plains for Garden City.

**1870**—St. John's College established in Brooklyn. Jamaica campus opened in 1955.

**1870**—Long Island City incorporated.

**1872**—Steinway Piano factory and village established by German immigrants in Astoria.

**1874**—Queens County Court House moved from Minneola to Long Island City.

**1874**—Prospect Park, designed by Frederick Law Olmstead and Calvert Vaux, completed in Brooklyn.

**1883**—Brooklyn Bridge opens.

**1885**—Brooklyn's first elevated railroad becomes operational.

**1883**—Suffolk County Historical Society founded.

**1885**—New York State establishes fish hatchery at Cold Spring Harbor. 1986 becomes Cold Spring Harbor Fish Hatchery & Aquarium.

**1890**—Biological Laboratory established at Cold Spring Harbor, forerunner of Cold Spring Laboratories.

**1891-1903**—William Merritt Chase conducts Shinnecock Summer School of Art in Southampton

**1891**—Shinnecock Hills Country Club founded. First private eighteen hole golf course.

**1899-1905**—John H. Holland Torpedo Boat Company operates out of New Suffolk. First United States Submarine base.

**1897**—Brooklyn Public Library established. Brooklyn Museum opens.

**1898**—Steeplechase Park opens at Coney Island.

**1898**—Camp Black at Mineola and Camp Wikoff at Montauk serve as training grounds for soldiers preparing for Spanish American War. Theodore Roosevelt's Rough Riders return to Camp Wikoff. 1898—City of Greater New York created including Kings (Brooklyn) and the three western Queens towns (Newtown, Jamaica and Flushing.)

**1899**—Nassau County created from the eastern three towns of Queens (Hempstead, North Hempstead and Oyster Bay.)

**1901-1908**—Theodore Roosevelt's presidency. Sagamore Hill functions as the summer White House.

**1901**—Guglielmo Marconi,

inventor of wireless telegraphy, transmits first wireless radio message from Babylon.

**1903**—Williamsburg Bridge opens, another link between Brooklyn and Manhattan. Manhattan Bridge opens in 1909.

**1904**—Mineola Flying Field—Long Island's first—opens.

**1904**—Carnegie Institution establishes station for experimental evolution at Cold Spring Harbor, immediate forerunner of Cold Spring Laboratories.

**1906**—First Vanderbilt Cup race held on Long Island.

**1908**—Vanderbilt Motor Parkway opens; first modern toll road in United States.

**1909**—Queensborough Bridge opens, linking Queens and Manhattan.

**1909**—Glenn Curtiss makes pioneering flights on the Hempstead Plains. International Aviation Meet at Belmont Park in 1910.

**1910**—Doubleday publishers move to Garden City.

**1910**—Francis Hodgson writes *The Secret Garden* at Plandome.

**1910**—East river tunnels and electrifies trains provide rapid transit between Brooklyn, Queens and Manhattan.

**1911**—Brooklyn Botanic Garden opens.

**1911**—Moisant School opens on Hempstead Plains, trains Harriet Quimby, the first licensed woman pilot.

**1912**—New York "Ashcan" school of painters discovers Bellport.

**1912**—New York State School of Agriculture founded at Farmingdale becomes four-year SUNY College of Technology.

**1915**—Queensborogh subway begins operations.

**1917-18**—World War One aviators train at Hazelhurst, Mitchel and Roosevelt Fields. Troops train at Camp Mills (Garden City) and Camp Upton (Yaphank).

**1922**—First transatlantic radio telephone transmittal station built by RCA at Rocky Point.

**1922-24**—F. Scott Fitzgerald resides at Great Neck giving him the source material for *The Great Gatsby*.

**1923**—KuKluxKlan rally in East Islip attracts 25,000 people.

**1924**—Sunnyside Gardens, a planned apartment complex, opens in Queens.

**1924**—Long Island State Parks Commission organized under Robert Moses.

**1927**—May20, Charles Lindbergh takes off from Roosevelt Field to Paris.

**1927**—Southern State Parkway opens as limited access road to state parks. Serves as model for later Moses' Parkways.

**1929**—Jones Beach State Park opens. Connected by Southern State and Wantagh State Parkways.

**1929**—Adelphi College relocates from Brooklyn to Garden City. Originally a women's college, it becomes co-ed after WW II.

**1929**—Grumman Aircraft Corporation begins in a garage in Baldwin.

**1930**—Michael Cullen opens the first "King Kullen" supermarket in Jamaica.

**1930**—Brooklyn College founded.

**1930-31**—"Big Duck" built in Flanders, enduring example of vernacular fantasy architecture.

**1933**—Grand Central and Northern State Parkways open.

**1935**—Hofstra opens as a two-year extension branch of New

*Gates of Hempstead House at Sands Point, NY. Courtesy, SPLIA*

York University. In 1940 it becomes an independent four-year college. 1963 it becomes a University.

**1936**—Triborough Bridge connecting Queens with the Bronx and Manhattan opens.

**1937**—Queens College founded.

**1937-39**—Camp Siegfried, run by the German-American Bund, active in Yaphank.

**1938**—Severe hurricane causes extensive damage and seventy deaths on eastern Long Island.

**1939**—Pan American inaugurates overseas air flights from Manhasset Bay.

**1939**—La Guardia Airport begins operations as land and seaplane terminal.

**1939-40**—World's Fair held in Flushing Meadow Park, Queens.

**1940**—Queens Midtown Tunnel opens.

**1940**—*Newsday* begins publication under Alicia Patterson and Harry Guggenheim.

**1940-45**—World War II—Long Island prominent in defense industry with companies like Republic, Grumman, Brewster, Hazeltine and Fairchild.

**1942**—German saboteurs landed from a U-Boat at Amagansett. They are quickly captured.

**1945**—The "Miracle Mile" shopping center opens along Route 25a in Manhasset.

**1947**—archetypical post-World War Two suburban development at Levittown begins.

**1947**—Brookhaven National Laboratory set up at former Camp Upton n Yaphank.

*Beaux Arts Casino interior. Courtesy, SPLIA*

**1951**—Roosevelt Field ceases aviation activities. Sold for development as a shopping center.

**1957**—Brooklyn Dodgers move to Los Angeles. Ebbett's Field converted to an apartment complex.

**1958**—Long Island Expressway begun. 1972, reaches present terminus near Riverhead.

**1961**—The Throgs Neck Bridge opens, connecting Queens and the Bronx.

**1962**—SUNY/ Stony Brook established on land donated by Ward Melville.

**1962**—Cold Spring Harbor Laboratories established.

**1964-65**—World's Fair held at Flushing Meadows Park.

**1964**—Verazzano Narrows Bridge opens connecting Brooklyn with Staten Island. The longest suspension bridge in the world.

**1964**—Fire Island National Seashore created.

**1966**—Long Island Rail Road purchased by Metropolitan Commuter Transit, forerunner of Metropolitan Transit Authority.

**1969**—The lunar module, built by Grumman, lands on the moon.

**1971**—Federal government designates Nassau-Suffolk a Standard Metropolitan Statistical Ares, the first such without a core city.

**1971**—Gateway National Recreation Area created along Jamaica Bay in Kings.

**1973**—LILCO begins construction of Shoreham Nuclear Plant. Regional opposition leads to its closure in 1994 without ever having operated.

**1980-83**—*New York Islanders*, whose home ice is at Nassau Coliseum, win four Stanley Cups.

**1981**—Alphonse D'Amato of

Island Park elected United States Senator. Serves until 1997.

**1983**—Barbara McClintock receives Nobel Prize for her work in genetics at the Cold Spring Harbor Laboratories.

**1984**—Geraldine Ferraro of Forest Hills (Queens) becomes the first woman nominated for vice-president by a major political party.

**1986**—Queensborough President Donald Manes commits suicide in wake of corruption in Koch Administration.

**1988**—Republic Aviation, which had been acquired by Fairchild, totally out of business.

**1993**—December 7, Colin Ferguson massacres riders on Long Island Rail Road.

**1994**—Grumman Aerospace bought out by Northrop. Most Long Island operations ended.

**1994**—Nassau County voters approve a County legislature.

**1995**—Major forest fires in Pine Barrens of Brookhaven and Southampton Towns.

**1996**—July, TWA 800 explodes off East Moriches, 230 killed.

**1999**—November, Nassau voters give Democrats majority in County legislature.

---

$2.50 Per Annum

Number 9

# Huntington Hails War's End With Tumultuous Demonstration Tuesday; War Plants Preparing To Pare Jobs

## THOUSANDS OF WAR WORKERS AFFECTED IN RECONVERSION

**Approximately 75 Per Cent of Employees In Aircraft and Other Type Plants Will Be Dropped.**

Following closely the news of Japan's surrender, thousands of Suffolk and Nassau war workers were being laid off pending the announcement of more definite plans for reconversion to peace-time production.

The bad news was tempered somewhat by the aircraft and other war plant announcements of reconversion plans which will make it possible for them to employ substantial numbers of their employees. Most of the plants declined to be definite about the numbers of those who will be dropped, but if Long Island follows the statistical trend throughout the United States approximately 75 per cent will be laid off. Nationally it has been estimated that 5,000,000 to 6,000,000 out of a total of 8,000,000 will lose

### WAR'S END SHOWS CASUALTIES HERE

That Huntington has a great and solemn right to be proud of its contribution to the winning of World War II was indicated this week when the American Legion's Official Honor Roll Committee thru its chairman, Walter Resler, made known the extent of the township's participation.

Approximately 3,600 names of men and women from this township appear on the Honor Roll. Out of these, 82 were killed in action, 23 died in service and 129 were wounded in action. Some 17 were reported missing in action.

### NASSAU-SUFFOLK CIO CALLS A CONFERENCE FOR MONDAY NIGHT

**Electrical and Machine Workers Group Announces An "Emergency" Meeting to Save War Plants.**

Announcement of an "Emergency" Conference to save the war plants, provide jobs and maintain public purchasing power in the Nassau-Suffolk counties" to be held Monday evening, August 20, at 8

## CHEERING CITIZENS IN MOTOR CAR PARADES GREET CAPITULATION

**Spontaneous Celebration Exceeds 1918 Armistice Observance In Noisy Enthusiasm of Townspeople.**

Huntington, mild and conservative and generally most placid, kicked over the traces Tuesday night to celebrate the end of the war in a boisterous spontaneous and hectic manner that lasted several hours and seemed almost unbelievable. The townspeople had been going on their regular business during the day without much apparent excitement, but when the sirens sounded, church bells rang, horns honked, pots banged and people shouted, Huntington blew her top. Persons who remembered the demonstration after World War I said it was much less tumultuous.

Steady streams of cars with an ever-increasing crescendo of blaring horns started from the various sections of the town on the official announcement of the capitulation

*The end of World War II is formally announced to the citizens of Huntington. Courtesy, Richard F. Welch*

# Bibliography

Bailey, Paul. *Long Island, A History of Two Great Counties, Nassau and Suffolk.* New York: Lewis Historical Publishing Co., 1949.

Bangs, Charlotte. *Reminiscences of Old New Utrecht and Gowanus.* Brooklyn, 1912.

Barber, John. *Historical Collections of the State of New York.* New York: Tuttle, 1841.

Barck, Dorothy, ed. "Papers of the Lloyd Family of the Manor of Queens Village, Lloyds Neck 1654-1826." *Collections of the New-York Historical Society.* New York: 1926.

Bassett, Preston. *Long Island: Cradle of Aviation.* Amityville: Long Island Forum, 1950.

Brasser, T.J.C. "The Coastal Algonkians: People of the First Frontiers." In Eleanor Leacock and Nancy Lurie, eds., *North American Indians in Historical Perspective.* New York: Random House, 1971.

Carpenter, James. *The Mineola Fair.* Uniondale: Agricultural Society of Queens, Nassau, and Suffolk County, 1965.

Ceci, Lynn. "The Effect of European Contact and Trade on the Settlement Pattern of Indians in Coastal New York, 1524-1664." Doctoral dissertation, CUNY, 1977.

_____ . "Method and Theory in Coastal New York Archaeology: Paradigms of Settlement Pattern." *North American Archaeologist* 3(1982):5-36.

Christ Church Parish Records. Oyster Bay, New York.

Clark, Stephen. "Gabriel Furman: Brooklyn's First Historian." *Journal of Long Island History* 10(Spring 1974):21-32.

Colonel Josiah Smith Account Book for 1776. Society for the Preservation of Long Island Antiquities, Setauket, New York.

Conkey, Laura, E. Boissevian, and I. Goddard. "Indians of Southern New England and Long Island: Late Period." In Bruce Trigger, ed., *Handbook of the North American Indians, Vol. 15: The Northeast.* Washington: Smithsonian Institution, 1978.

Cory, David M. "Brooklyn and the Civil War." *Journal of Long Island History* 2(Spring 1962):1-15.

Cummings, John. "The Dorflinger Glass Works." *New York History* 34(October 1953):468-74.

Daggett, Marguerite. *Long Island Printing 1791-1830.* Brooklyn: Long Island Historical Society, 1979.

Dankers, Jasper, and Peter Sluyter. *Journal of a Voyage to New York* (1679-80). Translation by H.C. Murphy, 1867. Reprint. Ann Arbor: University Microfilms, 1966.

DeLeat, John. "Extracts from the New World: A Description of the West Indies" (1625). In H.C. Murphy, ed., *Collections of the New-York Historical Society.* 2nd Series, Vol. 1. New York: H. Ludwig, 1841.

Denton, Daniel. *A Brief Description of New York: Formerly Called New Netherland* (1670). Ann Arbor: University Microfilms, 1966.

DeVerazzano, John. "The Voyage of John DeVerazzano Along the Coast of North America" (1524). In H.C. Murphy, ed., *Collections of the New-York Historical Society.* 2nd Series, Vol. 1. New York: H. Ludwig, 1841.

Dillard, Maud. *Old Houses of Brooklyn.* New York: Richard R. Smith, 1945.

Dobriner, William. *Class in Suburbia.* New York: Prentice Hall, 1963.

Dunn, Richard. "John Winthrop, Jr., Connecticut Expansionist, The Failure of his Designs on Long Island 1663-1675." *New England Quarterly* XIX (1956).

Dwight, Timothy. *Travels in New England and New York.* New Haven: S. Converse, 1823.

Eberlein, Harold. *Manor Houses and Historic Homes of Long Island and Staten Island.* Philadelphia: J.B. Lippincott, 1928.

Failey, Dean. *Edward Lange's Long Island.* Setauket: Society for the Preservation of Long Island Antiquities, 1979.

_____ . *Long Island is My Nation.* Setauket: Society for the Preservation of Long Island Antiquities, 1976.

Flick, Alexander. *Loyalism in New York During the American Revolution.* New York: Arno Press, 1964.

Floyd Family Papers. Society for the Preservation of Long Island Antiquities, Setauket, New York.

Fullerton, Edith. *History of Long Island Agriculture.* Jamaica: Long Island Rail Road, 1929.

Gabriel, Ralph. *The Evolution of Long Island.* New Haven: Yale University Press, 1921.

George Weekes Day Book. Raynham Hall Museum, Oyster Bay, New York.

Gibbs, Alonzo. "New Year's Calling." *New York Folklore Quarterly* 16:295-97.

Gosnell, Harold. *Boss Platt and his New York Machine.* Chicago, 1924.

Gwynne, Gretchen. "The Late Archaic Archaeology of Mount Sinai Harbor, New York." Doctoral dissertation, SUNY-Stony Brook, 1982.

_____ . "Pipestave Hollow Ideography." *Expedition* 24(1982):14-19.

Hammack, David C. *Participation in Major Decisions in New York City, 1890-1900: The Creation of Greater New York and the Centralization of the Public School System.* Ann Arbor, 1973, 1975.

_____ . *Power and Society: Greater New York at the Turn of the Century.* New York, 1982.

Hazelton, Henry. *The Boroughs of Brooklyn and Queens, Counties of Nassau and Suffolk, N.Y., 1609-1924.* 7 vols. New York: Lewis Historical Publishing Co., 1925.

Hedges Family Papers and Account Books. East Hampton Public Library.

*Hofstra University Yearbook of Business.*

Horne, Field, ed. *The Diary of Mary Cooper.* Oyster Bay: Oyster Bay Historical Society, 1981.

Horton, Azariah. "Azariah Horton's Letters to the Scots Mission" (1742). *Christian History* V:21-67.

Howell, George. *History of Southhampton.* New York: J.N. Hallock, 1866.

Huntington Town Meeting Records. Office of the Town Historian, Huntington, New York.

Idzerda, Stanley J. "Walt Whitman, Politician." *New York History* 37:171-184.

Jacob, Albert C. "Schooldays in Brooklyn in the Early 1900s." *Journal of Long Island History* 8(Summer-Fall 1968):30-38.

Jameson, J. Franklin, ed. *Narratives of New Netherlands.* New York: Charles Scribner's Sons, 1909.

Jaray, Cornell, ed. *Historical Chronicles of New Amsterdam, Colonial New York, and Early Long Island.* Port Washington: Ira J. Friedman, 1968.

Johnson, Henry. *The Campaign of 1776 Around New York and Brooklyn.* New York: De Capo Press, 1971.

Jones, Thomas. *History of New York During the Revolutionary War.* New-York Historical Society, 1879.

Judd, Jacob. "The Administrative Organization of the City of Brooklyn, 1834-1855." *Journal of Long Island History* 5 (Spring 1965):39-50.

_____ . "The Administrative Organization of the City of Brooklyn, Part II." *Journal of Long Island History* 5(Fall 1965):39-49.

_____ . "Brooklyn's Changing Population in the Pre-Civil War Era." *Journal of Long Island History* 2(Spring 1964):9-18.

_____ . "Brooklyn's Volunteer Fire Department." *Journal of Long Island*

*History* 6(Summer 1966):29-34.

_____ . "Brooklyn's Health and Sanitation, 1834-1855." *Journal of Long Island History* 7(Winter-Spring 1967): 40-52.

_____ . "A City's Streets: A Case Study of Brooklyn, 1834-1855." *Journal of Long Island History* 9 (Winter-Spring 1969):32-43.

_____ . "Policing the City of Brooklyn in the 1840s and 1850s." *Journal of Long Island History* 6(Spring 1966):13-22.

_____ . "Water for Brooklyn." *New York History* 47(October 1966):362-71.

Juet, Robert. "Extract from the Journal of the Voyage of the Half-Moon, Henry Hudson, Master, from the Netherlands to the Coast of North America" (1609). In H.C. Murphy, ed., *Collections of the New-York Historical Society.* 2nd series, Vol. 1. New York: H. Ludwig, 1841.

Kaiser, William, and Charles Stonier, eds. *The Development of the Aerospace Industry on Long Island.* Hempstead: Hofstra University, 1968.

Kurland, Gerald. *Seth Low: The Reformer in an Industrial Age.* New York, 1971.

LeBoeuf, Randall J., Jr. "Fulton's Ferry." *Journal of Long Island History* 10(Spring 1974):7-20.

Leiter, Samuel L. "Brooklyn as an American Theatre City." *Journal of Long Island History* 8(Winter-Spring 1968):1-11.

Log of the Schooner *Bayles.* Society for the Preservation of Long Island Antiquities, Setauket, New York.

Log of the Whaleship *Ontario.* Society for the Preservation of Long Island Antiquities, Setauket, New York.

*Long Island: America and Sunrise Land.* New York: Long Island Rail Road, 1933.

*Long Island Directory of Manufacturers.* New York: Nassau Department of Commerce and Industry/Suffolk County Office of Economic Development, 1981.

*Long Island Fact Book of Nassau and Suffolk Counties.* Garden City: Long Island Association of Commerce and Industry, 1965.

Mabee, Carleton. "Brooklyn's Black Public Schools: Why Did Blacks Have Unusual Control Over Them?" *Journal of Long Island History* 11(Spring 1975):23-36.

_____ . "Charity in Travail: Two Orphan Asylums for Blacks." *New York History* 55(January 1974):55-77.

McCullough, David. *The Great Bridge.* New York, 1972.

Ment, David, et. al. *Building Blocks of Brooklyn: A Study of Urban Growth.* Brooklyn, 1979.

_____ . *The Shaping of a City: A Brief History of Brooklyn.* Brooklyn, 1979.

*Nassau County Historical Journal.*

O'Callaghan, Edmund. *The Documentary History of the State of New York.* Albany, 1849.

Occum, Samson. "An Account of the Montauk Indians, on Long Island" (1761). *Collections of the Massachusetts Historical Society.* Vol. IX. Boston: Hall & Hiller, 1804.

Onderdonk, Henry. *Hempstead Annals 1643-1832.* Hempstead: L. Van De Water, 1878.

_____ . *Revolutionary Incidents of Queens County.* New York: Leavitt and Co., 1884.

_____ . *Revolutionary Incidents of Suffolk and Kings Counties.* New York: Leavitt and Co., 1849.

*Orderly Book of the Three Battalions of Loyalists.* Baltimore: Geneological Publishing Co., 1972.

Ostrander, Stephen M. *A History of the City of Brooklyn and Kings County.* Brooklyn, 1894.

Papers relating to the Sag Harbor Custom House. Society for the Preservation of Long Island Antiquities, Setauket, New York.

Pelletreau, William. *A History of Long Island.* New York: Lewis Historical Publishing Co., 1903.

Pomerantz, Stanley T. "The Press of A Greater New York, 1798-1893." *New York History* 39(January 1958):50-66.

Prime, Ebenizer. *Records of the First Church in Huntington, Long Island, 1723-1779.* New York: Scribner's, 1899.

Prime, Nathaniel. *History of Long Island to 1845.* New York: Carter, 1845.

Proceedings of the New York State Agricultural Society 1848-1869. Nassau County Research Library, East Meadow, New York.

Proceedings of the Queens County Agricultural Society 1842-1860. Nassau County Research Library, East Meadow, New York.

Queens County Wills. Surrogate Court, Jamaica, New York.

Randall, Monica. *The Mansions of Long Island's Gold Coast.* New York: Hastings House, 1979.

Rattray, Jeannette. *East Hampton History and Geneology.* Garden City: Country Life Press, 1953.

Roff, Sandra Shoiock. "The California Gold Miners from Brooklyn: As Viewed by the Local Press." *Journal of Long Island History* 9(Spring 1973):7-22.

Rossano, Geoffrey. "Suburbia Armed." In Roger Lotchin, ed., *The Martial Metropolis: American Cities in Peace and War.* New York: Praeger, 1984.

Salwen, Bert. "Indians of Southern New England and Long Island: Early Period." In Bruce Trigger, ed., *Handbook of the North American Indians, Vol. 15: The Northeast.* Washington: Smithsonian Institution, 1978.

Sclare, Donald, and Lisa Sclare. *Beaux Atres Estates.* New York: Viking Press, 1975.

Seyfried, Vincent. *The Long Island Railroad: A Comprehensive History.* Garden City: Privately Printed, 1961-1971.

Simon, Donald E. "Brooklyn in the Election of 1860." *New York History* 51(July 1967):248-262.

Slave Manumission Records 1793-1827. Office of the Huntington Town Historian.

Smith, Robert P. "Heroes and Hurrahs: Sports in Brooklyn, 1890-1898." *Journal of Long Island History* 11(Spring 1975):7-18.

Smits, Edward. *The Creation of Nassau County.* Mineola: Nassau County, 1962.

_____ . *Nassau-Suburbia U.S.A.* Garden City: Doubleday, 1974.

Statistical Abstract of Nassau and Suffolk Counties. Garden City: Franklin National Bank, 1962.

Statistical Reports on Age, Marital Status, Housing, School District Populations, Land Use, Farmland, Manufacturing, and Office Space. Hauppauge: Long Island Regional Planning Board, 1976-1982.

Statistical Reports on Social, Economic, and Housing Characteristics. Mineola: Nassau County Planning Commission, 1963.

Stiles, Henry. *History of the City of Brooklyn.* Brooklyn, 1867-1870.

_____ . *History of the Kings County Including the City of Brooklyn.* New York: Munsell, 1884.

_____ . et. al. *The Civil, Political, Professional and Ecclesiastical History and Commercial and Industrial Record of the County of Kings and the City of Brooklyn.* New York, 1884.

Stone, Gaynell, ed. *Readings in Long Island Archaeology and Ethnohistory.* 7 vols. Stony Brook: Suffolk County Archaeological Association, 1977-1984.

Stoutenburgh, Henry. *A Documentary History of the Dutch Congregation of Oyster Bay.* New York: 1902.

Syrett, Harold C. *The City of Brooklyn, 1865-1898: A Political History.* New York and London, 1944.

*The Airplane Industry of the New York Metropolitan District.* New York: Merchants Association of New York, 1920.

*The Beauties of Long Island.* New York: Long Island Rail Road, 1895.

*The Corrector.* 1826. East Hampton Public Library.

*The Future of Nassau County.* New York: Regional Plan Association, 1969.

*The Long Islander.* 1839-1841. Huntington Historical Society.

*The Portico.* 1826-1828. Huntington Historical Society.

Thomas, Samuel. *Nassau County: Its Governments and Their Expenditure Patterns.* New York: City College Press, 1960.

Thompson, Benjamin. *History of Long Island.* New York: E. French, 1849.

Townsend Family Papers. East Hampton Public Library.

Townsend Family Papers. New-York Historical Society.

Townsend Family Papers. Raynham Hall Museum, Oyster Bay, New York.

Tredwell, Daniel M. *Men and Things on Long Island, Part I* (1839). Brooklyn: C.A. Ditmas, 1912.

United States Census Returns, 1800-1860. Nassau County Research Library, East Meadow, New York.

Vagts, Christopher. *Suffolk: A Pictorial History.* Huntington: Huntington Historical Society, 1983.

Van Der Donck, Adriaen. "A Description of the New Netherlands" (1656). In H.C. Murphy, ed., *Collections of the New-York Historical Society.* 2nd Series, Vol. 1. New York: H. Ludwig, 1841.

Vanderzee, Barbara and Henri. *A Sweet and Alien Land.* New York: Viking Press, 1878.

Van Pelt, Daniel. *Leslie's Illustrated History of Greater New York.* New York: Arkell Publishing Co., 1901.

Vogel, Virgil. *American Indian Medicine.* Norman: University of Oklahoma Press, 1970.

Waller, Henry. *History of Flushing.* Flushing: J.H. Ridenour, 1899.

Ward, William. J. and Margaret C. "The Green-Wood Cemetery." *Journal of Long Island History* 12(Fall 1975):23-34.

Wassenaer, Nicholas. "First Settlement of New York by the Dutch" (1621-1632). In Edmund O'Callaghan, ed., *Documentary History of the State of New York.* Vols. 1-3. Albany: Weed, Parsons, 1850-1851.

Watson, Edward H. "One Hundred Years of Street Railways in Brooklyn." *E.R.A. Headlights* 16(July 1954):1-5.

Weld, Ralph. *Brooklyn Village, 1816-1834.* New York: 1938.

Winsche, Richard. "Echoes of Belmont Park." *Nassau County Historical Journal* XX(Spring 1964):15-33.

Wood, Silas. *A Sketch of the First Settlement of the Several Towns on Long Island.* Brooklyn: Alden Spooner, 1828.

Wyatt, Ronald J. "The Archaic on Long Island." In Walter Newman and Bert Salwen, eds., "Amerinds and Their Paleoenvironments in Northeastern North America." *Annals of the New York Academy of Sciences* 228(1977):400-410.

Sources, Chapter 10:

Brozan, Nadine, "For Vacation Homes, the Trend is Bigger," *New York Times,* April 9,2 000, 11,1.

"Counties in the United States with the largest population-1998" in Roy Fedelem, *Suffolk County Overview,*

Frank, Thomas, "On Island, Big Worries On Housing," *Newsday,* February 28, 2000. A3.

Hauppauge: Long Island Regional Planning Board, February 23, 2000.

Long Island Association WebPages, March 8, 2000.

Long Island Lighting Company, *Population Survey, 1997.* (Hicksville, NY: Long Island Lighting Company, 1997),

Long Island Power Authority, *Long Island Population Survey, 1999.* (LIPA: Uniondale, NY, October, 1999), 3.

Long Island Regional Planning Board, "Population by Age Group. Nassau and Suffolk Counties, New York. December 12, 1999.

Losciale, Alessandra, "Study: Stony Brook Has $1B LI Impact", *Newsday,* April 5, 1981.

Matorana, James and Hetter,Katia , "LI, Queens Ready to Share in Success", *Newsday,* April 3, 2000, C12.

"Moving Day for Two on the Isle," *Newsday,* March 15, 2000. A12.

Sengupta, Somini, "Bringing Asian Voice to the Council", *New York*

Sherwood, Terry, "Then One Day, Suddenly You Care, *Newsday,* November 11, 1999, A27.

Suffolk County Planning Department. "Population by Race and Hispanic Origin," 1999.

Suffolk County Planning Department, "Suffolk County Agricultural Statistics, 1987-1997"

Trager, Cara S., "To Sell or Hold Down the Farms", *Newsday,* November 12, 1999. C6.

# Index